Claire Trevor

Claire Trevor

*The Life and Films
of the Queen of Noir*

DEREK SCULTHORPE

McFarland & Company, Inc., Publishers
Jefferson, North Carolina

ALSO BY DEREK SCULTHORPE

*Brian Donlevy, the Good Bad Guy:
A Bio-Filmography* (McFarland, 2017)

Van Heflin: A Life in Film (McFarland, 2016)

Frontispiece: A publicity still from *Crack-Up* (1946),
set in the world of art.

LIBRARY OF CONGRESS CATALOGUING-IN-PUBLICATION DATA

Names: Sculthorpe, Derek, 1966– author.
Title: Claire Trevor : the life and films of the queen of noir / Derek Sculthorpe.
Description: Jefferson, North Carolina : McFarland & Company, Inc., Publishers, 2018 | Includes bibliographical references and index.
Identifiers: LCCN 2018003188 | ISBN 9781476671932 (softcover : acid free paper) ∞
Subjects: LCSH: Trevor, Claire, 1909–2000. | Motion picture actors and actresses—United States—Biography.
Classification: LCC PN2287.T74 S38 2018 | DDC 791.4302/8092 [B] —dc23
LC record available at https://lccn.loc.gov/2018003188

BRITISH LIBRARY CATALOGUING DATA ARE AVAILABLE

ISBN (print) 978-1-4766-7193-2
ISBN (ebook) 978-1-4766-3069-4

© 2018 Derek Sculthorpe. All rights reserved

*No part of this book may be reproduced or transmitted in any form
or by any means, electronic or mechanical, including photocopying
or recording, or by any information storage and retrieval system,
without permission in writing from the publisher.*

Front cover: still from the RKO production *Allegheny Uprising*, 1939

Printed in the United States of America

*McFarland & Company, Inc., Publishers
Box 611, Jefferson, North Carolina 28640
www.mcfarlandpub.com*

To my mother and father.

Acknowledgments

With thanks to Adolfo Fernandez Punsola de la Bodega for his advice and encouragement. Thanks to Joe L. Smith and Jon Whitehead for the opportunity to see so many obscure films. With thanks as always to my family for their constant support and patience.

Table of Contents

Acknowledgments	vi
Preface	1
1. Lady-in-Waiting	3
2. Broadway Sojourn	10
3. Hollywood "Vacation"	14
4. B-Movie Queen	25
5. Sophisticated Lady	41
6. The Queen Escapes from the "B" Hive	47
7. Radio Interlude	59
8. *Stagecoach*	64
9. "I'm not the Western type"	70
10. The War Years: *Street of Chance*	78
11. Femme Fatale	87
12. Queen of Noir	96
13. "Come on, Lady Bountiful!"	104
14. *Hard, Fast and Beautiful*	112
15. *The High and the Mighty*	125
16. The Small Screen	133
17. The Sixties	139
18. Swansong	145
Epilogue	150
Appendix: Appearances	153
Chapter Notes	163
Bibliography	179
Index	183

Preface

> Most of the performances I did came from my own feelings, my own heart...
> —Claire Trevor interviewed by Hank Whittemore for *Parade Magazine, Reading Eagle,* February 20, 1994, pp. 14–15

Claire Trevor, one of the finest actresses of her generation, appeared in two great films that I must have seen more than 30 times. *Stagecoach* (1939) and *Key Largo* (1948) are not only classics but contain two remarkable performances by Claire. She rightfully won an Oscar for the latter but was surprisingly not even nominated for the former. She enhanced every film by her presence and carved a niche as one of cinema's foremost *femme fatales* in a series of iconic and hugely influential noirs. For much of her career, she did not receive roles worthy of her talent, but she was one of a select band of actresses Oscar-nominated four times in four separate decades. Too versatile to be tied to one genre, she later extended her range on television, and once again proved her all-round worth by winning an Emmy.

If she had so desired it, she could have been one of the biggest stars of her time. She had the glamour, the sex appeal and the talent to eclipse everyone else. But she appeared to lack the ego and the overriding drive and ambition of her peers such as Bette Davis, Joan Crawford and Barbara Stanwyck. Crucially, she had endured no early struggles akin to those they had faced. Trevor was content to be the best actress she could be and less intent on being a star. "Let other girls have the leading roles and the top billing," she once declared. "I've always tried to make producers realize that I don't want to be a star—at least not straight stardom. It's the character parts that pay big dividends—make people talk."[1] As one observer rightly said, "It may be that she's too good-natured for real stardom."[2]

Her shortage of ego meant that she appeared in a lot of material that was not worthy of her time. However, she made them worthy by her presence and lifted otherwise forgettable ventures, making them seem so much better than they really were, the mark of a real actress. This was especially true during her early years, what she called her apprenticeship while under contract at Fox. A studio executive noted that she was that *rara avis*, a thoroughly reliable actress who was able to play any role. "She's absolutely dependable," he remarked, "she isn't temperamental and almost never blows her lines.... I don't believe I have ever seen her look at a script."[3] This same modesty, professionalism and adaptability led to her acquiescing to the diktats of bosses during her time as Queen of the Bs. When she branched out and went freelance from 1938, she had more control of her material and the standard improved markedly.

Trevor did beautifully on radio even though she disliked the medium; it made great use of her distinctive husky and seductive voice. Later she enjoyed great success on television, despite the brevity of her small screen career. She might have played more often on Broadway had she wished, but the thought of playing the same role night after night for several months did not appeal to her. Even so, she never abandoned the stage altogether and appeared at intervals on the so-called "straw hat" circuit and locally in California. In her fifties, she even tried to go on a national tour in a difficult British comedy with a background of lesbianism.

There have been a number of Trevor profiles over the years, but only one previous biography. My intention is to provide a comprehensive assessment of her. In this book, I discuss her career on film and put in context her theater, television and radio work. As far as possible, I delineate her personal life and show that although she may appear to be an underrated star, she was a well-loved actress whose acting contained an integrity few others have matched. Trevor is rightly cherished by true lovers of film and I hope my book stands as a fitting tribute to a consummate actress and a warm human being.

1

Lady-in-Waiting

> I'm going to be queen, or there ain't going to be a show!—William French,
> "The Lady Changes: Claire Trevor," *Movie Classic,* July 1936, 54

Claire Wemlinger was born on March 8, 1910, in Bensonhurst, near Brooklyn, New York. Bensonhurst (or in Brooklyn-ese parlance, Bensen*hoist*) is a suburb to the southwest of the city, established in the mid–nineteenth century when Brooklyn Gas company president Frank Benson began selling off parcels of land he had bought from the Polhemus family. By the time of Claire's birth, it still retained vestiges of a semi-rural appearance. It was home to a Jewish and Italian population, and some years later became known as Little Italy.

Claire's parents, Noel Benjamin Wemlinger, and Bea Edith Morrison, were married in Manhattan on February 19, 1902, when Noel was 33, Edith about 24. Noel was born in Paris, France, in 1868. Having been partly raised there, he and his brothers were all fluent French speakers. However, his family hailed from Germany. His father Benjamin (b. 1838) was born in Rust, near Ettenheim, Baden, and Benjamin's parents were Landelin Wemlinger and Helena (*nee* Schmider). Wemlinger is an unusual name which is of obscure origin; the family was established at Rust in Germany from at least the seventeenth century. The earliest known ancestor I discovered was Andreas Wemlinger, who lived there around 1640.[1]

Benjamin and his wife arrived in the U.S. about 1890 and settled in Westchester, New York. Noel had been a resident since the year before, and became a naturalized U.S. citizen in 1922.[2] The Wemlingers were tailors by trade and Noel continued in the family business, eventually catering to New York's smart set from a shop on 51st Street in partnership with a Mr. McGrane. Claire was named after her father's mother Clara (*nee* Sauter) (1842–1917).[3]

Claire's mother, often known as Benny or Benjamina, was a dressmaker and had been born in Belfast, Ireland. She was one of at least 11 children of Robert and Mary Chambers Morrison. Robert was a restaurateur and arrived in America in 1888, settling in Manhattan; his family joined him two years later, coincidentally around the same time as the Wemlingers.[4]

As a child, Claire took part in church social functions and enjoyed nothing better than dressing up to give stage shows for the grown-ups. When acting with the other children in the area, she was usually called on to be a lady-in-waiting, but she secretly longed to play the queen. One day she rebelled, insisting that she must be queen. "Be nice and be a lady-in-waiting like you always are," the other children implored, but she would not relent. "I'm going to be a queen, or there ain't gonna be a show!" she declared.[5] Thus her family and all the other children were required to sit down and watch her play the queen. After that, she remarked, "I became the outstanding neighborhood pest. But not for long, as, after I won my rebellion and wore my opposition down, my inspiration dimmed."[6]

Of her mother, it was observed that she too had always seemed to be like a lady-in-waiting and "always did the things other people wanted her to do and never the things she wanted to do most in the world."[7] Claire described her mother as being "full of life, humor and enthusiasm."[8] Her father was different; he was stern and disapproving. When he heard she wanted to be an actress, he was rather shocked and never really came to terms with the idea.

Claire first attended school at 116th Street and Broadway in the city. Her childhood seemed quite idyllic. As an only child of well-to-do parents, she had a privileged start in life. From an early age she was often taken to Broadway shows by her mother and collected a great number of theater programs. Before long, she fell in love with cinema too. At school she showed an interest in drama although she once said that at that point she really dreamt of being a ballerina.[9] When she was eight, she made her New York theatrical debut in a production of Maurice Maeterlinck's popular allegorical fantasy *The Blue Bird*. The exact date and venue is not known.[10] Although she had no speaking lines, she was paid the princely sum of $20 a week.[11] She observed, "I played, with a note of finality, one of the unborn children."[12]

Trevor recalled a fascination as a small child with other children and particularly with other baby carriages and their occupants. It was once reported that her "deepest childhood impression was the death of her best friend at the age of nine." This gave her, she said, a special outlook on life. "Later, she vowed she'd find out how to cheat death, if only by living her own life doubly rich—for the little girl who died and for herself."[13]

Around 1923, when she was 13, the family moved to Larchmont, an affluent village some 18 miles from the city. A long established settlement, it was a distinct social elevation from Bensonhurst, and even boasted its own yacht club. Claire went to the George Washington High School in Mamaroneck. Her chief memory of her high school days was the dancing. She always loved to dance although she said she never took formal lessons, she just improvised. When attending her first college prom, she said she was "petrified by so many college boys at once." She soon hit her stride and before long she was the toast of Princeton, which she described as "three times the size and three times as exciting."[14] She went to all the dances at Dartmouth, Annapolis, Harvard, West Point and many other colleges. "I just love Yale," she commented years later, when the college voted her one of the three most popular movie actresses. "For two or three years I don't think I missed a single prom at Yale."[15] She attended every prom she could, including those at U.S.C. and New York University, and kept all the programs as mementos.[16] One of the most memorable of the many dances she attended was the Winter Carnival at Colgate where she was voted Queen of the Carnival.[17]

She had many adventures during her prom years, some of which she shared in interviews. One time at a dance at Colgate, 17-year-old Claire was fixed up with a date by her cousin Frank. She found the boy incredibly dull and although she danced with him, feigned a headache so she could slip away to meet a more exciting youth she had met. With another couple, they "went tobogganing in the moonlight" and she instantly fell in love with him.[18] Her cousin and the "dull" date both found out. Frank was furious and wrote her a righteously indignant ten-page letter in which he told her in no uncertain terms that she would never be invited to another prom. She had three invitations in the following week alone.

By her own admission, her life then was one big social whirl. She loved life. She had many beaux and her dance card was always full; "Try to make a boy throw himself at your feet early in the game," she once advised the lovelorn. "Then you'll find it isn't so interesting, and there's less danger for you."[19] By her own admission, she lived impulsively and never asked for advice. "In all my crucial moments," she declared, "I've totally disregarded what was proposed to me as my best move."[20]

An oft-related tale concerned the time she wanted a new dress for a prom but her father refused to increase her allowance to pay for it. Determined to get her own way, she went out to get a job and worked for two weeks as a typist and filing clerk at the Underground Cable Company.[21] She bitterly hated the work and vowed never to do anything similar again, but at least the dress was a sensation.

At high school she had a mild interest in drama, and showed a talent for public speaking. At one time she entered a public speaking contest and won; she had to memorize a speech that lasted 35 minutes.[22] She had a great retentive memory which stood her in good stead for learning scripts with ease. She was naturally intelligent but, by her own admission, lazy. Her initial idea on graduation was to go to Smith College, or Vassar, like many of her school friends, but she lacked the necessary credits and did not feel inclined to study any further to earn them; "I decided that was too much trouble," she said.[23] Instead she took an extension course in art and design at Columbia University, to which she commuted every day. By then the family had moved to New Rochelle, an affluent city in the southwestern part of New York State. At that time, Claire specialized in conversational French and displayed an aptitude for the language. She was attracted to a career in art and had inherent talent. There were several artists in the family including her uncle Charles Morrison.

Her father, who she once described as "the best custom tailor in New York," counted some of the city's most successful businessmen as his clients.[24] At first his shop with McGrane was at 259 Fifth Avenue but from about 1920 moved to 435. Her mother was also a skilled dressmaker. It was no surprise then that Claire had a natural affinity for beautiful clothes, and entertained ambitions to be a fashion designer, particularly of dresses, cloaks and suits.[25] She never lost her love of fashion and always made an effort to look her best at all times.

Drifting somewhat, and feeling that she had not yet found her true vocation, she followed the advice of a man who had once been a theater manager for Ethel Barrymore, and one of her girlfriends: They both encouraged her to try for the American Academy of Dramatic Arts. However, when she was reading the Academy's prospectus, she was teased about her lofty theatrical pretensions by one of her college classmates. In her annoyance, she hurled the prospectus at her fellow student and it flew out of the window and fell several floors to the street below. Despite her attempts to locate it, she could not. This delay meant it was another term before she finally entered the Academy for real. Ever afterwards, she refused to throw anything again, even if a script required her to do so.[26]

Claire attended the American Academy of Dramatic Arts from 1928 to 1929.[27] Established in 1884 at the old Lyceum Theater, it is considered to be the oldest English-speaking acting school in the world. A list of past alumni reads like a Who's Who of Hollywood. Spencer Tracy, Rosalind Russell and Agnes Moorehead were among those who had attended in the 1920s. Claire realized that she had found her calling: "I hadn't been there more than a week when I knew I wanted to be an actress."²⁸ During her time there, she learned all aspects of acting technique and ways of thinking that stayed with her always. She once said that she got her principal dramatic training "by falling downstairs," commenting, "We learned diction, posture, breathing, fencing and dancing; but we learned to take our falls too."²⁹ There was a series of flights of steps there which students were required to practice on and she became adept at falling both up and down. She learned all about the use of hands, which is hardly something non-actors would think about. She explained:

> We had regular dramatic training to manage the hands. We had regular training in pantomime—had to sit before the class at an imaginary table and show the class, simply by use of the hands, precisely what we were doing. The sort of pantomime work with the hands will help any girl to use her hands gracefully and without needless gestures.³⁰

She spent two six-month terms at the Academy. In the second term, students took part in plays and were sent out to observe people at work, in stores, restaurants or in the street, and then to imitate them in class. She commented; "If the rest of the class could discern from your pantomime what you were supposedly eating or selling, you were showing some ability."³¹

She considered her first performance in a play at the school a disaster. She felt she was too self-conscious and began to feel she was not suited to acting after all. As she explained, "I was only there a short time when they handed me the difficult role of the child in *The Wild Duck*. I was a miserable failure. So much so I decided to give up all thoughts of theater then and there. Some time later, friends persuaded me to try again."³² Ibsen was the theatrical equivalent of being thrown in at the deep end, and has stumped many an experienced player.

A college friend, Gregory Deane, took her to a party where he introduced her to a number of theatrical agents. They were enthusiastic about her ability and convinced her that she would make an excellent actress, being both beautiful and expressive.³³ This boost to her morale was just what was required at that stage of her development. Deane became a stage actor and director and played some roles on Broadway in the 1930s.

Claire's life of ease came to an end with the Stock Market Crash of October 1929. The wealthy patrons of her father's business were the ones who suddenly lost most of their money. As a result, her father lost his business. He actually used the family's savings for several months before letting them know what had happened. Eventually he bluntly told Claire, "You'd better go to work."³⁴ She was always rather intimidated by her father, who she said was stern and unyielding. For instance, when she was 22 he caught her smoking. "If you must smoke, don't do it in my presence," he said, and she promptly went to her room.³⁵

She began modeling hats for a number of companies including Stetson. The Academy of Dramatic Art instructors had recognized her latent talent and encouraged her to join stock companies for experience. Armed with a list of fake credits, she trawled around theatrical offices trying to get work. An agent got her a job with Robert Henderson's repertory players, based at Ann Arbor, Michigan, for the spring and early summer of 1930.³⁶

At Ann Arbor, she gained valuable experience in seven plays and earned $75 a week. The star of the company was the legendary stage actress Margaret Anglin, then in her mid-fifties and still a force to be reckoned with; she had recently been decorated by the Greek government for her services to Greek theater. The year before, Anglin caused a stir when she walked away from Broadway after her demand for roles for her husband was not met. Among her supporting cast of New York "professional players" at Ann Arbor was one Claire St. Claire. At this stage, Claire was uncertain which name to go for. She had decided early on that Wemlinger would not look good in lights—if it was even possible to find enough light bulbs. After toying with Claire Morrison during her time at the academy and then Claire Sinclair or St. Claire, she finally settled on Trevor, chosen seemingly at random by an office boy with a telephone directory.

Although she gained valuable experience at the Ann Arbor festival, she mostly played small supporting roles such as a chorus member in *Antigone,* and had just a few lines in some of the others. The repertoire was effectively tailored for Anglin, a devotee of Greek tragedy. It ended with her favorite Oscar Wilde comedy *Lady Windermere's Fan,* in which Claire had a couple of lines. But she enjoyed working with a troupe in a new play each week, and fit in easily enough despite at times feeling out of her depth. It was a varied schedule that encompassed *Salome,* Wilde's tragedy, and *Excess Baggage,* a Vaudeville-style musical comedy that had been popular on Broadway a couple of years earlier. There was also *Serena Blandish,* a smart satire of the London social set by S.N. Behrman.[37] Completing the lineup was Edna Ferber and George S. Kaufman's *The Royal Family,* a parody of the famous Barrymore acting dynasty. These were all proven hits and were well-received by Michigan audiences hungry for culture.

In contrast to the "black memory" of her tussle with Ibsen at the Academy, at Ann Arbor Claire was adjudged a great success as Nina in Chekhov's *The Sea Gull.*[38] It was all new to her but she soon learned by doing. "I was so green," she recollected, "I didn't know you had to study for a part. I just thought you went on and tried to do the best you could."[39]

It was somewhat ironic that one of the first criticisms leveled at her during her early years in the theater was regarding her voice. She was once told that her acting was all right but that she would have to do something about her "terrible voice."[40] For many, it was one of her greatest assets and set her apart from all the other blonde actresses of the time.

Claire's next appearance on stage was in *The Stork Is Dead,* previously known as *Not Yet.* A satiric play by Hans Kottow, it originally played in his native Vienna and then in a number of other European cities. The American production was rather troubled and in September the first producer of the show, 21-year-old Harry Silvers, was replaced by vaudeville agent Peter Wells from St. Louis. The director was Kent Thurber. The North American debut took place in October 1930 at the Lyceum Theater in Paterson, New Jersey, in what was classed as the "first Broadway premiere in that town."[41] The production transferred to Bayonne, New Jersey, and marked the first time she was billed as Claire Trevor. Some members of her family came to watch her and were reportedly "shocked when she innocently spouted a debatable line."[42] The play was a bedroom farce of the kind that was in vogue some years earlier, especially in London and on the Continent. One critic described it as "a vulgar farce which is *Wife in Name Only* in modern clothes."[43] It did not go over well in New Jersey and once the show closed at the end of the week (Saturday, October 11), the promised full transfer to Broadway never came about.[44] After several other unsuccessful out-of-town tryouts, it eventually made its New York debut in September 1932 at the 48th Street Theater with only one cast member the same as the original production.[45] It was panned by the critics but managed to last three weeks.[46]

Trevor returned to modeling, and then looked for acting jobs around New York. In one theatrical manager's office, she met a director who invited her to make some films for the Vitaphone Company.[47] The first of these Vitaphone shorts was *The Meal Ticket*, set in some unnamed German town and featuring vaudeville comedian Jack Pearl as a baron. The baron constantly argues with his wife (Trevor) but she always runs rings around him. This was followed by *The Imperfect Lover,* a musical comedy billed as "the most complete and pretentious short turned out by the plant."[48] Trevor played a doctor opposite Jack Haley as an inventor. *Good Times*, "a satire on the unemployment situation," featured Claire as one of a group of girls who attempt to study the unemployed.[49] The last of the films was *Angel Cake*, a two-reel musical comedy, again starring Haley. Trevor appeared as the ingénue who "sweet talks a phony British aristocrat into funding a revue."[50] Although running at only 19 minutes, the short featured quite a few show tunes and popular songs of the day delivered by the Foursome and the Paige Sisters. The repertoire ranged from Offenbach's "Barcarolle" from *Tales of Hoffman* to the "Fats" Waller tune "I've Got a Feeling I'm Falling." Also included was the song "Black Maria" and one of the earliest renditions of "Walking My Baby Back Home," written a few months earlier.

"They were terrible!" Claire said of these films some years later.[51] However, she was noticed and on the strength of them she was invited to join the Warner Brothers stock company of players in St. Louis, Missouri. The group included such later famous names as Lyle Talbot, Wallace Ford and Albert Dekker in the days when he was still van Dekker. She would later appear in films with all three. "Naturally, everyone presumed I'd had much experience," she remarked. "I let 'em think so."[52]

She spent eight weeks with the company and did eight plays, giving ten performances weekly.[53] It was a terrific training ground for her as for all the players. Lyle Talbot became a friend and gave her some sound advice. "She was an ambitious novice," he recalled, "and out of my long experience I could help her and coach her a little. She had talent and quickly proved it."[54] She was popular at the stock company where at the outset, she played mostly ingénue roles. The season started with a Christmas night production of the David Belasco comedy *It's a Wise Child*, which was lauded as being "among the outstanding features of the Christmas Holiday season in St. Louis."[55] All the plays were unseen in the Midwest and were presented at an affordable price at the Grand Central Theater. The season continued into the new year of 1931 with *As Good as New,* "a light and sketchy comedy of infidelity." A reviewer called Claire "a charming addition to the company."[56] In the farce *Broken Dishes*, she played the youngest daughter of a harassed and henpecked man. A critic noted, "[S]he makes an attractive leading lady and in one fiery scene shows that she is capable of some difficult acting."[57]

Even in these early days, Trevor easily displayed her range. In *Broadway*, Trevor "made an attractive cabaret girl, the cause of most of the trouble in the play."[58] In the next, the light comedy *Jonesy*, she was different again: This time she was "very sweet and charming as the little girl who lives next door."[59] Belying her lack of experience, she played well with all the leading men of the company, especially Wallace Ford and Lyle Talbot. She later said that she felt she was not ready to play leads at this stage of her career, but proved herself wrong.[60] Having proved popular and shown plenty of promise, she got her big chance to shine when the director was casting Preston Sturges' *Strictly Dishonorable*. "Why not give the ingénue the lead?" suggested writer Thornton Sargent at a script meeting. The director was unconvinced because of her lack of experience, but was finally persuaded one day when he sat in the audience and heard for himself the positive response she received. "Everyone liked her," commented Sargent. "She was lovely and her throaty voice intrigued you."[61]

In the modern and risqué comedy *Strictly Dishonorable*, Trevor was the only woman in the cast. She was praised for her charm, and she and Talbot were commended for bringing "such breath of youth and lack of responsibility to their playing."[62] One reviewer noted, "Claire Trevor portrays, with charming naivety, and certainly with a large share of natural comeliness, the leading role, that of the innocent Southern girl whose 'intentions' wander astray from the precepts laid down in staid old Yokum [Mississippi]."[63]

The last production was *Gold Diggers*, a lively farce in which Trevor displayed a fine comedic sense as the "delectable and inexperienced Violet."[64] The season ended and the stock company was soon abandoned altogether. The attention that Trevor garnered brought her a three-month optional contract with Metro-Goldwyn-Mayer. Although she was paid a great salary—$1,000 per week—she was left idle for a long time.[65] Nothing seemed to transpire and before long she began to think it would never happen for her. During the lean periods, she haunted agents' offices and was repeatedly told, "Nothing for you today." She resolved to go to Cornell University if acting didn't work out for her, but really wanted to make at least one feature film first.[66]

2

Broadway Sojourn

> Nothing stands still. In a career, one goes up the ladder or goes down or vanishes altogether. It's the same in love.—Edith Dietz, "Notes on the 'Discovery' of an Actress: This Trevor Girl Makes Her Own Fame in Films," *The Long Island Sunday Press: Screen & Radio Weekly*, August 11, 1935, 5

After another stint at modeling, Trevor joined a stock company in Southampton, Long Island, for the 1931 summer season. She appeared in five plays with them, earning about $5 a week and a share of the company's profits. Most were comedies such as *Too Young to Love* and *No Money to Guide Her*. It helped that she knew the director, Hank Potter, a Yale man just out of college.[1] She admitted that she was not fired by searing ambition to be an actress, but simply enjoyed herself so much there. The company lived together in a large house, with the actors in the house and the technical crew in the barn where the scenery was assembled and painted. The camaraderie of a stock company appealed to her and the constantly changing schedule kept things interesting so a player could feel that they were progressing. All the plays took place at the Parrish Masonic Hall in Southampton, with some additional shows at other theaters and country clubs in Southampton and Northampton. In *Rhapsody in Black*, she was one of the cast members who it was said "gave satisfactory performances."[2] She played a caretaker's daughter in the mystery *Phantom Footsteps* by Walter Livingston.[3] She was especially praised for her "splendid bit of acting" in *Immodest Violet*, a lively tale of a rebellious girl in staid 1910 Oklahoma.[4]

The summer season in the Hamptons attracted a number of producers from New York. One of them, Alexander McKay, offered her a leading role when he was casting Broadway's *Whistling in the Dark*.[5] This was Claire's big chance and she readily accepted. Originally entitled *The Perfect Crime*, the play was described as a "jolly comedy"[6]: A mystery writer (Ernest Truex) starts to live his stories for real and gets involved with a gang of crooks holed up at a mansion in Spuyten Duyvil at the northwest tip of Manhattan. Edward Arnold was also in the cast. Claire played Truex's fiancée. She asked for $100 per week, and was given $85. She commented, "I thought that as long as I was going to make money, I might as well make plenty. The only way you can get anything is to expect it."[7]

The bright new comedy had many great reviews, hailing it as well-paced and appealing. There were also a few decidedly lukewarm notices. Failed actress Alice Alworth, writing her column in *The Bronxville Press*, declared that "except for the presence of the vibrantly alive Ernest Truex, little can be said for *Whistling in the Dark*." Alworth called Trevor "pretty enough, but unfortunately—as an actress—she is just another girl."[8] Alworth was in the minority, as most considered the play entertaining and inventive.

One observer called lively young ingénue Trevor "a delicate wisp of a blonde."[9] Another perceptive reviewer wrote: "Claire Trevor, making her first appearance in the Big Leagues, shows herself to be an expert comedienne. She is a comely young lady with a nice future before her. She, too, will probably go to Hollywood."[10] Trevor once said that she considered comedy the hardest thing to do and felt that if she could master that, she could do just about anything in acting.

While she was in the play, her mind was on something else: love. A wealthy New Yorker who was never named was the object of her affection and most of her attention: "I was so preoccupied with him that I resented having to go to the theater every night."[11] But the play was as much a social as a cultural event, and there were many of her friends and family in the audience watching her and rooting for her. Before each performance began, there were cocktails, and afterwards supper and dancing, a pattern that was replicated in most of the cities they visited. Still only 22, she was very much the social butterfly and she had numerous cousins across the country.

When her suitor proposed, she turned him down because she was not ready for marriage at that time. Later she found herself half-regretting her response but he never asked her again. If she had married then, it is likely she would have been lost to the acting sisterhood for all time and become part of the social set.

Her performance in the play brought her a lot of attention from the movie studios, and several of them made tests of her when the tour reached Los Angeles in June. She did one for MGM opposite Lionel Barrymore which made such a big impression that Irving Thalberg called her to his office one night and offered her a seven-year contract. "I told him I didn't want it then," she recalled. "I wasn't ready for the screen I preferred to remain on stage. At first he wouldn't believe I was serious."[12] He tried hard to convince her, describing how it normally took seven years to make a star, to "groom, train and create popularity," citing the examples of Marlene Dietrich and Joan Crawford. But seven years seemed like an eternity to Trevor at that time. Thalberg spoke to her for 45 minutes. "I still said no," she recalled, "and I've hated myself ever since."[13]

When the tour of *Whistling in the Dark* reached San Francisco the following month, she met a broker and would-be actor, Alfred C. Read, and as a result was unwittingly drawn into a court case. Read, described as "the debonair Lochinvar of the bay district and God's gift to women,"[14] entertained her lavishly and told her that he would soon be accompanying her to Hollywood to try his luck as an actor. Shortly afterwards, he was involved in a $100,000 alienation suit brought by his wife against another actress, Claire Windsor, who in court was labeled a "love thief."[15] Having been seen places a number of times with Read, Trevor was also drawn into the melee; the press dubbed her "Claire No. 2" and splashed her photograph all over the front pages.[16] The two Claires knew and liked each other, having been introduced by Read. Trevor, annoyed to be dragged into the suit, said, "Mr. Read is a very nice young man but he means nothing more to me."[17] Nevertheless her name was mentioned quite often in court and evidence attesting to the many unpaid [sic] telephone calls he had made to her number excited the interest of the press if no one else.

Discussing *Whistling in the Dark* years later, Trevor said, "I remember that play because one critic said I got along by the simple expedient of not acting at all."[18] At the time, she felt that this was a criticism but realized in retrospect that it was more like a compliment.

The play was well-received in most of the cities in which it played during its lengthy tour, including Chicago, Cincinnati and St. Louis, where she had played in the Warners stock company. Playgoers called the show "hilarious" and its two leads' performances were described as "scintillating."[19] The most commonly used adjective applied to Claire was "charming."[20] One reviewer commented that she "is easy on the eyes and crisp and amusing in her presentation of the fiancée."[21] But the tour eventually began to run out of steam; by the time it reached Milwaukee, there were perhaps 50 people in the audience.[22] It was a struggle for her just to get back to New York and she began to rue turning down the offers that Thalberg and two other studios had made. By that stage, her living allowance was down to about $3 a week and she was sending home all the rest she earned.

When the tour finished, she made it back to New York and was without a play for two months. In that interim, she modeled hats again. Eventually she was cast opposite Brian Donlevy in *Far Away Horses,* due to open at Broadway's Martin Beck Theater in February 1933. The play was built around an Irish-American family in New York. Claire tried hard to master a convincing Irish brogue but was dissatisfied with the results and withdrew not long before opening night. Donlevy was also busy with other projects and could not take part.[23] It was fortuitous for both of them that they missed out on the debacle, which only ran for four nights. "It was so deadly and fatiguing," wrote one critic, "so unskilled and unnecessary, so half-baked and irritating that it is fated to occupy a prominent place on any list of the season's more unfortunate offerings."[24]

In *The Party's Over*, Claire played the third lead role as frowsy New Haven hash-house waitress Betty Decker. The story revolved around a young man who is the sole supporter of his whole lazy family. His youngest brother, home from college, had a brief romance with Betty and got her into trouble and is eventually persuaded to do the right thing by marrying her. He finds that he is jealous of the attentions of her hash-house boss. *Variety* commented that it provided "a fair diversion with doubtful chances of registering."[25] One of the main drawbacks was that there were too many selfish and unlikable characters, but the dialogue got a few laughs. Another reviewer noted that Claire and others "all do nicely in their roles."[26] The show lasted throughout April but struggled into May and did not tour after losing two of its main cast members. "I hated the play," she declared. "But it was all I could get."[27] She was stricken with tonsillitis a week before it was due to open, but recovered in time. Her mother had it too, and Claire spent most of the first week of the play's run ministering to her.

According to reports, Trevor came close to marriage with an advertising executive around this time, and was only waiting for him to get a legal separation from his wife. It never happened.[28]

She was at something of a low ebb, but it was then that she received a telegram from Fox with the offer of a film contract, and asking her to come to Hollywood on April 30. She and Harvey Stephens (a fellow cast member from *The Party's Over*) were signed by Fox agent Mike Connolly on behalf of the Jenie Jacobs-Pauline Cook agency.[29] Fox was on the lookout for another Mae West, and seemed to imagine that because Trevor was blonde, she might fit the bill. But there was no comparison, and Claire had no intention of aping anyone else. She remarked, "After a star becomes famous like Mae West, it isn't difficult to find others to mimic her well—but who wants to see imitations?"[30] She didn't want to be the next Mae West; she was quite content to be the first Claire Trevor.

It was with an air of anticipation that Trevor made the trip west with her mother, imagining that she would not be required to do any actual work for the first six months. When she had been given a contract in 1930, she was left without an assignment for virtually the whole three months, and she had heard similar stories from other girls she knew. As she told her mother, "We'll go, but it'll be just a vacation for us."[31]

3

Hollywood "Vacation"

> I was going to be another Lynn Fontanne, you know. I wasn't going to chase the movies, they were going to chase me. But then something called the Depression came along.—Lucie Neville, "She's Too Busy to Be a Star," *The San Bernardino County Sun,* June 26, 1938, 32.

Claire imagined that the trip west would be a sinecure for the first six months, but it proved to be anything but. She reached Los Angeles on the evening of May 2, 1933, and was met by two men who gave her a script, told her to "learn the first 14 scenes" and report to the studio at 10 a.m. the following day.[1] As soon as she arrived at the studio, she was whisked off to makeup and made screen tests with co-star George O'Brien. After that, she posed for stills for an hour, and then she had her hair "experimented with" for the rest of the day.

Early the next morning, she was taken to Fox Hills where her teeth were examined and then she was "paraded before a battery of fault-finders who looked for defects."[2] This was followed by more stills and more tests. It was not until four a.m. on Monday morning that she began filming *Life in the Raw* (1933), a western based on a Zane Grey novel. Half-asleep, she was bundled onto the studio bus and taken on a rough drive 125 miles into the desert to the Victorville location. Once there, she was expected to ride a horse—something which she had never done before. She had to rehearse a lot with O'Brien, and was more than a little saddle sore after the day's shooting. Next she had to contend with a wind machine that blew the desert sand in her face, leaving it feeling like it had been sandpapered. This was for a scene in which her underwear had to blow into the Joshua trees, but the director wasn't satisfied with the way they were falling until the seventeenth attempt. For all that, she was billed as "The Girl" on the cast list. So began Trevor's career at Fox. For the next five years she was on the Fox treadmill grinding out movies of varying quality and feeling increasingly frustrated. "Of course when you're working on a picture, you can't call your soul your own," she once observed.[3]

Quickly she was slotted in another western, *The Last Trail* (1933), consoled that the shooting schedule would not begin until 6:30 a.m. this time. This was another routine Zane Grey affair, similar to *Life in the Raw,* and again she played opposite George O'Brien, who became a friend (they often played tennis). A contemporary reviewer drew attention to "the comely and capable Claire Trevor," and continued: "[L]et it be stated here that she is surely on her way to screen celebrity. There is an ease and assurance about her performance that speaks volumes for her ability."[4] In her second Fox feature, she showed a spirit that made her seem a distinct personality, immediately making her stand out from other screen blondes. Perhaps it was her enticing voice or the warmth in her eyes, but she seemed full of feeling and insouciant humor. Even at this early stage, she had the ability to make far more of her lines than seemed to be there, along with her instant believability.

Her on-screen assurance was at odds with the bundle of nerves she was off-screen. Her over-eagerness in her first films was especially noticed by O'Brien; she was constantly pacing about and hyperactive on set. "Sit down, Claire. Rest," he advised. "Conserve your strength. Save your energy for the camera."[5] She never forgot his advice. Later she found that knitting also helped to relax her on set during the seemingly endless times spent waiting around.

She was penciled in to play opposite Spencer Tracy in *Shanghai Madness*, then switched to another picture. The two great actors were teamed for the first time in *The Mad Game* (1933), a kidnapping yarn. Tracy played an imprisoned ex-bootlegger who is recruited to help track down his own gang after they kidnap the daughter and son-in-law of the judge who sent him up the river. Plotlines about kidnapping were not encouraged by the Hays Office at that time in light of the case of the Lindbergh baby's March 1932 abduction. The subject was well-handled in a fast-moving and engaging drama which gave Trevor a role she could get her teeth into as a reporter who falls for Tracy.

She was praised for her authenticity. *Variety* commented, "Miss Trevor impels an exciting interest. [Hers is] about the best portrayal of a newspaper gal which the studios have submitted."[6] In only her third film, she was singled out for most of the applause. One reviewer observed that she was "casual, with a precious knack of reading her lines as if she thought them up herself; interesting, because there's fascinating unpredictability to the pitch of her voice and the tempo of her performance."[7] *Picture Play* raved about the "discovery of a striking newcomer. ...[S]he is crisp, intelligent and pretty."[8] *Hollywood Filmograph* declared, "We cannot speak too highly of Claire Trevor. Her dialogue is delivered with clearness and sincerity and a few clever mannerisms that are charming."[9] Although *The Mad Game* was not an A-picture, it had some quality and was elevated by its two leads. It was far better than most B pictures of the time. It was also popular with the public, who immediately recognized her worth.

In the movie, Trevor sashayed with an air of supreme nonchalance, rolling her own cigarettes and striking matches on her carved jet ring. However, she revealed that the cigarette-rolling and match-striking routine took her eight or nine weeks' practice.[10] She was struggling to master the cigarette-rolling, but then one morning she noticed one of the hundreds of extras milling about the gates of the studio had it down pat, and she spent the day studying the art with him. By evening, she could roll them one-handed.[11]

Trevor enjoyed working with Tracy, and the feeling was mutual. "He liked the way I delivered lines, tossed lines away. He really liked my style," she recalled. Tracy admired his co-star in more ways than one, and made a play for her. According to his biographer, Trevor responded to his overtures with "I don't go out with married men." After a pause, Tracy flashed her a smile and said, "Stay that way!"[12]

Trevor admired Tracy as an actor and found herself emulating his casual style, which appealed to her greatly. Tracy and Trevor were soon announced for *Work of Art*, a proposed adaptation of the latest Sinclair Lewis novel.[13] This was considered one of Lewis' lesser works and was never adapted for the screen. Although Trevor was later due to appear opposite Tracy again in *Gold Rush of 1934*, he was moved to another project. The title was changed to *Wild Gold*.

After Sally Eilers refused to do *Jimmy and Sally* (1933), the part of Sally was given to Trevor, and it seemed as though it was her first stroke of luck. Star James Dunn was a popular, breezy leading man with a winning personality who had proved highly successful when teamed with Eilers in romantic comedies. The "plot" revolved around Dunn as a puffed-up publicity man for a large meat packing corporation and his romance with Trevor, the intelligent girl who lives across the hall from him. They want to get married but don't have sufficient funds, and go through the expected adventures before all ends predictably. It was hardly new but it was well-liked. "A highly diverting piece of nonsense with no pretensions to be anything else," wrote one reviewer, who also said that the involvement of the two leads "was sufficient to ensure the success of any film, for both these young people have an irresistible sense of fun and delightful stage personalities."[14] There were some charming songs by Jay Gorney including "It's the Irish in Me," "You're My Thrill" and the ditty "Eat Marlowe's Meats." Although the plot was pure hokum, one reviewer called her a "bright, capable" actress and commented that she "does everything possible to make these implausible events in which she is involved seem as if they could actually happen."[15] At the height of the Depression, this was just the kind of uplifting, escapist film that was badly needed and the studios provided. "Guaranteed to drive away the 1933 blues," commented one reviewer.[16]

One of the key elements that made the film a success was the wisecracking dialogue, which co-writer William Conselman worked on. An ex-newspaperman, he had an ear for

After two formulaic westerns, Claire (right) scored a hit when she replaced Sally Eilers in *Jimmy and Sally* (1933), a charming comedy opposite James Dunn (left).

The appealing *Hold That Girl* (1934) capitalized on the growing popularity of Trevor and James Dunn.

colloquialisms, but felt he was getting stale and so took to the streets and listened in on conversations at prizefights and in ballrooms. Dialogue is often an overlooked element of filmmaking, but he commented on its importance to film and the wider cultural influence of the movies on popular culture: "Our language ... is filled with colloquialisms which change almost daily. When some dialogue is written for a film, it must not only be current speech but it must, of necessity, anticipate the trend and go a step ahead."[17]

By the time Trevor had made just a handful of films, many observers already recognized that she stood out from the crowd. "[Trevor] serving notice that though blond, she was not 'just another' of the near-platinum sisterhood, but a capable young actress of individuality and charm," wrote one reviewer, who continued, "One hopes that before too long she will have opportunity to display the talent of which her two screen appearances give promise."[18]

Jimmy and Sally was so successful that Dunn and Trevor were immediately reteamed in *Hold That Girl* (1934), which was said to be "even better than their last picture."[19] This time detective Dunn and reporter Trevor clash when they both work on the case of a gang of jewel thieves. Trevor witnesses a murder and is kidnapped by the gang, but the erstwhile detective saves the day. There was little new in the plot but the two worked with ease, making a sprightly couple and capturing exactly the right tone. One theater manager commented that Trevor "threw everything she had in this picture and was well-liked by the audience."[20] There was a particularly fun scene in which she poses as a fan dancer in a club which is raided by police. In the courtroom, Dunn spots her and asks her to do the fan dance, much to her embarrassment, but she is funny in all her attempts. The film was popular with the public. A theater manager in Lebanon, Kansas, declared it "the kind of show that sends them out smiling and not sorry they spent their all-too-scarce dimes for a show."[21] Another in Florida observed; "That Claire Trevor gal is becoming very popular, more so with each picture."[22]

Dunn and Trevor worked well together and while chatting on set one day realized that their paths had crossed a few times without them knowing. Trevor had been due to take a film test on the same day as Dunn but she had cancelled when she signed a theatrical contract that morning. Both New Yorkers, they were also "inveterate first-nighters" and had often attended the same shows.[23] "It's easy to do scenes with Claire," observed Dunn, "because you can't help believing what she's telling you and your response is spontaneous."[24]

Sol Wurtzel, the head of production of Fox's B unit, announced that he had "ambitious plans to promote the little unknown."[25] At the beginning of 1934, she had been declared one of the five debutantes at the studio (the others were Alice Faye, Pat Paterson, Drue Leyton and Rosemary Ayres).[26] At this stage of her career, she seemed to be on the rise and many new projects were lined up for her. Some never came to pass. She was listed as co-star with Victor Jory and Preston Foster or Spencer Tracy in *Woman and the Law,* which seems not to have been made.[27] *The First Baby* would have reunited her with James Dunn, but neither appeared in the film which was not made until 1936.[28] Trevor had appeared in the original stage play of *The Party's Over* (as the third lead) and she was briefly considered for a role in the big screen version.[29] There was the prospect of her appearing in an adaptation of Nathanael West's controversial novel *Miss Lonelyhearts,* but the eventual film *Advice to the Lovelorn,* with Sally Blane, was not the indictment of the newspaper world that West had delineated.[30] Trevor was to have starred with Alice Faye and John Boles in *Redheads on Parade* (1935), described as "a new kind of musical."[31] There was nothing especially new about it, and Dixie Lee had the

Claire was often credited with doing her own singing in films but with only a few exceptions she was dubbed. The real singers were not credited. Trevor's image adorned the cover of the sheet music for *Wild Gold* (1934), a forgettable B-movie about a modern-day search for gold in California's old mining boom towns.

lead female role. Nor did Claire feature in the all-singing all-dancing *Fox Movietone Follies of 1934*, which was later retitled *Stand Up and Cheer* (1934).[32]

Another project was *Lady Cop*, with Lew Ayres and eight-year-old Jane Withers.[33] The story by Judith Raven was bought as a vehicle for Trevor but it appears to have been abandoned altogether.[34] She was to have co-starred with Warner Baxter in *Maximilian and Carlota* with John Blystone as director.[35] A historical romantic tragedy would have been a welcome change for Trevor at this time and would have given her a chance to display her range. However, this version of the story of Mexico's ill-fated monarch and his wife was never realized. Both the Mexican film *Juarez and Maximilian* (1934) and Warner Brothers' *Juarez* (1939) went over some of the same ground but with a political rather than personal emphasis. Bette Davis played Carlota in *Juarez*.

The projects that came to fruition were a mixed bag. *Wild Gold* (1934) was inspired by the fact that gold had recently doubled in value when the value of most everything else declined. As a result, there was said to be a new gold rush to the old California mining towns that had seen most of the action in 1849. One such was Kernville, to which cast and crew decamped to film the location scenes. All the locals were eager to get involved as extras. John Boles played an unsuccessful drink-addicted engineer hopelessly in love with nightclub singer Trevor. As soon as gold is discovered, there's the expected mad rush to the towns, not to mention a traveling show led by Harry Green and his showgirls. The movie tried to resurrect the same sense of excitement as the old days but somehow it didn't seem the same in 1934. Not many struck it rich and in the end everything is washed away in a spectacular flood. Despite all the action, the result was rather lackluster and for many reasons did not engage audiences. Two songs were featured, "I've Got You at the Top of My List" and "Cute Little Rumba." The former, by Jay Gorney again, reportedly marked Claire's singing debut—not for the first or last time. She was featured prominently on the cover of the sheet music, reclining provocatively. The real singer was uncredited; it could have been Grace Saxon. Over the years, Trevor was often billed as the singer but with the exception of her unforgettable rendition of "Moanin' Low" in *Key Largo*, it is doubtful if she sang any of the songs credited to her. The half-spoken rendition of "Swing Low, Sweet Chariot" she sang to the dying sailor in *Navy Wife* could have been her. She often played nightclub singers, and although most of her songs were sung by others, the two songs in *King of Gamblers* (1937) were said to have been adapted to suit her range. There was also her memorably askew duet with Broderick Crawford, "You're My Ever Loving," in *Stop, You're Killing Me* (1952) which if it wasn't her was someone remarkably like her! It was curious that many of her obituary writers referred to her as a singer even though she once said that she was the world's worst.

A well-liked Shirley Temple vehicle, *Baby, Take a Bow* (1934) that teamed Trevor with Dunn again, this time as the poppet's parents. Eddie Ellison (Dunn) comes out of prison and vows to go straight after marrying his fiancée Kay (Trevor). Six years pass and his pal Larry (Ray Walker) comes out of jail, but is constantly thwarted in his attempts to find work by the intervention of a parole officer, Welch (Alan Dinehart). When a valuable necklace is stolen, Welch is determined to pin the blame on both men, but doesn't reckon on the interference of Eddie and Kay's little daughter Shirley (Temple). There were some charming moments between Trevor, Dunn and Temple but it was hard to engage with the enterprise, which seems trapped in its era. However it would undoubtedly appeal to fans

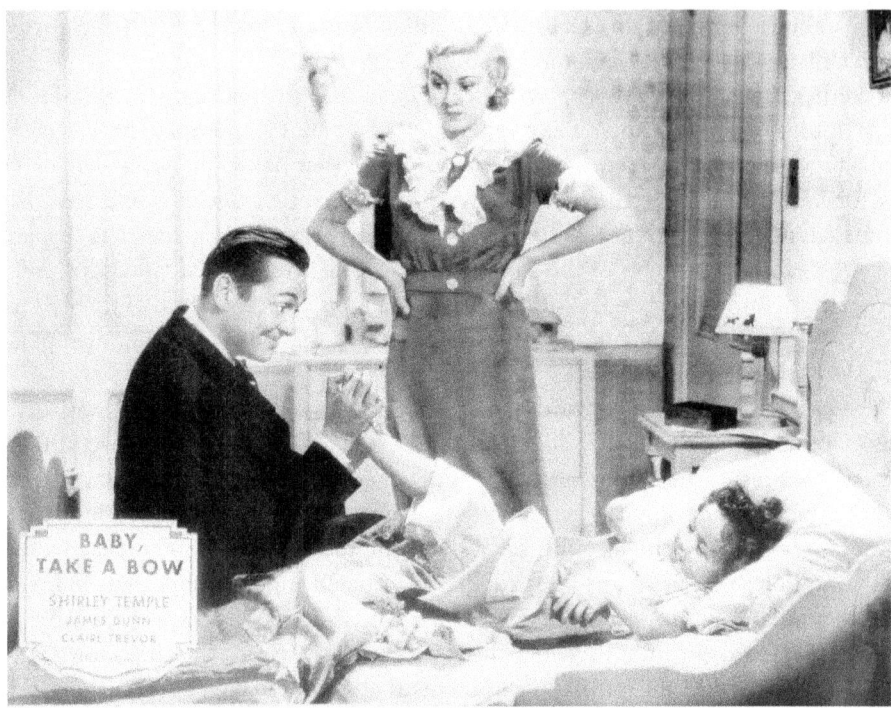

Baby, Take a Bow **(1934) marked the third and final time Trevor and James Dunn were teamed on screen. But this movie belonged to Shirley Temple (on the bed), a true phenomenon of the Depression years.**

of the child star. As usual, Temple took top billing in what was her tenth feature film that proved popular at the box office. She was a phenomenon and in essence represented Fox's answer to the Depression. For some reason the film was banned in Germany.[36]

Claire was again cast as Shirley's mother in *Bright Eyes*, but was pulled out of it and put into *Elinor Norton* instead.[37] It was a custom at Fox that if a formula proved in any way successful or popular, then it was immediately repeated—ad infinitum. This lack of imagination spoke of desperation to find a winning formula that precluded experiment in either casting or story. Hence, Claire was often teamed with the same actors and put in the same kind of situations as before. Having made such a striking impression as an ace reporter in her third film, Fox called upon her to repeat the role—with slight variations—time and again. This same want of vision dogged her throughout her career which followed a pattern: She made an impression, was thereafter always cast in the same kind of part, disappeared for a while, reappeared to effect in another kind of role, and was expected to repeat *that* role henceforward. Perhaps casting directors were to blame for being so eager to typecast everyone and put them neatly into pigeonholes.

The sheer volume of movies made was another factor. Films were churned out at a rate of knots and there was a lack of care and attention to many which were merely program fillers. Perhaps also her lack of acumen and ambition meant that her career moved forward in fits and starts. She initially had the studio boss at Fox on her side, and Sol Wurtzel too, but when Darryl Zanuck arrived, she had no real support there. Wurtzel tried to help but he had less sway and only ran the B-movie department. With imagination and a little support, she could have easily moved into A-pictures and been given more adventurous assignments. She was never given a role in a historical epic, or in any of the most prestigious films at Fox. Admittedly she was not suited to the big musicals of the day.

Trevor was kept so busy that several of the other projects announced for her fell by the wayside. She might have appeared yet again with Dunn in the auctioneering farce *What Am I Bid?* starring Will Rogers.[38] There was also the prospect of the lead in *Twenty Four Hours a Day*, slated to be directed by Irving Cummings, director of *The Mad Game*.[39] *The Dice Woman* with Victor Jory, based on a play by Wilson and Anzonetta Collison, appears to have been shelved.[40] *365 Nights in Hollywood*, taken from a novel by gossip columnist Jimmy Starr, was announced as a starring vehicle for Trevor, but was never made.[41] Trevor was first listed as the star of the screwball comedy *Highway Robbery* opposite Spencer Tracy. The film was retitled *It's a Small World*, and she was replaced by Wendy Barrie.[42]

Painted Lady was called an upcoming Trevor vehicle, constructed around her, but in the event the film was retitled *Wanted* and Rosemary Ames was handed the female lead.[43] Another was director George Marshall's comedy *She Learned About Sailors* (1934), but Alice Faye was cast in her place.[44] *Farewell to Fifth Avenue*, based on the autobiography of millionaire Cornelius Vanderbilt, Jr., was one of many projects abandoned when Darryl F. Zanuck became head of production in June 1935.[45]

Apparently almost every Fox contract actress tried for the lead role in *Elinor Norton* (1934), and "agents for freelance players buzzed for weeks around [Sol] Wurtzel's office."[46] It was reported that around 50 actresses had been tested, and Helen Twelvetrees was first announced for the part.[47] But Wurtzel decided to give the role to Trevor, who, he said, was "destined to be the next star on the Fox lot as a result."[48]

Upper class girl Elinor (Trevor) marries Tony Norton (Hugh Williams), who is prone to mood swings and is of a jealous nature. He goes to fight in France during the First World War and is injured, and also begins to drink. Elinor meets and falls in love with a Brazilian, Rene (Gilbert Roland). On his return from the war, Tony suspects her of having an affair with family friend Bill, but she confesses all about Rene. Tony threatens to shoot himself but she prevents him and they reconcile for a time. A doctor suggests that they should go away to the country and says that Tony needs to stop brooding. They go and live on a ranch but their

Trevor did well playing the coveted starring role in *Elinor Norton* (1934). But this rather turgid drama did not engage audiences greatly and failed to advance her career.

problems follow them there, and Tony again tries to shoot himself. As she grapples with him for the gun, she is accidentally wounded in the shoulder. It is clear that Elinor's future is with Rene and not Tony.

The film was loosely based on Mary Roberts Rinehart's novel *The State vs. Elinor Norton*, but was watered down from the original, which was considered racy in its time. The author wrote many mystery novels and has been dubbed the American Agatha Christie. The character of Tony was dour and complex, and the contrast between him and Rene was stark; the whole mood lightened when she was dancing with Rene. It seemed hard to believe that in real life there would have been any incentive for her to stay with Tony. At times the film seemed like a case study of psychology. The traumatic effect of war and its psychological impact was one of the underlying themes, but not one that was brought out. Tony goes to war for a number of reasons; one is to escape his unhappy marriage. He is suspicious by nature, and the war only exacerbates his psychological problems. The happy ending didn't match the tone of the rest of the screenplay. Trevor did remarkably well in the difficult central role and made Elinor a credible and empathetic character.

Wurtzel was so pleased with her performance that she was allowed to keep her entire wardrobe from the film.[49] However the public was not so impressed with the movie, which proved highly unpopular at the box office. Theater managers were not queuing up to show it: "One of the worst," declared one. "No entertainment to it. Failed to get by on 10 cent night."[50] Perhaps it was the absence of some of the more sensational aspects of the novel, or perhaps it was the heaviness of the story that marred its chances. A rather turgid feeling pervaded, but Trevor did remarkably well in a dramatic role of the kind she needed. Some reviewers recognized her worth, one commenting, "Her role is an exacting one and demands the display of emotion to a nicety. An excess or lack of it would make the film valueless, but Claire Trevor is equal to it, and the success of the film is hers in large measure."[51] Director Hamilton McFadden was under contract at Fox but he was not retained after Zanuck took over. Few of McFadden's pictures troubled the scorers, but he directed two of the Charlie Chan series and also appeared as an actor in small roles. Trevor's stand-in for the horse-riding scenes at the ranch was Ione Reed, a veteran rider and master horsewoman of the silver screen.[52]

Altogether more suitable for Trevor was *Black Sheep* (1935), an entertaining adventure set aboard a luxury liner. The urbane Edmund Lowe stars as Dugan, a professional gambler who discovers that fellow passenger Fred (Tom Brown) is in fact his son that he has not seen since his birth because the boy's mother's family did not approve of him (Dugan). Fred is being blackmailed by an adventuress with whom he is besotted. With Trevor's help, Dugan he plans to seek restitution from the woman and restore his son's reputation. Trevor breezed through the film with unconscious ease, her timing and delivery of lines now honed to perfection. Her scenes with the adventuress (Adrienne Ames) on the deck were a sheer joy. "How do you manage to snare so many millionaires?" she asks blithely. "Tell a dumb and struggling sister how you do it." She had such delicious fun with her lines and obviously realized the absurdity of the whole thing. Although the screenplay relied on a series of coincidences worthy of a Dickens novel, the amiability of the players ensured that the plot was immaterial to enjoyment of the film. In the supporting cast, the redoubtable Eugene Pallette with his distinctive frog-like voice added great value as a card sharp. This was the first of six movies that Trevor made for director Allan Dwan. Lowe and Trevor were lined up to appear again in *Kiss and Wake Up,* another Dwan project, but that too was dropped when Zanuck took over. Also shelved was the western adventure *Hawk of the Desert* with Warner Baxter.[53] Trevor was one of the first to be cast in directed Raoul Walsh's *Under Pressure* (1935), a story about the hazardous construction of an underwater tunnel. She was replaced by Florence Rice.[54]

Spring Tonic (1935), which had the working title *Man-Eating Tiger*, was based on a 1920s Broadway play by husband-and-wife team Ben Hecht and Rose Caylor. The flimsy premise involved Betty (Trevor) leaving her lackluster fiancé Caleb Enix (Lew Ayres) the day before the wedding because she is bored with him. A circus comes to town and a tiger escapes. After many shenanigans, Enix eventually helps to capture the tiger and then Betty begins to think he is exciting and wants to marry him after all.

Production did not go smoothly. The director first assigned, Melville Brown, withdrew after less than a week because "he was dissatisfied with the treatment of the story and felt some of the principal roles were miscast."[55] Composer-songwriter Jay Gorney contributed a song "Tonight There's a Spell on the Moon." Gorney was most famous for the Depression anthem "Brother, Can You Spare a Dime?" The cast members were not easily assured that the tiger was tame and harmless. When told that it was in fact toothless, Jack Haley quipped, "Toothless, yes, but can he gum you to death?"[56] Trevor played the familiar role of a independent-minded, bored debutante who craves excitement and the best parts were when

Black Sheep (1935) was a distinct improvement on some of Trevor's early films. She was in great form as a wisecracking actress who falls for the urbane Edmund Lowe, seen here lifting her over a partition after a night in First Class.

she took off with her maid (ZaSu Pitts) in the car. She brought her usual verve to the role, as did Pitts and other reliable players such as Haley and Marx Brothers stooge Sig Ruman. However the film was distinctly lacking as a whole. It's essentially a lesser screwball comedy; the humor of *Spring Tonic* and its ilk has not aged well. "The picture has every appearance of having been ad libbed while the director's back was turned," commented *Variety*, which lamented that it had "zero entertainment" and "no production values. ...Miss Trevor struggles bravely against great odds."[57]

"A new low, even for Fox," commented one disgruntled theater manager. "On the second night we grossed an even $1.50 and were glad to get it."[58]

4

B-Movie Queen

> I've grown to love my work. I want to stay in Hollywood in the profession I know I prefer. I like the people here, they're so stimulating. Kind also. The breadth of the country out here has won me. I stumbled into the work I'm cut out for instead of the social life I anticipated. It's so gratifying.—"A Lark That Lasted," *Modern Screen,* May 1937, 81

Trevor's first two years at Fox had seen her make some progress, but it was often a case of one step forward and two back. She had graduated to leading dramatic roles, albeit in B-movies. She had done her level best in *Elinor Norton,* but the film itself had seemed like a lost opportunity to establish herself in the kind of parts she had dreamed of at the beginning. She still craved the kind of dramatic roles Miriam Hopkins and Marlene Dietrich played. The films she made in the next two years were generally uninspiring and it was not until she made something happen herself that she was able to escape from her contract. The arrival of new production head Darryl F. Zanuck coincided with her being sidelined, as she saw it, in favor of those actresses he wanted to promote.

Off-screen, she continued to live with her mother in their old Spanish villa on a San Fernando Valley hillside. She preferred to put some distance between herself and the studios after spending hours each day there. Her mother appeared to relish the Hollywood life, but her father only ever visited her once in the mid–1930s, completely out of the blue; it seemed that he wondered what had become of his wife. Claire said the house was "big, gloomy, mustard-colored and leaked in five places."[1] Away from the hectic schedule at the studio, she tried to find time to relax and made the most of free weekends when she went sailing and liked to go antique-hunting. The house contained eighteenth-century furniture and tapestries, but she combined the old with the new by using modern fabrics. Her boudoir was done in the French Empire style, with "more mirrors than Mae West" and a bed that measured ten feet across.[2] She preferred a wide bed with no pillows, and her blankets were powder blue, her favorite color. She also preferred to wear pajamas.[3] Her unusual collection of perfumes included many rare and imported brands.[4] Her favorite scent was Caron's Sweet Pea, which she had problems finding.[5] She reportedly did fine French embroidery and could "whistle in two keys at once."[6] She once tried to cultivate orchids in a greenhouse, but none of the bulbs came up and she thought they must have been old. She abandoned the idea and her mother sold the greenhouse for $5.[7]

She had a number of collections at various times; since the 1920s, she had accumulated a large number of carved ivory figures of animals. In 1936, she shipped them all to Germany to exhibit at the renowned Leipzig Fair where she hoped to win a prize.[8] She collected handkerchiefs and was even persuaded to buy one made of lace and linen that was reputed to be over 700 years old.[9]

Her tastes were for fine foods such as venison or partridge with pate de foie gras, and she was fond of chicken livers en brochette.[10] Her Filipino cook Marcalo Canania was a magician in and out of the kitchen. Last thing at night, Trevor drank a half cup of pure honey.[11]

At first, she tended not to socialize with other stars. "About the only people I know well are the friends I've made on the sets," she said. "You meet many others at parties, but you know how it is—an introduction, and then you don't see the same people again for months. Everybody is busy working."[12] She did have a number of female friends including Sally Eilers, June Lang and Inez Courtney. At a party in San Diego, she went for a moonlight swim with a group of other actresses including the divine Simone Simon. She said she had no time for "phonies, snobs or all-round stupid people."[13] She was sociable but in some ways an outsider in Hollywood. She remained a wide-eyed movie fan, always keen to watch the latest film, and only too happy to attend premieres. She once tagged along with a newspaperman just to get an autographed photo of matinee idol Ramon Novarro.[14]

Whenever she had time off, she returned to New York, where she sometimes liked to live extravagantly, staying in expensive hotel suites. She liked to reside at the Sherry-Netherland Hotel on Fifth Avenue, in a suite on the twenty-ninth floor.[15] At other times, she stayed at the Waldorf.[16] During long vacations, she would take off to Mexico, Honolulu, Bermuda, Panama or Havana.

She was never short of dates but maintained that only one of the relationships in her early Hollywood days was in any way serious; she declined to say which one. During the summer of 1934, she was linked romantically with agent Vic Orsatti, but they had stopped seeing each other by the following February.[17] There were six Orsatti brothers and she was also friends with Vic's brother Ernie, a baseball player for the St. Louis Cardinals. She and Mrs. John Boles, another keen baseball fan, watched him play in several matches of the World Series that year (1934).[18] She said it was unlikely she would ever fall in love with her leading men, finding them far more vain than women as a rule, nor did she feel that acting was the right profession for a man. Of her male co-stars, she once commented, "The interesting ones are too old. The young ones are stupid."[19]

She was a regular in the Hollywood tennis crowd, and was considered a good enough player to have become a champion with enough practice, according to tennis pros.[20] She was an all-round sportswoman, particularly in the water, winning a number of medals for swimming and other prizes for water polo, high diving and underwater swimming.[21] Her piano was always perfectly tuned, and she sometimes entertained for a few close friends. One of her favorite memories was meeting the great Arthur Rubinstein at an intimate gathering at which she first tasted vodka.[22]

She admitted to a number of foibles and phobias. One report highlighted a fear of anything to do with aviation.[23] She also refused ever to throw anything, and if a script called for her to do so, she would refuse. This went back to the time she threw the American Academy of Dramatic Arts prospectus out of the window in annoyance at the taunts of a friend, and then could not locate it outside.[24] She hated the sound of bells; she had a telephone that made a musical chime, preferred a doorknocker to a bell, and could not countenance an alarm clock. Her fear of the sound was so pronounced that when she watched

An all-around sportswoman, Claire was especially fond of tennis and was a regular in the Hollywood tennis crowd.

the French version of *Crime and Punishment,* she had to leave the cinema when the murderer returned to the scene of the crime and rang a door gong.[25]

All things considered, she was happy with her lot. "I love life and every day I live it, I love it a little more," she declared. She was a grounded personality with a sense of humor and a sense of proportion, unaffected by fame and fortune. As she once observed; "I have enough to eat, a nice place to live, comfortable clothes, and a little money put away—why should I worry? Everything is comparative."[26]

Dante's Inferno (1935) was the first release by Twentieth Century–Fox, formed by the merger of the Fox Film Corporation and Twentieth Century Pictures. The film was a suitably ambitious attempt to create a modern version of Dante's fourteenth century masterwork. Jobless ex-stoker Jim Carter (Spencer Tracy) is invited to work for Pop McWade (Henry B. Walthall), who owns a small concession in a fairground containing art and artifacts depicting scenes from *Dante's Inferno*. Jim falls in love with Pop's niece Betty (Trevor), and they are married. He proves successful, making a going concern of the curious collection; he buys up other lots and in time owns the whole fairground complex. One of the concession sellers is aggrieved and on the grand opening night of Jim's big new attraction, Dante's Inferno, the man throws himself to his death in the grotto. Jim is undaunted and buys into other interests. There is a court case when Dante's Inferno collapses and Jim and Betty perjure themselves by claiming they were not forewarned that the construction was dangerous. They decide to split up and share custody of their son. Disaster strikes when there is a fire on Jim's ocean liner on its maiden voyage. Jim is attacked by the drunken crew, but manages to turn the ship around and return to safety.

Dante's Inferno certainly had its moments; it was different from the run of trite romantic comedies churned out by the studio. It was well acted by a fine cast, especially Tracy, Trevor and Walthall. A great deal of time and money went into the venture. The makers made a heroic attempt to capture the spirit of Dante and specifically to recreate the illus-

Director Harry Lachman's *Dante's Inferno* (1935) was an ambitious attempt to transpose Dante's classic to a twentieth century setting. Spencer Tracy and Trevor did well but the film was not a success. Scotty Beckett played their son.

trations of a number of artists including the muralist Willy Pogany. Director Harry Lachman was an artist who moved to France in 1911 and had great success as a post-impressionist painter; he was described as a "friend and contemporary of Picasso, Renoir, Matisse and Monet."[27] He was awarded the Cross of the Legion d'Honeur by the French government for his artistic achievements. He became a set designer and directed some films in France and England, including *Under the Greenwood Tree* (1929) and *The Outsider* (1931). He returned to the U.S. in 1933 and made a variety of films, notably the Laurel and Hardy comedy *Our Relations* (1936). He had also been at the helm for Trevor's *Baby, Take a Bow*. On *Dante's Inferno*, his visions sometimes overshot his budget. One scene, for instance, called for the use of $150,000 worth of jewelry which required the services of a police guard.[28] Due to its inflated budget, *Dante's Inferno* was given a bigger-than-usual publicity build-up, and the caption writers went into hyperbolic overdrive for the occasion: "Trapped in the Hell of modern life they fight AS YOU DO for the right to love!" screamed the posters. Rita Hayworth appeared in one scene as a dancer under her original name Rita Cansino.

Despite all their best efforts, *Dante's Inferno* was not well-received and lost a substantial amount of money. The special effects during the famous ten-minute "Hell" sequence were lauded and derided in equal measure. "We depart gratefully," wrote one critic, "having seen papier-mache photographed in more ways than we thought possible."[29] A more recent observer, John Baxter, called it "one of the most unusual and effective films of the '30s."[30] Trevor later remarked:

> They gave him [Lachman] a lot of time and a lot of money but it was not an A-picture. Harry Lachman was a dreamer, really a creator, an artist, but crazy, you know? The picture had no boundary, no spine, no foundation. It may have had an A-picture budget, but it was a B-movie script.[31]

When she took a vacation in Honolulu, the film cameras followed her. It appears that Sol Wurtzel "had a terrific yen for her" and persuaded studio bosses to make a film there purely because he knew it was a place she often visited.[32] Director Allan Dwan was assigned to the project, *Navy Wife* (1935), in which Trevor was to play the starring role—under certain conditions. Fox executives made it known that they were not happy with her efforts thus far. A studio official took her to one side to have a little talk. He spoke in a manner described as a "kindly but stern parent rebuking a spoilt child," telling her in no uncertain terms that she would have to mend her ways if she wanted to get ahead: "You are too careless ... inclined to be lazy: you are slipshod in your work.... You will have to improve your diction—it is too sloppy. You'll have to take the slouch out of your walk and acquire some poise." He continued to tell her where she was falling down, encouraged her to read good books, be more discriminating in her dress, and to cultivate charm. He criticized her mannerisms and lack of grace. After hearing all this, she remarked brightly, "Apart from those few faults and 20 or 30 other things, I seemed to be quite all right."[33] Although she took some of his observations to heart, it is hard to imagine that she was ever lacking in charm, poise or dress sense. With the aid of voice coach Nina Moise, she "lowered the pitch of [her] voice and removed the hint of nasal twang that the loudspeakers revealed."[34] Her voice was full of character, and one of her greatest assets, so the vocal coach cannot have done too much harm.

Navy Wife was loosely based on the best-selling novel *Beauty's Daughter* by Kathleen Norris. Trevor played a nurse in a naval hospital in San Diego who falls in love with a doctor (Ralph Bellamy). She accepts his proposal of marriage but is hurt by his apparently undimmed love for his first wife. She goes away for many months to seek a cure for his crippled daughter, and on their return she believes he has found someone else. The "other woman" turns out to be a spy, but all ends happily enough once everything is explained. The screenplay made detrimental changes to the novel, and particularly to Bellamy's character to make him more sympathetic. In the original novel, he was a far less cut-and-dried "good guy." But whatever changes were made, the film was poor in execution and noticeably a B-movie, if not a C. It was difficult to get involved in the story, and the film had a disjointed feel to it. For instance, the scenes of horseplay among the three sailors coming to port riding on motorbikes looked like an outtake from a Keystone Cops routine and jarred with the somber death scene of a young seaman during which Claire sang a snatch of "Swing Low, Sweet Chariot."

It was reported that filming partially took place in Hawaii. There was a surfeit of rear projection and an overriding impression of cheapness—it was no surprise to learn that Fox was practically bankrupt by the time it was made, and soon to be swallowed up by Twentieth Century. In the supporting cast, Jane Darwell provided good value as always. The script was weak, and although Claire emoted well, she seemed more remote than usual. She was playing a character who was required to live inside herself to a great extent, and the script gave her virtually nothing to work with. Actually she was looking forward to a break in New York and hoping to catch several shows, but was ordered to Honolulu instead by her studio to make the film. While there, she picked up an infection and soon began to suffer from tonsillitis. She had to undergo a tonsillectomy, and it took her a while to recover. It could have been a strong emotional role for her if it had been better conceived and executed, and as such represented another lost opportunity.

Marginally better was *My Marriage* (1936). It's set in the world of high society, which Carol Barton (Trevor) entered when she married John De Witt Tyler III (Kent Taylor). After Carol's late father is revealed as a gangster, her mother-in-law Mrs. De Witt Tyler II (Pauline Frederick) makes things almost impossible for her. While pretending to be on her side, she uses her influence to ensure that her son cannot get work, and is determined to get rid of Carol whatever the cost. Tyler's brother confesses the truth about her father's death and a family friend straightens everything out, including Mrs. De Witt Tyler II, who is contrite in her apologies. It was a sometimes overwrought drama, with veteran stage actress Frederick a standout as the mother-in-law from Hell. The director was French émigré George Archainbaud whose long Hollywood career stretched back to 1916 and who was mostly remembered for westerns. The screenplay was based on a short story by I.A.R. Wylie which had appeared in *Good Housekeeping* three years earlier, and both provided an occasionally pointed satire of the upper echelons of the Long Island social set. As the most admirable character in the piece, Trevor held the attention as always. She was sick during production, her temperature rising to 104.[35] She was suffering from pneumonia, according to one report, which also let it be known that her week away from the set while ill cost the studio about $19,000.[36]

She was announced as co-star with Paul Kelly in *The Black Gang*, described as a dramatic story about a ship's stoker.[37] The film was later retitled *Here Comes Trouble* (1936) and the female lead went to Arline Judge. Trevor's next was opposite Kelly in *Song and Dance Man* (1936), George M. Cohan's popular and oft-repeated tale of Hap Farrell (Kelly), a "ham-and-eggs hoofer" who thinks he is another Fred Astaire, but who is in reality holding back his talented young vaudeville partner Julia Carroll (Trevor). A drunkard and gambler, he loses everything they earn. When she tries to sell a gun to buy bread, she is spotted by a big producer (Michael Whalen) who, naturally enough, falls for her and gives her a shot at the big time. Realizing that he is standing in her way, Hap feigns drunkenness one night in order to break up the act. Originally planned as an A-movie starring Alice Faye and James Dunn, the project stalled when Dunn backed out and asked to be released from his contract.[38] It was handed to Wurtzel, and from then on was strictly a B-feature. A number of songs were featured including "Join the Party," "On a Holiday in My Playpen" and "Let's Get Goin' Baby." The backstage insights were especially good, and redoubtable scene-stealers Ruth Donnelly and James Burke were in top form. Although the tale seemed over-familiar, the players held the interest. Few contemporary critics thought much of it, but Trevor came in for what praise there was, one commenting, "The poise, charm and sincerity of Claire Trevor, her mellow voice and grave beauty give to *Song and Dance Man* what distinction it possessed."[39]

During filming, a fire started as the result of an electrical short circuit. The blaze was soon brought under control by extinguishers but the set Trevor and Kelly were working on was completely destroyed, which meant that another had to be hastily constructed.[40] Trevor learned a new dance routine for the production under the tutelage of Klayton Kirby, who said he had never encountered a woman with such inherent dancing ability. "In three days she learned a complicated dance that would try the efforts of professionals who have been

The sentimental melodrama *Song and Dance Man* (1936) was convincingly played by a capable cast. This publicity shot features Paul Kelly (left to right), Trevor and Michael Whalen.

dancing for years," he said. "She not only learned the steps, but performed with a grace that made her dancing a beautiful thing. She has a natural sense of grace and rhythm that instantly gives her the ability that others must acquire in long hours of practice."[41] The new dance, a cross between the tango and the rhumba, was known as a tarumba. Claire thoroughly enjoyed the experience. She was already a big fan of the rhumba and even put in a standing order for all new rhumba records at a local shop.[42]

Trevor appeared as yet another reporter in *Human Cargo* (1936), this time a debutante desperate for some excitement. She finds it after teaming with rival reporter Packy Campbell (Brian Donlevy) to investigate a gang of people smugglers. They make their way aboard one of the boats from Canada and although they are discovered, they manage to get the story out and expose the gang. An improvement over some of the previous Fox offerings, it was enlivened by quick-fire banter between the two leads, and a swifter execution. It was based on the novel *I Will Be Faithful* by Kathleen Shepard, a little-known writer who enjoyed brief fame in the 1930s as the author of several racy tales of life among the social elite.

One day on set, the actors were compelled to work virtually the entire day surrounded by man-made fog. Claire asked Donlevy why he was chewing gum; "It takes away the taste of the fog," he replied. This gave her an idea and she arranged with a technician, Lou Witte, to vaporize peppermint oil in with the mineral oil which was used to generate the fog, thereby creating pleasant peppermint fog.[43]

Towards the end of filming, Claire fell ill, which meant that work had to be postponed

Trevor and co-star Brian Donlevy have a go with a Ouija board during the making of *Human Cargo* (1936).

Trevor played a subsidiary part in *To Mary—with Love* (1936) but she impressed in a fine cast. This was one of the few films in which she felt satisfied with her performance. Left to right: Warner Baxter, Trevor, Ian Hunter and Myrna Loy.

for a week, costing the studio $10,000 for the electricians and prop men to reconstruct the set.[44] She was so taken with the clothes she wore in *Human Cargo* that she persuaded the costumier William Lambert to design new dresses and suits for her in an "ultra-feminine" style.[45] After this film, Trevor and Donlevy were suddenly noticed by Zanuck and were promised the starring roles in a big new feature, but this never transpired.[46] Both had become disillusioned at Fox. Donlevy asked for his release in 1937 and Trevor the following year. *Human Cargo* did attract the attention of Gaumont-British, who were impressed by her performance and sounded her out with a number of offers which she apparently did not take up.[47]

To Mary—with Love (1936) was at least an A-picture, headed by a top cast: Myrna Loy, Warner Baxter and Ian Hunter. This told the story of the first ten years of a couple's (Baxter and Loy) marriage, beginning in 1925, following all their personal problems and along the way encapsulating some of the big events of the time. Hunter played to perfection the thankless role of the loyal best friend and Trevor was once again the "other woman" who causes several of the upsets in the marriage. The movie began brightly and looked initially like another featherweight romantic comedy of the kind with which Loy in particular was long associated. However, the screenplay took a different approach thereafter and was actually a good commentary on the whole period it delineated. After all, the postwar boom of the 1920s and the 1929 stock market crash was very recent history in 1936, in a world which had only just begun to recover. At one stage, a graph starkly showed that the low of '29 was followed by much further lows well into the early 1930s, despite all the politicians' optimistic talk. Jack (Baxter) leaves his job as an architect to become a promoter and, like millions of others, believes that he can get rich quick and that the boom will never end. After the crash, he loses his job and it takes him a long time to get back on track, which adds to their personal difficulties. The recurring use of the song "The Best Things in Life Are Free" was a piquant and sometimes poignant comment on the story. Trevor was natural and assured in her scenes, especially at the wedding where it is immediately established that she has eyes for Jack and will cause problems in his marriage. She was sassy and knowing, delivering her lines with wit in that sultry, irresistible voice. She was not seen as much in the latter half and only reappeared near the end, but the scenes at the Dempsey fight and on the train ought to have caught a talent-spotter's eye if they were not already well aware of it by now.

A visitor to the studio during rehearsals observed the four leads at work and gave an insight into the seemingly blasé but insecure young actress: "Claire Trevor reminds me of Miriam Hopkins somehow," she noted. "And then again, there is a bit of a [Constance] Bennett about her. She's very pretty and was very scared. You could almost hear her thinking 'I won't be scared, I won't be scared.' She looked awfully nice in a Redingole affair."[48] Trevor's obvious jitteriness was a complete contrast to her nonchalant on-screen appearance. She

A likable drama well-played by a good cast, *Star for a Night* (1936) featured Trevor as a nightclub singer-dancer. Front, left to right: Susan Fleming, Lynn Bari, Trevor, Joyce Compton and Chick Chandler.

Clockwise from bottom left in this shot from *Star for a Night* (1936): Evelyn Venable, Dean Jagger, Jane Darwell, Trevor, Arline Judge and J. Edward Bomberg.

once commented that the film was one of the few in which she actually felt satisfied with her work.[49]

Star for a Night (1936), originally called *The Holy Lie*, starred Jane Darwell as Frau Martha Lind, a blind woman living in Austria. She believes that her three grown children in New York are all doing well in their careers; in reality, Nina (Trevor) is only a chorus girl, Fritz (Dean Jagger) is a cab driver, and Anna (Evelyn Venable) is a song-plugger for a record store. Martha arrives in America and her children concoct various ploys to keep up the pretense of their success. Nina is given a spot in a hit show. However, after an operation to restore Frau Martha's sight is a success, the truth is soon apparent to her, and all's well that ends well; she is happy no matter what they are doing.

It may sound corny, but the actors made it humorous, believable and sometimes moving. The backstage scenes between all showgirls were well-realized, and the part where Trevor breaks down during a big number was effective, especially because of the bickering that ensues between the other girls wanting to take her place. Songs including "Over a Cup of Coffee" and "Down around Malibu Way." Some of the numbers were recycled from *Song and Dance Man*, including "You're My Favorite One." The real singer was, as usual, unbilled. Singers at that time were hired on a contract basis by the studios.[50]

An adventure about jewel thieves, *15 Maiden Lane* (1936) was based in the famous district that had been the center of the New York jewelry business since the mid–nineteenth century.

15 Maiden Lane (1936), a fast-moving, unpretentious yarn about jewel thieves, starred Claire as an undercover insurance agent, seen here with police captain Lloyd Nolan.

Constance Bennett was initially cast in the leading role, but she was switched to *Ladies in Love* and Trevor replaced her here.[51] She played an insurance investigator (working for her uncle), who poses as a buyer from San Francisco. Using her feminine wiles, she inveigles her way into the gang of Frank Peyton (Cesar Romero). When her identity is discovered, she is in great danger, but she manages to escape and expose the gang and is awarded a captain's badge from Police Chief Walsh (Lloyd Nolan). The breezy if formulaic tale was well-acted by the principal players and held attention despite the familiarity of the situation. Director Allan Dwan was dissatisfied with the way paste jewels looked under the lights and so the emerald seen in the heist was a real one borrowed for the occasion. Worth $100,000, it was accompanied on its journey to and from the studio by a police escort. When time came for the emerald to be returned to the jewelers, it was nowhere to be found. Panic ensued for a while, with no one allowed to leave the lot, until it was discovered that Nolan still had it in his pocket.[52] The film was shot on location in New York. Trevor looked right at home in the uptown setting, lounging in satin gowns, while Romero made a suitably charming villain with his suave manner and silk hats. One night Trevor went to watch Tallulah Bankhead in *Reflected Glory* on Broadway wearing an evening gown borrowed from the wardrobe department.[53]

Trevor hardly gave *15 Maiden Lane* a second thought once it was finished, but many years later she was at a party and met the broadcaster Alistair Cooke, whose *Letter from*

America was one of the longest-running and most highly regarded programs on British radio. Cooke told her that *15 Maiden Lane* was one of his favorite films. "I was amazed," she remarked.⁵⁴

Better than many of her other Fox films was *Career Woman* (1936), in which she starred opposite Michael Whalen for the second time. They made a bright pair, she as the earnest student lawyer, he as the cynical city man with a bag of courtroom tricks for every case. Gracie (Isabel Jewell) inadvertently causes the death of her tyrannical father and is accused of murder. She is reluctantly defended in her home town by Carol Aiken (Trevor), who struggles against the bigotry of the small town until Barry Conant (Whalen) comes to her rescue. Apparently based on a real-life case, the film had moments of genuine power, such as when Conant railed against the townsfolks' narrow-mindedness, and when Carol made an emotionally charged but heartfelt case for reason to prevail. Trevor made effective use of her voice. The small town was usually held up in film as a paragon of virtue, the repository of all the good and decent values of a humane society and the bedrock of American life. Here was a glimpse of the other side of the coin; here the small town was a place of fear, moralizing, religious intolerance and a stifling lack of career choice. The opening scenes were slow, but the movie picked up pace when the action moved to Clarkstown. Trevor was noticeable in a good cast. She was equally adept in the scenes of light banter as she was in the wholly dramatic scenes, and her final summation to the jury was moving in its sincerity.

Career Woman (1936) provided Claire with a good dramatic role as a lawyer defending a girl accused of murdering her father. Left to right: Gene Lockhart, Trevor, Edward Brophy.

The dramatic high of *Career Woman* was followed by lightweight comedy in *Time Out for Romance* (1937), in which she was once again teamed to good effect with Whalen. This had a typically silly 1930s plot but was nicely played by all concerned and enhanced by the efforts of the supporting cast including the ever-reliable William Demarest. At her wedding rehearsal, society belle Barbara Blanchard (Trevor) discovers that she has been tricked into her forthcoming marriage by her scheming mother for money. She dyes her hair blonde and goes on the run, joining a caravan of car testers on their way to California. She meets and naturally falls for Bob Reynolds (Whalen), hiding out in his car until her presence is revealed. This jeopardizes his chances of getting paid on reaching their destination, because they are not allowed to carry passengers. There is a wanted man with the caravan; Barbara and Bob help expose him and all ends happily. The film was pleasant enough with some fine moments if one could get past the ridiculous plot. Whalen possessed a charming personality with a distinct lightness of touch, but could also be dramatic when the occasion demanded. But he was cast in B films for most of his career.

One cannot help but think that Trevor was wasted in such fare and that by now she was champing at the bit to escape her Fox contract. "I'd be willing to play a bit, just a bit, in a big picture, to show I can act," she commented around this time, but no one appeared to be listening and she was stuck in yet more Bs.[55] Incidentally, her stunt double on the film was Bob Rose, who did "four car skids in one for $100." Rose was a movie veteran who had stood in for other women on occasion, even doubling for Pearl White in silent days.[56] It was also reported that Trevor refused to accept a stand-in for the scene in which she drove a car into Malibu Lake.[57]

Trevor was next loaned out to Paramount for *King of Gamblers* (1937), which starred Akim Tamiroff as a gang boss with control of a crooked slot machine racket. In love with showgirl Dixie (Trevor), he sets her up in a luxurious apartment and showers her with gifts, but she does not know about the source of his income. Ace reporter Jim Adams (Lloyd Nolan), trying to break the racketeers, enlists the help of Dixie, who falls in love with him.

Time Out for Romance (1936) was a typical product of the Fox B-movie unit. By this time, Claire was fed up with being told how necessary B-movies were for the studio economic health. "I know all about why they are necessary," she remarked, "I just don't want to be in them!"

This was a vast improvement on some of the fare Trevor had been given by Fox. The film was lifted from the commonplace by its breezy cynical tone, excellent cinematography and its fine cast. An underrated actor, Nolan could play good and bad with equal conviction. Tamiroff was excellent in every role, but after appearing in *King of Gamblers* said he was sick and tired of playing the bad guy. "For 18 years I was a comedian. Now they want me to be a villain. I don't want to be hissed," he explained.[58] The slot machines seen in the film were borrowed from the Los Angeles Sheriff's Office as props. The cast tried their luck on them, and true to form each in turn lost their money on the crooked 25-cent machines.[59]

To save time and money on studio rehearsals, a three-way telephone hook-up between the principals was arranged one night between eight and ten o'clock during which each sat by their phones and did their lines.[60] Notable was the distinctly European expressionist influence of German-born art director Hans Dreier. who set the tone for much of the look of Paramount's films of the time. Director Robert Florey made a number of influential B-movies in a similar vein to *King of Gamblers,* and also some other interesting films such as the horror flick *The Beast with Five Fingers* (1946) and underrated noirs like *The Crooked Way* (1949).

Trevor essentially played a prototype femme fatale. Although she is on the side of the law, she proves at least unwittingly lethal to Tamiroff. After accepting his bounty, she not only betrays him but falls in love with the man who seeks to bring him to justice. No wonder he ends up by vowing to be avenged.

Trevor was required to sing two songs in the film, "I Hate to Talk About Myself," written by Richard Whiting and Leo Robin, and "Feelin' High" by Burton Lane and Ralph Freed. It was stated in the press that this would mark her singing debut on screen, and that the songs had been especially adapted to suit her range.[61]

Back at Fox she was cast in the timid melodrama *One Mile from Heaven* (1937). This concerned the maternity of a white child (Joan Carol) of a colored mother (Fredi Wash-

On loan to Paramount, Trevor made *King of Gamblers* (1937), playing a nightclub singer set up in a swanky apartment by gang boss Akim Tamiroff (standing). The film was much better quality than she was used to at her home studio and displayed a distinct German Expressionist quality that later came to play in what became known as film noir.

ington). Trevor starred as Tex, a reporter desperate for a story. She discovers the child by chance when she is sent on a fool's errand by rival newspapermen. The girl is surrounded by love and looked out for by "Uncle" Bill (Bill Robinson), a local policeman. Even so, Tex is determined to uncover the child's true parentage and in the process make a name for herself as an ace reporter. In time she finds out that the real mother is a white woman who believed her child had died in an accident. The story was based on a true case which Judge Benjamin B. Lindsey heard in Denver, Colorado, while working in a juvenile court.[62] He told the story at a party, and the news filtered back to Sol Wurtzel who asked Lindsey to write it down and then bought the manuscript from him. This manuscript was embellished by Robbin Harris and Alfred Gold.[63]

As in the actual case, the screenplay's solution to the conundrum of two mothers was to let both be involved in the child's upbringing, but the colored mother could only be the child's nurse. One cannot help but think that mother and child were doing quite all right until the nosey reporter appeared on the scene. In her debut, Joan Carol made a delightfully unaffected child, and Fredi Washington was touching as the mother. Washington, a pioneering African-American actress with fair skin and green eyes, made a distinct impression in the 1934 *Imitation of Life*. She preferred stage work and *One Mile from Heaven* marked her final film appearance. The movie's real saving grace was the tap dancing of Bill Robinson, who brought a welcome spark to the proceedings.

Trevor's studio next assigned her to *The Great Diamond Robbery*, but illness prevented her from starting the film and she was replaced by Phyllis Brooks.[64] The same illness cost her the lead in *Dangerously Yours* (1937) with Cesar Romero, which also devolved to Brooks.[65] Claire was due to co-star with Ralph Bellamy again in *With Kindest Regards*, but her role was given to Betty Furness and the 1937 film was retitled *It Can't Last Forever*.[66] She was also one of a number considered for the lead in *Marry the Girl*, which eventually went to Barbara Stanwyck.[67] Nor did Trevor appear in *Wake Up and Live* which starred Alice Faye instead.[68]

Claire had a dedicated fan following characterized by their "tone of fantastic loyalty."[69] With increased fame came unwanted attention from some of her more eccentric admirers. A private detective was so impressed by her cinematic ability as a reporter that he "offered her a lifelong partnership in marriage—plus—crime detection." He made the same proposal upon the release of every new Trevor film.[70] Less humorous was the man who managed to slip past studio security and "concealed himself in her dressing room for a day and a night claiming to have lost a wallet containing $30 in her room and asking her to return the money." He kept harassing her, sending her letters, and the postal authorities were asked to investigate him.[71] Another time there was a man in New York who went around claiming to be her brother.[72] She once made the mistake of announcing in the press that she was on the lookout for a husband. Unsurprisingly, she was besieged by offers from all over the country when too many lonely men took her literally.

5

Sophisticated Lady

> She needs, you sense, no cosmetic veneer of manner or mystery to spin enchantment.—Louis Reid, "A Really Good Bad Girl," *Screenland*, June 1950, 45

Claire believed she was getting nowhere fast during her five years at Fox, grinding out one B-picture after another. But her name had become known in a fairly short period, and she was one of the most popular young actresses of the time—her mailbag was always full. In addition, she had become something of a trendsetter during the 1930s, a decade when high style was within reach of millions of ordinary young women. These women, like the screen characters Trevor often played, were independent and career-minded but still romantic.

Winnie Sheehan, Fox's head of production when Trevor began at the studio, noted that she "personifies the self-reliant modern girl," and this set the tone for her roles and seemed to jive with the perception of her off-screen persona.[1] The studios were essentially selling a lifestyle, a concept then in its infancy. The mass appeal of movies brought awareness of fashion and image to a huge audience in a way that had been unknown just a few years earlier.

She acknowledged that she was well-paid, earning far more than she could in any other profession. Her earnings for 1937–38 were reportedly $27,655, which was actually substantially lower than many. She was well behind such established stars as Madeleine Carroll ($288,000), Marlene Dietrich ($200,000), Shirley Temple ($121,000), and even Shirley Temple's mother ($68,000).[2] However, her salary compared favorably with other actresses of similar age. And it was supplemented by income from advertising. Over the years, she hawked everything from Max Factor Super-Indelible Lipstick to Royal Crown Cola; Ry-Krisp Cereal to Lux Soap; and Woodbury Beauty Night Cap cold cream to Serval Gas Refrigerators. She even sold Rheingold beer and cigarettes. For most of the Depression years, she was supporting both of her parents.

To put it all in perspective: At that time, the average annual salary for a single woman was about $525. There was a big gender pay gap; a man was typically earning $1027.[3] However, many women chose to marry later, or not to marry at all, relishing their independence and ability to control their own finances. In the decades following the First World War and universal suffrage, there was a spirit abroad that inspired women with a newfound confidence. Some of the greatest icons of the age were women who rivaled and surpassed men in their endeavors in such previously male-dominated areas as aviation, particularly Amelia Earhart and Amy Johnson.

Claire said she wanted to marry in time, but was not in any rush: "I still want to make enough money first to be independent," she maintained. "I've earned my own money for too many years now ... to ever be content to ask a man for money every time I wanted a new hat."[4]

Unlike the more remote icons of the era (Garbo, Dietrich and Hepburn), Trevor had a warmth and naturalness that made her seem real to audiences. Although her natural look appeared effortless, she worked hard to maintain it. She was usually referred to as a natural blonde, but once revealed that her real hair color was mousy, and admitted that she had been bleaching it since she was 18.[5] As a child she had been blonde but it had darkened as she got older.[6] Within a short time of her arrival in Hollywood, she was known as a beauty and her advice was considered worth following. In the 1930s, image became almost everything. This was the zenith of the highly stylized Art Deco movement which influenced the design of everything from clocks to cinemas to ocean liners. Everything had a streamlined, geometric look which reflected the overriding faith of the age in industrial and technological advance. The whole ethos of this era was summed up neatly by the refrain of the song "Keep Young and Beautiful If You Want to Be Loved." In tune with many, Claire espoused the importance of regular morning exercise and the ability to relax thoroughly. Apart from tennis, she played golf and was an expert sailor, ice skater, swimmer, surfer and aquaplaner. She enjoyed walking and sometimes went fishing.[7] She adored dancing most of all. (After dancing, she would rub her feet in witch hazel.) She always drank eight to ten glasses of water a day, and took a bath each day, reflecting her motto "water within and without."[8]

Glamour publicity still, circa 1938.

Former Ziegfeld Girl Gladys Glad (wife of writer Mark Hellinger) wrote a syndicated newspaper beauty column in which she often mentioned Trevor. She revealed some of the young actress' secrets, such as which creams she used and tips on how to care for the hair and nails. Claire once said that she favored long nails but because she was so keen on tennis and played the piano regularly, she could not have them long herself. She preferred red or dark shades for painted nails, although observed that this was frowned upon when she was playing in stock, as only suitable if playing a fast woman.[9] Once a week she put on an egg-white facial which she said "closes the pores and stimulates the circulation." She also contributed her own fashion and beauty articles to papers and film magazines. When filming for long hours under the arc lights, maintaining that naturalness was a feat in itself. She reckoned that she had only a short time to impress on screen, so when making a film she would be single-minded and put everything into it, going to bed early, avoiding dinner dates and not entertaining friends. She was determined to look and act her best: "In 40 minutes I must make an impression that will last for weeks until my next picture comes along," she said.[10]

In common with other actresses, her costume in each of her films was featured in the pages of *Photoplay*. She was said to be one of the first in Hollywood to favor the "be tailored before noon" idea.[11] Whether modeling the autumnal shades of "dark green wool with green-brown and beige plaid" from *The Last Trail*, or an "aqua blue summer silk frock ... with white mousseline de soie frills at the collar and sleeves" in *Wild Gold*, her latest was always eagerly awaited.[12] Most of these outfits were designed by Louis Royer, the resident Fox costumier, but she was seen in other creations by the B-movie designers Herschel McCoy, Helen Myron and the Russian stylist Rega. Her "smart swagger tweed coat with the Johnny collar and ... merry widow hat" which she wore in *Hold That Girl* was deemed ideal for the independent girl about to go on a motorboat ride.[13] She loved the "feminine, sporty and dashing" Royer designs for that film so much that the studio made her a present of them.[14] She often modeled swimwear by the leading Fox designers, such as a white satin number with a haltered neck. "Swimming is swifter in satin," she noted.[15] She took her morning dip in the Pacific at Malibu Beach all year round, with the exception of January when it was too cold. An exact replica of her sportswear costume in *The Mad Game* was made available in stores of the Dayton Company of Minneapolis, as were many of her other costumes. She had been used to modeling since her earliest days but hated the chores of a Hollywood actress' life, particularly when she had to spend hours in a hot photo studio posing for Christmas and holiday promotional handouts. Her personality came across strongly on screen but the stills seldom captured her, and in some she was hard to distinguish from other actresses. These stills were too posed and with their false backgrounds appeared too contrived.

She liked to dress well for dancing—her favorite pastime over many years. An observer vividly described a typical ensemble: "Claire Trevor's latest dance frock has the new 'waltz' length, reaching just above the ankles. Made of 'sweet pea' rose tulle, it features a voluminous skirt topped by a bodice with loose taffeta ribbon in shades of Chartreuse, deep rose, white and mauve. To match those shades she wears a bouquet of sweet peas in her hair."[16] Another noted her outfit at the Coconut Grove where she wore a "dress of soft gold lame tissue with a low cut décolletage and the narrowest of straps," the ensemble completed by scarlet slippers.[17] When doing her daily dancing exercises, she preferred a suit of raw silk crepe.[18] Although not a trained dancer, she was considered one of the ten best in Hollywood by Cesar Romero, who was a good man to judge because he had begun his career as a professional dancer.[19]

In such a stylish era, women looked to Hollywood for inspiration. Despite the Depression, or perhaps because of it, ordinary women dressed well, or at least tried to. Even young women of limited means made an effort, and most were handy with a sewing machine. Many endured privations but maintained their self-respect and kept up appearances.

Trevor's dress sense reflected her personality, nothing too exotic, but a discerning ability to use color combined with her own unique style and attention to detail. In an article about fashion that she contributed to a movie magazine, she noted that she "prefers wearable, tailored things," and admitted that she "splurges on perfume depending on the mood of the moment."[20] She was not a slave to fashion but had a timeless elegance that was neatly summarized as sophisticated simplicity. A reporter once asked her if she dressed for women or men; "I dress for both," she laughed. "When I'm going to a luncheon I definitely dress for the women who are going to be there. But when it is an evening party the last thing I think about is impressing a woman."[21]

She was undoubtedly noticed and had a large following of both sexes. In February 1935, *Screenland* voted an image of her in a bucolic setting from *Elinor Norton* as the "Most Beautiful Still of the Month," calling her the "original Stetson girl."[22] Fashion diarists of the day noticed what she was wearing when she was seen out; "Wheels within wheels, in antique silver, button the princess frock which Claire Trevor wore to dinner at the Trocadero recently," wrote one.[23] One commented on her "gown studded with tiny white stones like star-shine on snow."[24] She even managed to look chic when playing tennis in a "red and white polka dotted playsuit."[25] Another outfit in green and white linen with a playful red stripe on the belt was deemed ideal "for a round of tennis or an afternoon of loafing."[26] Once she wore a gypsy frock "of white brizette crepe" which was described as a "provocative blend of the hoyden and the lady."[27] She preferred playful feminine fashion and eschewed slacks; "According to my experience, diaphanous and clinging frocks make even businesslike businessmen react pleasantly," she avowed.[28]

She was featured regularly on the highly collectable cigarette and bubble gum cards of the time for most of the big names including Gallaher, Godfrey Phillips, Greiling, Abdulla, Carreras, the B.A.T. "Modern Beauties" series and an impressive embossed range for Aurelia and Garbaty. In common with most of her contemporaries, she smoked for most of her adult life. Smoking was a major industry for much of the twentieth century and was often glamourized on film. Claire was once depicted in a famous painting with cigarette in hand, and also advertised them like many others. The cigarette cards that came free in packets were much sought-after, even by non-smokers and children who used to swap them. These were manufactured from the 1870s onwards and only disappeared entirely by the 1950s. Among the sets of sports legends and prominent people featured, Hollywood stars were some of the most popular in the U.S., Britain and much of Europe.

Like many of her contemporaries, Claire was often featured on cigarette cards. Here is an impressive embossed example by the Aurelia Company of Dresden, circa 1936.

Claire also appeared as a popular paper doll, and endorsed a range of sewing patterns which were produced by the Hollywood Pattern Company based in Greenwich, Connecticut. She was also featured on a series of charity fund-raising stamps for her studio. She supported the California Fruit Growers Exchange by promoting Sunkist lemons both as fruits and to use as a shampoo rinse.

Inventive designers such as the prolific Milo Anderson, famous for his *Mildred Pierce* creations, came up with some ingenious ideas for costumes. For instance, although *Valley of the Giants* was a rugged adventure set among the California redwood trees, he still managed to dress Claire in a green satin number trimmed in marabou adorned with 28 spiders of varying sizes made of green rhinestones and gold.[29]

She was an admirer of the work of Elsa Schiaparelli, a leading personality of the time. Schiaparelli was once described by her archrival Coco Chanel as "that Italian artist who makes clothes."[30] Schiaparelli's most famous creations were directly inspired by the surrealist movement, notably the tear dress, the shoe hat and lobster dress designed in collaboration with Salvador Dalí. She co-designed with other artists including Jean Cocteau. She eventually made her way to Hollywood and worked on several films including *Moulin Rouge* (1952). Claire seldom modeled her creations; "I'm afraid I'm just not the exotic type," she said wistfully.[31]

Claire endorsed a range of sewing patterns in the 1940s when many women made their own clothes.

Over the years she continued to be admired for her sense of style, and her outfit in *Murder, My Sweet* (1944) was included as part of a four-way fashion show to promote the film. She had a direct input into the design of the white dress in that film by Edward Stevenson. All the designs for the RKO noirs of the 1940s with which she was identified have become iconic in their own right, and inseparable from discussions of the genre. Undoubtedly the fashions of the era are a large part of the appeal to those who adore old films; this was a time when even maids were well turned out when they were off duty, and gardeners wore ties. Hats were *de rigueur*, the smart set still dressed for dinner and ladies always wore white when playing bridge.

Ray Driscoll, nicknamed "Hollywood's bad boy designer," had views on many of the leading ladies of the day.[32] In typical iconoclastic style he listed Judy Garland and Ginger Rogers among the five worst-dressed stars in the film capitol. He listed Claire among the top five best-dressed, on a list that included Rosalind Russell and Ann Sheridan. He declared Claire to be "an odd combination of blonde and blasé with simplicity."[33] Observers often remarked that she was one of those actresses who dressed well on- and off-screen. She believed she had a duty both to her audience, and to herself, to look as good as possible at all times. As she explained, "Being well-groomed, chic and smart takes very little extra effort and it's well worth while in inner satisfaction. A woman owes it to her sex to be charming, dainty, well-groomed and well-dressed wherever she is."[34]

Throughout the years, she maintained the same unaffected personality as she had to begin with. Despite the tenor of some of the roles she played, society columnists noted that she was "as friendly and natural as one of the girls in the afternoon bridge club."[35] She declared that her own wardrobe was modest, with only a few coats and around 15 dresses—but 35 pairs of shoes.[36]

She saw the absurdity of fame and her delightful sense of humor was never far from the surface. One time when she visited an upmarket dress shop on 57th Street in New York with her aunt, the assistant invited her to try on the latest design. "This is a Claire Trevor frock," said the assistant helpfully, "only $150." Claire tried it on but it didn't quite suit her; "Who is this Claire Trevor? She doesn't strike a responsive note in my memory," said Claire mischievously. "Don't you know?" replied the assistant. "She is playing over here at the Rialto right now in *Black Sheep*." Claire's aunt let the assistant in on the joke and before long she asked her for her autograph.[37]

Her sense of style extended to her house. The interiors were designed by Helen Franklin, who had designed the homes of many other Hollywood stars, including Irene Dunne and Alan Ladd.[38] Even into her seventies and eighties, Trevor was still stylish and elegant, often favoring the designs of Arnold Scaasi and Pauline Trigere. Some of them she knew personally; she sometimes attended Florence Klotz's parties.[39] In later years, many people remarked on her eternally youthful appearance, something she said was partly genetic; both her parents remained active into their eighties. She said that her mother had wonderful skin and very few wrinkles for her age. Her father was a big advocate of a raw vegetable diet, but Claire admitted that "all that sort of thing bores me to death," and she was not watchful of her diet.[40] She cited worry and boredom as the two things that aged a person most, and advised not worrying about age and to try and keep interested and busy. She never lied about her age. In fact, reporters were fond of adding a year to her age. She once took a New York newspaper to task for getting her age wrong: A caption under her picture read, "Claire Trevor: Still radiant at 73." "How dare they!" she retorted, "I was 72 last March"[41]

Despite all the adulation, Trevor was never content with her appearance. "I hate myself on the screen," she once commented. "I never look the way I'd like to—like Joan Fontaine, for instance. I like tall, thin people. I look short and fat most of the time."[42] But at five foot three and 110 pounds, she was always petite, slim and attractive. No male member of the audience had any complaints and she was always immensely popular with them. In 1939, she was voted the first sweetheart of the 20–30 Club on Sunset Boulevard and attended a dinner in her honor.[43] It was not simply her looks but her winning personality that always shone out from the screen. In an age of glamour, she created her own distinct style and became a role model to millions of women all over the world.

6

The Queen Escapes from the "B" Hive

I'm sorry, Miss Trevor, but I don't know your work. Have you made any pictures?—William Wyler, quoted in Sheilah Graham, "Claire Trevor Got Her 'Oscar' and with It Leading Lady Roles," *The Milwaukee Journal,* May 30, 1949, 48

After four frustrating years at Fox, Trevor took a chance and played a small role in *Dead End* (1937) for United Artists. Despite the size of the part, she made a big impression and was nominated for an Academy Award as Best Supporting Actress. It was exactly the boost her career needed. But although she had marginally better roles thereafter, it was still not the final breakthrough she was hoping for.

Sidney Kingsley's *Dead End* was a successful Broadway play in 1935. The Hollywood version brought some of the cast along from the original, most notably the Dead End Kids, augmented by Humphrey Bogart, Sylvia Sidney and Joel McCrea. Although director William Wyler wanted to shoot on location on the Lower East Side, studio boss Sam Goldwyn, who had paid $165,000 for the rights to the play, insisted it be shot on one set, utilizing an inventive stage design by Richard Day. This added to the theatricality of the piece. It was reworked for the screen by Lillian Hellman, who was required to "water down [the] street language and soften the characters" in the process.[1]

Escaped gangster "Baby Face" Martin (Bogart) and his partner-in-crime Hunk (Allen Jenkins) return to the neighborhood where they grew up. Martin is there to see his ex-fiancée Francey (Trevor) and his mother (Marjorie Main). During the course of the day, he meets both but does not receive the homecoming he imagined. He is slapped by his mother and told to go in no uncertain terms, then finds that Francey has fallen on hard times and become a prostitute; what's more, she has contracted syphilis. After their soul-destroying meeting, Francey walks wearily away up the street as the electric tingalary cynically plays the plaintive melody "Girl of My Dreams," which seems intensely ironic and mocking to him. Martin has traveled all the way across country, risking everything to see his mother and the girl he once loved and gets slapped in the face—once literally, the other metaphorically; rejected, as he says, "twice in one day." Before the day is out, things get worse for him.

The story goes that Trevor turned down the offer of a $30,000 role opposite James Cagney in *Great Guy* in order to appear in the small part in *Dead End* for $10,000.[2] On the face of it, this might have seemed a retrograde step but Trevor was a canny judge of material, and relished her escape from the Fox treadmill: "At last I'll have a chance to do something besides wear clothes and smile," she remarked. "I was tired of doing routine heroines in routine romances. I needed something to give me a break and I think Francey is the answer."[3] She was right. The part of Francey took only a day and a half to shoot and essentially consisted of just a few lines of dialogue. But somehow this small role stayed in the minds of audiences, and soon she was Oscar-nominated. When he first interviewed her, Wyler blithely asked her if she had ever made any films. "I was crushed," she remarked. "I had played the sweet young thing in 28 pictures and Wyler never had seen one of them."[4] Convinced she was not wanted, she turned to go and casually asked who would be playing Francey. "You are," replied Wyler.[5] He offered her one of the more prominent roles and was surprised when she chose instead the smallest part. "He said he'd be glad for me to do it," she remarked, "but that he would be ashamed to offer it to me. It looked like a good role to me even though it was brief."[6]

Despite the acclaim and Oscar nomination, she admitted that she was unhappy with her performance when she saw the film: "I hadn't given it what I thought I had. Or else they didn't use the shot where I gave the most," she observed.[7] The scene took nine takes before meticulous director Wyler was satisfied with it.[8] Trevor was attracted

Poster for William Wyler's *Dead End* (1937), in which Claire appeared in a small role as the ex-fiancée of Baby Face Martin (Humphrey Bogart). Although she had little screen time she made a big impression and was nominated for an Academy Award for Best Supporting Actress.

to the character, who she felt was an idealist and a dreamer. Those kinds of roles appealed to her, she said, because "they are emotionally exciting and absorbing."[9]

Due to the success of the movie, there were several ideas to reteam the Dead End Kids with others in the cast. Bogart and Trevor were to have both featured with them in *Hell's Kitchen* (1939), but in the event neither appeared in the film.[10]

In the wake of Trevor's nomination, her name was to the fore more than it had ever been, and she was considered when studios were casting big films. She was sought by Paramount for the female lead in *Spawn of the North* (1938) which starred George Raft and Henry Fonda as rival Alaska fishermen. Although Carole Lombard and Frances Farmer were also mooted, the role went to Dorothy Lamour.[11]

6. The Queen Escapes from the "B" Hive   49

Being young, attractive and unmarried, Trevor was often the subject of the gossip columnists, who construed a romance with any male she happened to be spotted with more than once. One such was her dentist Dr. MacDonald, with whom she went bowling in Beverly Hills. Her name was also linked with that of western actor Allan Lane and notorious ladies' man Greg Bautzer.[12] Watchers on the sidelines implied she was involved with some of her co-stars including George O'Brien, with whom she played tennis frequently, and Michael Whalen, who accompanied her to see a Los Angeles Philharmonic Symphony Orchestra concert.[13] Other names mentioned included Clay Adams (a Fox executive and the head of Pathé Newsreels), Billy Bakewell and attorney Anthony Bentley Ryan.[14] She always maintained that none of these romances was serious, and besides she admitted that she preferred men as companions rather than women.[15]

Her love of tennis brought her into contact with a number of players and she became friends with Wilmer Hines from South Carolina.[16] Hines was an All-American champion who competed twice at Wimbledon in singles, doubles and mixed doubles.[17] During his successful European tour of 1935, he won the Italian Open. Trevor and Hines were seen so often together for much of 1937, either dancing at the Trocadero or playing tennis, that by September there was talk of marriage in the press.[18] It was said that he "thinks she is so beautiful that he'll scarcely let her out of his sights."[19] She often watched him on tour and bought a box to see him play in the Pacific Southwest tournament. When asked about the

Left to right, Trevor, J. Edward Bromberg, Tyrone Power and Loretta Young in *Second Honeymoon* (1937), a minor, forgettable screwball comedy. It was a showcase for its stars, audience favorites Power and Young, but Trevor and Bromberg made the most of all the chances that came along.

romance, she replied, "He is very charming, and we are very companionable. No, I'm not wearing a ring, but he is a wonderful person."[20]

Shortly after the release of *Dead End*, Trevor was all dressed for a dinner date when she received a call from Fox with news of a chance in a big new A-picture starring Tyrone Power and Loretta Young. Full of optimism that here was her big break, she hurried to the studio, only to find that her role was actually a small one that "required a girl who knew how to stand about."[21] *Second Honeymoon* (1937) was a minor screwball comedy that revolved around Power and Young, who had once been married and predictably find themselves falling in love again over a weekend in Honolulu where they had first honeymooned. A typical 1930s scenario was presented in which the better social set could dine, dance, gamble and play to their hearts' content against false scenery. The film served as an excuse to show how much the camera loved the two leads; it was easy to understand why everyone was captivated by Power. There was excellent support from Lyle Talbot as Young's steady businessman husband and Stuart Erwin as Power's nervous valet. There were lively performances from J. Edward Bromberg and Trevor as a seemingly more contented married couple. They matched each other for dry humor and casual asides. Unfortunately, they had little to do but made what they could of the material. They had a brief slapstick scene in which they swatted mosquitoes in bed: He swiped one that landed on her behind and she immediately slapped him in the face. Such bright moments were scant and although the running time was only 78 minutes, it felt like much longer. The pacing was uneven; the

In *Big Town Girl* (1937), Claire went on the run from her gangster husband and posed as a singing French countess. Here she is persuaded by a fast-talking agent (Alan Dinehart) that she could make a great career as a singer.

scenes between Power and Young were far too long and did not hold the attention. The role of Marcia had been handed to Trevor after Phyllis Brooks withdrew because of illness.[22] Director Walter Lang had a long and varied career but was mostly remembered for musicals such as *The King and I* (1956). In his early days, he had once directed a version of the rarely filmed *Alice Through the Looking Glass* (1928).

Working on the picture, Trevor observed that Loretta Young used to finish at noon and then called the publicity department to tell them that she was ready for an afternoon of posing for stills. This was something Trevor could never countenance. "I want to act— I didn't want to do puff publicity," she remarked.[23] It was reported that Zanuck was impressed with Trevor's *Second Honeymoon* performance and planned to give her a starring vehicle with Brian Donlevy as a reward for both of them. However this never came to pass.[24]

One of her last engagements with Fox was *Big Town Girl* (1937), an entertaining comedy drama which employed a good cast and a lightness of touch. She played a nightclub singer whose unwanted gangster husband escapes and makes straight for her place. She gives him the slip and goes into hiding, taking a job in a department store. A big-talking agent hears her sing and convinces her that he can make a great singing star out of her on the radio. She reluctantly agrees but is desperate not to be recognized and adopts a disguise. Wearing a mask and a black wig, she is billed as a mysterious French countess. In time her husband discovers where she is but a newspaperman helps her out.

Claire and the cast seemed to enjoy themselves. The film was fast-paced and had some appealing character sketches along the way. On the downside, it was too roughly edited and the end was particularly abrupt in the print I watched. Three songs were featured, plus one of the most adventurous dance routines in which she ever took part. This was the "Argentine Swing" number in which she was surrounded by a dozen men dressed as gauchos and hoisted aloft on a round platform while still dancing. Actually the sequence was filmed for *Star for a Night* but not used in that.[25] She had fun with a cod French accent; it was a good tongue-in-cheek role for her and made a refreshing change. Whether it was because she knew that she would soon be free of Fox or just sheer enjoyment of the part, she played with a sense of joy as though a weight had been lifted from her shoulders. At one stage it seemed as though the film would become an all-out musical, but then it veered off into comedy-drama territory. Although she was undoubtedly doing the dancing, she was not the one singing.

Walking Down Broadway (1937) followed six Follies girls who, one New Year's Eve, agree to meet a year hence to see how they have all fared. They go their separate ways; some are successful, some not, and one of the group does not live that long. The bittersweet tale was based on a Mark Hellinger story, "Six Girls and Death." The film was well executed considering the many complex plot strands of the six stories. It followed a similar template to that of the almost contemporary *Stage Door* (1937). *Walking Down Broadway* was built up by the studio as a showcase for "six stars of tomorrow."[26] The other girls were Phyllis Brooks, Dixie Dunbar, Leah Ray, Lynn Bari and Jayne Regan. Only some of those made successful careers; Bari was the one who received the mantle of "Queen of the Bs" which Trevor was only too eager to bequeath when she left the studio.

Trevor played the most level-headed of the girls: She gives up on a stage career to be a dress designer and becomes a kind of mother-confessor to the other girls. On screen, rather a lot happened to them all in the course of the year, stretching credulity, when it

Walking Down Broadway (1938) was a tale of the fluctuating fortunes of six girls trying to make it on the Great White Way. Left to right: Phyllis Brooks, Claire (sitting), Leah Ray, Jayne Regan, Dixie Dunbar and Lynn Bari.

might have had more credence if it had been set over the course of several years. One critic called it confusing and cheerless, chiefly blaming the lack of depth in the writing. He also noted, "[The] best acting is done by the always reliable Miss Trevor, whose every screen appearance causes this reviewer to wonder why Mr. Zanuck fails to give her one of his spectacular star-making build-ups."[27] Many observers noted that she stood out in the cast and some said she was considered "a likely candidate for Academy honors for her distinguished work."[28] She was not nominated.

Trevor was aware of a lack of support from the management at Fox, and grew increasingly discontented. "What burns me up is to see them put inexperienced girls in big roles, or to bring girls from Europe who aren't any more glamorous than I am," she remarked. "The worst is to see them borrow actresses for a part I know I can do."[29] She tried to arrange a meeting with Zanuck to discuss the situation, but could not get past his secretary. Nor could she reach him by phone. In the end, she let him know of her grievances through Sol Wurtzel. Zanuck's rather condescending response was that he "didn't think he could do much for Miss Trevor. For one thing he regarded her as a character actress, for another ... the studio just didn't make big budget pictures of the type that would be most suitable for her talents."[30]

That was the straw that broke the camel's back: "Mr. Zanuck never had faith in me," she said. "Why, I don't know. Perhaps he may even have been justified. If he hasn't confidence in a player, said player might just as well up and leave from the outset. And that's what I did."³¹ After *Walking Down Broadway*, it no longer mattered what Zanuck thought; she had seen out her Fox contract. She "turned down two studio offers of long-term contracts" and went freelance.³² "I decided that freelancing might really give me a new life in movies," she observed. "While I couldn't select my roles, at least I had the authority to reject unsuitable parts."³³ Once again her judgment was sound, and it proved a positive turning point in her career. The films she made from then on were not all classics, but they reflected her own choice, and were a vast improvement on those that had gone before.

It had been decided that Trevor and June Lang would star in a series of four films "based on the experiences of modern girls."³⁴ The first was *Meet the Girls* (1938) but Trevor had quit by then and was replaced by Lynn Bari. (Only one other film of the series was completed, 1939's *Pardon Our Nerve*.) Apart from a promised starring role in an A-feature with Brian Donlevy which never materialized, the only other project Zanuck ever announced with Trevor specifically in mind was *I Love the Author*. A comedy by Gregory Ratoff, this would have teamed her with Don Ameche. Retitled *You Can't Have Everything* (1937), it was handed to Alice Faye instead.³⁵ Wurtzel acted as Trevor's agent once she began freelancing, and reportedly formed a new producer-star company with her. He arranged financing for three films, two to be made in Hollywood and one in New York. The budget for each film was announced as $500,000.³⁶

Full of sardonic humor, *The Amazing Dr. Clitterhouse* (1938) had the unmistakable Warner Brothers hallmark of quality. Boasting a great cast and a script co-written by John Huston, it was streets ahead of anything Claire had been given at Fox. This Italian poster shows (left to right) Humphrey Bogart, Edward G. Robinson, Trevor, Maxie Rosenbloom and Vladimir Sokoloff.

Trevor let her hair down at in-house events such as a private showing of the Broadway hit "The Drunkard" in which she played with Michael Whalen at a party for the Screen Actors Guild. Her mother was among those watching in a capacity audience composed of her fellow actors, including Alice Faye and Sterling Holloway.[37]

For Warner Brothers she appeared in Barre Lyndon's *The Amazing Dr. Clitterhouse* (1938). This had started life as a stage play, first in London, where it had much success, and afterwards on Broadway, starring Cedric Hardwicke. The story concerned a respected society doctor whose investigations into the criminal mind and modes of behavior lead him into crime himself. He joins up with a gang of jewel thieves led by "Rocks" Valentine (Humphrey Bogart) and Jo Keller (Trevor), a fence. The doctor effectively takes over the gang and masterminds a number of robberies. When he returns to his respectable life, Valentine tracks him down and attempts to blackmail him, but Clitterhouse poisons him. At the trial, he is acquitted on account of insanity.

The opening titles showing sinister-looking chemistry bottles bubbling away were rather misleading. Allied to the title and the dramatic score by Max Steiner, they gave the distinct impression that this was something akin to a Universal horror on the lines of *Dr. Jekyll and Mr. Hyde*. The trailer promised "a thousand thrills" but although that proved to be something of an exaggeration, there were quite a few laughs. The film was rather deliberate in its pacing. It picked up when the doctor met Jo, who he first assumes is Joe, a man. Claire made a nonchalant fence and this was an excellent role for her. The movie sometimes came to a standstill at awkward times; this may have been a hangover from its stage roots. John Huston and John Wexler worked on the screenplay, and there were some touches which showed Huston's mark. Bogart even says at one stage, "You'll take it and like it," a familiar line to those who know *The Maltese Falcon*. Producer Robert Lord first sought Ronald Colman for the title role and he would have been a good choice, because Robinson was already associated so much with crime that it was no stretch to imagine him turning criminal.[38] However, Robinson was at his best and Bogart featured prominently. (Bogart despised his role, which he called ludicrous and said was his least favorite.[39]). Trevor did superbly in her role, ably reflecting the varying feelings of her character and handling the dry humor with aplomb. The Warner Brothers stock players (Allen Jenkins, Thurston Hall, Victor Sokoloff *et al.*) gave valiant support and Donald Crisp was an unusual but effective choice as a police inspector. Russian émigré director Anatole Litvak had a varied Hollywood career that encompassed *The Sisters* (1938) and two versions of the *Mayerling* story 20 years apart (1936 and 1956). He also made some intriguing noirs such as *Sorry, Wrong Number* (1948) and a groundbreaking film about the treatment of the mentally ill, *The Snake Pit* (1948).

The Amazing Dr. Clitterhouse was an entertaining film, essentially a black comedy. Some of the best moments were in the witty dialogue such as when the police lieutenant questions Clitterhouse in the thieves' hideout and ends up having to show the doctor his credentials. The court scene at the end was especially telling when the psychiatrist is asked for his opinion on the sanity of the doctor and of course confuses everyone with his circulatory response. The gang hides out in a music conservatory and poses as the Hudson River String Quintet, each pretending to play instruments while a record plays. Perhaps this was the inspiration for the gang in the Ealing comedy *The Ladykillers* (1955). In fact a similar strain of ironic and mordant humor was at play in *The Amazing Dr. Clitterhouse*.

At one stage, a member of the gang is concerned that the doctor is not looking too well; "Maybe he ought to see a doctor" is the nifty response of Valentine.

There was fine cinematography by Tony Gaudio, who had previously worked on *The Adventures of Robin Hood* (1938) and whose later credits included *The Letter* (1940) and *High Sierra* (1941). He used some effective camera angles and played with light and shadow in some sequences, particularly the one in which Valentine is poisoned. The film had that strong Warner Brothers look. Everything about the production spoke of its quality; the attention to detail in the background sets alone was a cut above anything she had been given at Fox, and showed how much more at home she would have been at Warners.

Impressed with Trevor, Warner Brothers offered her a seven-year contract at double her present salary, in a deal estimated to be worth almost $1,000,000. She was thankful for the offer, but politely refused, explaining, "I feared that if I tied myself up for that length of time it might interfere with my marriage."[40] She had only recently married radio producer Clark Andrews. She was set to star opposite Robinson again in *Murder for Two Cents* with Pat O'Brien but the film was never made.[41] She was also sought for *East Side of Heaven* but her role went to Joan Blondell.[42] Although penciled in for *Shanghai Deadline*, she was replaced by Dolores del Rio and the film was retitled *International Settlement* (1938).[43]

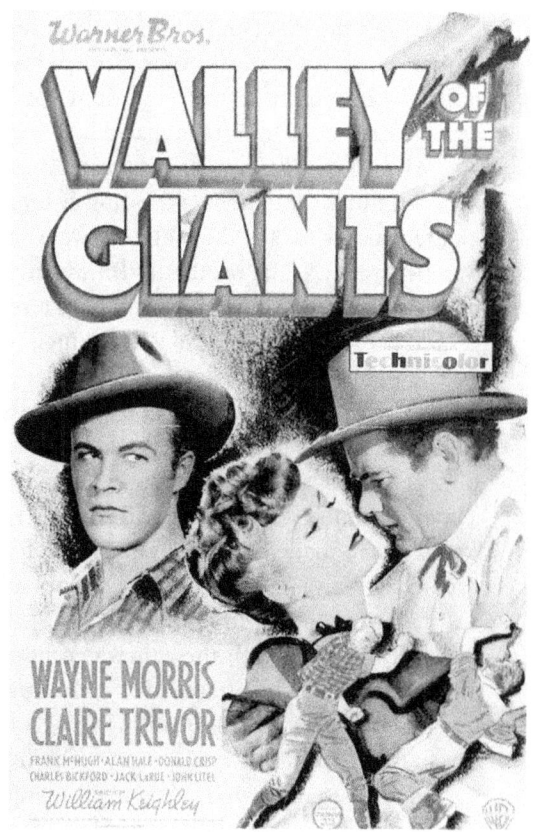

She had plenty of admirers, many of whom could not be taken seriously. One of her most ardent followers was "Slapsie" Maxie Rosenbloom, a boxer who later became an actor. He reportedly asked her out seven times to shows, prizefights and nightclubs, but was politely rebuffed. One time when Trevor appeared at a soiree with Andrews, Rosenbloom announced her arrival and called for drinks all round. Although he was not a gifted singer, he asked her which song she would like to hear; "Thanks for the Memory," she replied smartly. Although this was not in his repertoire, he had a go. Afterwards he asked her what she thought of his rendition; "It's very— interesting," she replied tactfully. Some days later, when he was on the set of *The Amazing Dr. Clitterhouse* (in which he had a fairly prominent role as one of the gang), he was still wondering what exactly she meant by that. He was a game one, and said he would keep asking her out no matter what.[44]

When Bette Davis turned down the lead in Warners' *Valley of the Giants* (1938), Trevor was assigned the role.[45] Originally Humphrey Bogart was listed as the star but

A rousing Technicolor adventure set among the California redwood trees, *Valley of the Giants* (1938) was the third of five screen versions. It was done with brio and featured a fine cast of familiar faces.

was replaced by Wayne Morris. This was a vigorous Technicolor adventure set among the California redwood trees, based on the bestselling novel by Peter B. Kyne. The story concerned a group of unscrupulous lumber merchants from the east headed by Charles Bickford, who seek to despoil the forests with their greed. Trevor was the saloon gal who is initially on the side of the merchants but who decides to stand up to the ruthless men and is almost killed by a runaway caboose. Along the way there were the expected explosions, chases, crashes and gunplay. Once all the studio work was complete, the cast and crew decamped to the remote town of Eureka for four weeks to shoot the outdoor scenes. A special train was laid on to transport the whole shebang, and Trevor traveled with fellow cast member Frank McHugh. The entire company took over three floors of the local inn, much to the chagrin of some of the residents, because the film men were up and about at 4:30 a.m. each day. Most of the cast took the only freight car to the location 20 miles away, which left at five a.m., but Trevor preferred to sleep till seven, which meant using the railway handcar that she and Wayne Morris boarded at the lumber town of Cranell.[46]

Shooting the film was a major event for the local population, who unwittingly added to the problems of Joe Barry, the location manager. Huge traffic jams built up on the surrounding roads when some of the big scenes were about to be filmed, such as the destruction of a dam on the Van Duzen river and a freight train wreck. Sightseers swarmed from miles around to catch a glimpse of the filmmakers at work. Schoolchildren at Orick, 60 five miles north, "went on strike" so they could see Trevor and Morris. The teacher compromised and took the class in Eureka instead.

All in all, it was a major logistical operation. Seven hundred dollars a day was spent on food, and the total cost of the month-long stay was estimated to be $100,000. The eagerly awaited rushes for the day's filming were shown every evening in a Eureka theater, which was also a first.[47] The resultant film was rather formulaic and tried to include everything, but it boasted appealing color and gave a real sense of the majesty and sense of awe of the giant redwoods. This may have accounted for much of its box office popularity. Trevor was excellent, but the role did not advance her career any. There was good support from Bickford, Alan Hale and others. The scenario seemed too familiar, which was unsurprising because the subject had been filmed twice before and would go on to be filmed twice more; the most famous version was probably *The Big Trees* (1952). Director William Keighley did a competent job but there was no comparison to his other work such as *The Adventures of Robin Hood*, made the same year. Adolph Deutsch provided a decent score and goggle-eyed comedian Jerry Colonna gave a suitably tongue-in-cheek rendition of the old music hall favorite "A Bird in a Gilded Cage." There were some accidents during filming; for instance the scene with the runaway caboose was too close for comfort, and both Trevor and Frank McHugh suffered cuts and bruises when the train came off the tracks.

Five of a Kind (1938) was the last of three films built around the Dionne Quintuplets, the first known to survive infancy. The five girls became a kind of tourist attraction in Callander, Ontario, where they lived in a privately run compound opposite the house of their parents. Set in the fictional Moosetown, *The Country Doctor* (1936) was the first in the series, followed by *Reunion* the same year. *Five of a Kind* was a further attempt to cash in on them, four years after their birth. The "plot" consisted of Trevor and Cesar Romero as reporters for rival newspapers who constantly try to outdo each other in their search for a story. Trevor signs the quins for a radio broadcast but Romero invents a story that

Five of a Kind (1938), one of three films exploiting the Dionne Quintuplets of Canada, starred Claire and Cesar Romero as rival reporters. Front, left to right: Trevor, Inez Courtney and Romero.

sextuplets have been discovered and Trevor is discredited when she falls for the ruse. Needless to say, all ends happily, and although the girls are not allowed to leave their compound to appear in person in a New York theater, the magic of television comes to the rescue.

There were some satiric moments such as when the false news of the discovery of sextuplets is announced, customers in the quins' gift shop drop their souvenirs and exit en masse, leaving the girls' father (John Qualen) crestfallen. The sequence involving the fake sextuplets was not without humor; the "mother" was none other than Esther Howard, who went on to appear in two great noirs with Claire. The shenanigans were geared to engineering sequences in which the girls could be seen playing in their isolated nursery. Of the actors, only Jean Hersholt was allowed to interact with them, and the radio broadcast was achieved with the aid of back projection.

The contrivance of the screenplay underlined that the film was purely an extension of how best to exploit the girls, who had arguably already been exploited to the full by their parents and even the government. The quins appeared in segments interspersed throughout: having breakfast, playing on toy pianos, bathing dolls, getting dressed, riding hobby horses, dancing a minuet and attired in alpine garb singing "Frere Jacques." The whole thing culminated in a grand fourth birthday party with mountains of presents and cake. Hersholt played the avuncular Dr. Luke, based on the real guardian of the children, Dr. Dafoe. After the release of *Five of a Kind,* Dr. Dafoe declined to allow any further films to be made, and the girls were regularly seen in newsreels for many years.

This was the last film in which Trevor appeared in the costumes of Herschel, who had designed those for *Career Woman, 15 Maiden Lane* and *Star for a Night.* She sported a fine array of stylish hats and a striped jacket which enhanced her character's sophisticated air. His elegant simplicity and tasteful use of blocks of color and fine details such as collars especially suited the kind of modern and independent-minded characters she played. In fact, the costumes were more successful than most of the films she made during all her years at Fox.

7

Radio Interlude

> Radio is worse than pictures, and pictures are worse than poison. I wish I could get a good play.—"What Should Claire Trevor Do?" Interview with Malcolm H. Oettinger, *Screenland,* April 1938, 54

Although Trevor maintained that she did not enjoy doing radio programs, she nonetheless made an excellent contribution to the genre. It was no surprise that her best roles were in dramas and mysteries, where she could use her remarkable voice to great effect. Hers was one of the best voices of any actress, able to convey all kinds of emotions: anger, despair, warmth, ruthlessness, fear, joy. There seemed no end to her facility, and perhaps radio helped her develop her natural speaking voice into a very effective instrument. The medium raised her profile, doubled her salary and directly led to her appearance in *Stagecoach*.

She made her debut in 1936 on the syndicated series *Hollywood Hotel,* which featured short scenes from her films *To Mary—with Love* and *Career Woman.* She was often interviewed and in 1937 and '38 she was a regular on the series *Big Town*, in which she played society reporter, Lorelei Kilbourne of *Illustrated Press.* Edward G. Robinson played crusading editor Steve Wilson. The format was highly successful and the show ran on radio until 1952, giving rise to four Paramount films, a television series and a comic book. The radio show's producer Clark Andrews became her first husband. Her appearance on this popular show and the hike in her "box office pull that ... accrued" was cited by film producer Walter Wanger in *Variety* as the main reason he gave her the lead female role in *Stagecoach*.[1] She was undoubtedly a hit, and stayed with *Big Town* for 20 months, the longest run in her entire radio career. When negotiating her new contract in February 1939, she was unhappy with her agents, Rockwell-O'Keefe, whom she dismissed, and negotiated her own contract.[2] She was making about $1500 for each broadcast and had to fight to receive the full amount. If a player was under contract, he or she was required to give part of their radio check over to their film studio; it was a kind of stipend for the privilege of recording for the medium. Trevor refused to go ahead with the broadcast at all if she was not awarded the whole value of the check, and the studio reluctantly agreed.[3] At that time, Robinson was the highest paid dramatic actor on radio, making $5500 per show. When he asked for a raise, the program's makers approached Trevor to take a cut; naturally she refused, and quit the show. Robinson got his raise (to $6000) and she was replaced by Ona Munson.[4] The show continued to be a great success but Trevor had no regrets about leaving. She was happy for Munson, commenting, "She's a swell actress and deserved the break."[5]

While working on *Big Town*, she met producer Andrews and they got engaged in April 1938. Described as an intelligent, quiet-spoken gentleman with a "swell sense of humor," he had the same sort of social background as Claire. The product of a good family, he graduated from Yale, "sampled Cambridge and studied a spell at the Sorbonne," spending much of his time with novelist Thornton Wilder."[6] He was also a friend of Orson Welles. Clark shared her love of tennis, and they often played together. She wanted a quiet wedding with just immediate family and a few close friends. She even hoped they could elope to Yuma without a word to anyone and dig up a justice of the peace at two a.m., but her parents and the press disapproved of the idea.[7]

Their July 27, 1938, wedding at the Bishop Episcopal Church in Beverly Hills was witnessed by 300 guests. She had just finished making a film and admitted that the wedding happened "in a whirl." She wore a "pearl-embroidered medieval gown of white brocade," with a bouquet of white lilies and orchids.[8] "All the pews were candlelit … and all the candles were entwined with gardenias," as she wanted them to be. The reception took place at their Westwood home. The couple honeymooned for a month in Honolulu, where they stayed at the Royal Hawaiian Hotel.[9]

Trevor once appeared in a playlet written by her husband. In "The Story of Ruth Taylor" on *The Kate Smith Hour*, she played a nurse who believes she has given a sick child the wrong medicine and is tortured by a nightmare. It was a suitably emotive performance and displayed her warmth and ability to move an audience. A spectator noted that Andrews directed his wife "in a genteel tone, invariably addressing her as Miss Trevor."[10]

Another likely winner on the airwaves was *Results, Inc.*, a romantic comedy-mystery series in which Trevor played the assistant to Lloyd Nolan of the Springboard Detective Agency. It was a familiar format but featured excellent work from the two leads. Mutual had high hopes for the show and invested $2200 in each weekly episode.[11] It appears not to have captured the public imagination in the same way as *Big Town*; maybe the problem was that there were too many similar detective shows. Whatever the reason, only 13 episodes were made. Of these, only three are known to have survived, all available on mp3 download and cd formats from many online sources.

Following the success of the radio series *Big Town*, Trevor became a popular airwave star and graced the cover of *Radio Mirror* in June 1938. She made a significant contribution to the medium in a 20-year career and her distinctive voice was perfect for mystery series.

Acknowledging that radio work was well-paid, Trevor once explained that her dislike of the medium was on artistic grounds: "There is no artistic satisfaction to be derived from a radio program in the making. A scene lasts three or four minutes, then there's a commercial or station announcement. You can't even get warmed up before the thing is over."[12]

But if radio wasn't popular with her, she was popular with radio. She even made the June 1938 cover of *Radio Mirror,* and the following year was voted the most popular radio actress in a nationwide fan poll.[13] The medium was in its heyday and her voice became familiar to millions. In the years between 1925 and 1955, most people had a radio and they were heard generally in cafés, bars and shops. Some shows had huge followings.

Trevor joined her friend Don Ameche in early 1940 for his *Don Ameche Old Gold Radio Show.* Ida Lupino had first been considered.[14] Trevor was featured in small dramas within the show's variety framework. The initial stories, serious in tone, were written by Mark Hellinger. Before long, he asked for his release from his contract; he objected to the lighthearted treatment of his often tragic tales that he considered unsuitable for the Ameche style.[15] A big hit with audiences, the show had an entertaining mix of material and Trevor was considered an integral part of its appeal. The stories ranged from "The Bribe," about a policeman who takes a small bribe from a motorist and goes into a downward spiral, to "The Life of Stephen Foster," an operetta based on the great composer's life; Trevor played his wife.

Trevor contributed to a number of shows for Pittsburgh's local station KDKA as part of the all-day ballyhoo to celebrate the premiere of her RKO film *Allegheny Uprising.* RKO had promised a number of stars and starlets would attend, but in the event she was the only one who turned up. She entered into the spirit with gusto, took part in several interviews, a live broadcast of some dramatized scenes and even inaugurated a new radio transmitter at Allison Park under which was buried a time capsule containing a microfilm copy of the film script.[16]

At various times she tried to negotiate terms for her own show, and was reportedly in talks with Parliament Cigarettes to act as sponsors, but the show never came about.[17] She once auditioned a western show with Randolph Scott, but although they had sponsors interested, that too did not happen.[18] In May 1943, she joined the cast of *The Mayor of the Town,* a long-running saga starring Lionel Barrymore in the title role. Set in the fictional small town of Springdale, this popular show also featured Agnes Moorehead as his housekeeper; Claire played his resourceful secretary Toni McCafferty, but only for a brief time. The series ran for most of the 1940s, and was spun off into a short-lived Thomas Mitchell TV series.

Trevor was heard regularly on air in charity appeals. One for the Red Cross in 1940 was an all-star affair which drew a capacity audience with a further 4000 packed in the street outside the studio.[19] The two-hour program was also broadcast to Central and South America, parts of Europe, Australia and New Zealand.[20] She showed her sense of humor and guested on the popular programs of Jack Carson, Abbott and Costello, Bob Hope and Martin and Lewis. She had a flair for comedy as evinced by such plays as "One Last September" in which she played a restless woman who feels she has missed out on something in life. She returns to the scene of her happy girlhood hoping to find meaning but is cruelly disillusioned. The piece displayed a typically ironic humor shot through with sentiment but she made it live.

She was a regular on *Lux Radio Theater*, *The Lady Esther Screen Guild Theater* and others. She usually appeared in adaptations of her film hits such as *Murder, My Sweet* and *Stagecoach*. Occasionally she popped up in interesting items made famous by her leading contemporaries such as *Mildred Pierce*, *All About Eve* and *Destry Rides Again*. Her portrayals illustrate just how easily she could have played these roles on screen. Sometimes she had a chance to work with performers she had not worked with previously, such as Edmond O'Brien who played the Humphrey Bogart role in a radio version of *Key Largo*. This was the only time these two film noir greats met. She was due to appear alongside Errol Flynn in a version of *Trade Winds*. Unfortunately she had too many studio commitments and at the eleventh hour her place in the cast was taken by Mary Astor.[21]

Trevor was excellent as a schoolteacher accused of being un–American for attempting to teach history from a realistic perspective in Marc Connolly's "The Mole on Lincoln's Cheek." The fine cast also included Robert Young as the principal, Charles Bickford as an investigator and Elizabeth Patterson as the kindly wife of a trustee. A 1941 episode of the series *The Free Company*, this quietly potent but unheralded tale raised important issues about censorship and blacklists and seemed in many ways prescient considering the rise of McCarthyism in postwar America.[22]

Often the radio roles Trevor played explored deep emotional problems. She was drawn to such interesting projects as "Father's Day," an ironically titled play about a woman who suffers after making two mistakes in life, one being an early marriage to a moral weakling, from whom she attempts to gain custody of their adopted child.[23] In "The Sun Comes Up," she played a mother who grieves so much over the loss of one of her children that she shuts all the others out.[24]

Trevor made five episodes of *Suspense* and they are all worth seeking out. She shows just what a real actress can do with an interesting script, some eerie music and the odd sound effect. Her later screen narrations had a strength few other actresses could match, and maybe the focus required for radio helped in this regard. The stories, psychological in nature, were ideally suited to the medium. "The Plan" was an unusual tale about a convicted murderer who escapes from the asylum and goes to visit his brother and his wife, but all is not what it seems. "The Light Switch" was a beautifully narrated story in which she played a woman who plans an explosive surprise for her philandering husband when he returns home and switches on the light. "Every window was locked now, every jet of gas was on full..." she intones. "I moved as if guided by subconscious force. For an instant the naked little wires that made up the filament seemed to hypnotize me..." However, things don't quite work out as she hopes in this clever and engrossing tale which also contained elements of humor.

Sometimes she understudied other actresses such as Bette Davis. For one *Screen Guild Theater* presentation in 1941, Davis had a sore throat so could not attend rehearsals. Trevor was assigned the lead in "Jane Eyre" and spent the whole day rehearsing, only to be told that Davis would be all right after all. But despite all the work she put in for no credit, Trevor "took it with a smile" and was voted the best sport by radio technicians for that season.[25]

When not rehearsing, she would sit in the control room and knit rugs. An observer commented, "She's one of the best dressed women in Hollywood and always shows up for the broadcast in a new and stunning costume, usually featuring a smart hat."[26] Even with the decline of radio in the early 1950s, she was still seeking a vehicle as a female detective, but was unsuccessful in persuading producers on radio or television to back her idea.[27] One of her most fascinating abandoned radio projects was *Petticoat President,* a series based on the life of Victoria Woodhull, the first woman to run for the U.S. presidency. A radical, she was an early advocate of free love and women's rights and first ran for president against Ulysses S. Grant in 1872 on behalf of the Equal Rights party. She was ineligible because she was under 35. Thereafter she unsuccessfully ran twice more for the nomination. The series was devised by writer-producer Irving Wallace, and although there was the promise of an eventual television serial, it would appear that neither project was realized.[28]

Trevor found a surprising fan of her voice in Dr. Frenz Fodor, a radio and TV engineer and cousin of Albert Einstein. He called her an "oral strip teaser" and said her voice was "sensuous and enchanting." He continued: "Miss Trevor is the personification of what a mistress of coquetry and romance can accomplish through mastery of the voice. She is sensitive to the power of inflection. She possesses expert craftsmanship in using the flexibility of the larynx so that it can disarm, bewilder and enchant."[29] When she heard his comments, she quipped that she would "keep him posted," but said that she was "not doing any stripping today" because she was suffering from laryngitis.[30]

Ida Lupino made a point of using radio actors in her films, and once observed, "Next to the legitimate stage, radio still offers the best training for dramatic performances."[31] Radio gave many players of the era a lucrative income; Trevor acknowledged that it had bought her a new car. Despite her dissatisfaction with the medium, it gave her career a boost at a crucial time, and may have helped to hone her considerable vocal skills. "It was *Big Town* which finally put me across," she once acknowledged. "I never realized how much it did for me until after I gave it up."[32] The old shows that are available today provide an insight into a bygone time and give a different slant on the great actors and actresses we think we know so well. Trevor's airwave career lasted 20 years. A cd and mp3 recording is available that encompasses about two-thirds of her radio work, the length of which—23 hours—puts into perspective the importance of radio in properly assessing a performer's career.[33]

8

Stagecoach

"Maybe you'd like to ride a ways with the Kid."—Curly to Dallas in *Stagecoach*

For the *New Zealand Herald*, the forthright British film critic Freda Bruce-Lockhart wrote an excellent article entitled "Elusive Stardom" which lambasted Hollywood for its failure to give true talent its opportunity. In her entry "Mystery of Claire Trevor," she summarized the frustration of the young actress' predicament: "For four years she has been doing some of the most consistently fine acting on the screen at the rate of six pictures a year. Her efforts have not won her one inch of progress."[1]

Despite the acclaim that Trevor received after her performance as Francey in *Dead End*, this did not translate into significantly better roles. Not until *Stagecoach* (1939) two years later did she have a true breakthrough part.

Director John Ford first approached David O. Selznick with the project in 1937. Selznick wanted Gary Cooper and Marlene Dietrich for the leading roles and considered John Wayne and Trevor "too downmarket."[2] Ford turned to Walter Wanger instead. Wanger was uncertain about casting Trevor but he was finally persuaded by her success in the radio series *Big Town*. The role of Dallas was one she particularly wanted.

Although the *Stagecoach* script was ostensibly taken from Ernest Haycox's short story "Stage to Lordsburg," Ford readily acknowledged that his source was "really *Boule de Suif*."[3] Guy de Maupassant's tale, published in 1880, followed a group of assorted passengers traveling through France after the Franco-Prussian war. Each reflected a class of French society, and the concern with social comment mirrored that of *Stagecoach*.

The plot of *Stagecoach* is simplicity itself: Seven passengers travel from Tonto to Lordsburg. During the journey, they are constantly threatened with attack by Apaches, and an army captain's wife gives birth. Trevor played the prostitute Dallas, run out of Tonto with drunken Doc Boone (Thomas Mitchell) by the Ladies Law and Order League. Others on the journey include gentleman gambler Hatfield (John Carradine), a captain's wife Mrs. Mallory (Louise Platt), whiskey salesman Peacock (Donald Meek) and a banker Gatewood (Berton Churchill) absconding with the bank's money. Along the way, they are joined by the Ringo Kid (John Wayne), who has escaped from prison to get even with the Plummers who killed his brother.

Ford tells the tale simply in 90 minutes; the dialogue has a spare feel to it, as though it had been pared down to essentials. Ford did discard several pages of dialogue in Trevor's big romantic scene with Wayne and left her with just two lines. "I was crushed," she said. She also observed that the actors had no feeling at the time that they were involved in a great drama. "The scenes were too fragmentary," she noted. "But it was all shaping up in

In director John Ford's *Stagecoach* (1939), Claire has great on-screen chemistry with John Wayne. The two became lifelong friends.

Ford's mind."[4] He used image to such effect and relied to a large extent on the actors to convey everything without words. One especially successful sequence was when they were well into their journey and there was a sandstorm. No one speaks inside the coach and they are all alone with their thoughts. Dallas and Ringo glance at each other. A lot was said in these moments without the need for words, and the driving music established the momentum of the journey. One of the key factors in the film's success, the score received a well-deserved Academy Award. Ford had fine judgment in songs and his choices were particularly apposite. From the opening strains of the stirring "Trail to Mexico," there is a real feeling of the spirit of the west. The old folk tunes "Lila Dale," "Rosa Lee" and Stephen Foster favorites such as "Jeannie with the Light Brown Hair" worked well with a few religious tunes and a Mexican song, "En Mi Soledad." Especially poignant was the scene when Dallas walks down the street in the red light district at the end with Ringo just after they reach Lordsburg. They are both tense and few words are spoken, but the sounds emanating from the rough houses seem like a commentary on the situation. "She's More to Be Pitied Than Censured" and "She May Have Seen Better Days" underscore Ford's essential humanity.

Louise Platt, who played the army captain's wife, felt that the film belonged to Claire: "I thought she was just wonderful in it," she remarked. Her favorite scene was at the adobe when Dallas enters carrying the child and says, "It's a little girl." Platt observed: "That scene was so beautifully lighted, with her eyes sparkly, and she did it so beautifully. You know she's going to be a warm and wonderful mother and wife, and any man would be lucky to get her—and it's just that one line. To me, that's magic."[5] The three-day-old baby was Mary Kathleen Walker, and the scene was filmed by cameraman Bert Glennon wearing a white gown, under the supervision of four nurses and two doctors. Only natural light could be used and filming took place in "four 15-second hits."[6] She is the last surviving member of the cast.

Trevor remarked: "For some reason, Ford was interested in me as an actress. I couldn't understand why. During the filming, Ford got the most out of all of us."[7] Ford was on record as saying that he never liked directing women in his films "except Claire Trevor."[8] The resultant film is such a warm and human story and retains its power because of the integrity of director and actors. "They're saved from the blessings of civilization," declares Doc Boone as he sees Dallas and Ringo ride off into the night. This expansive humanity is at the core of all Ford's finest films, the best of which are centered around journeys. (Another example: 1950's *Wagon Master*.)

The character of Dallas was essentially the prostitute with the proverbial heart of gold, which even then might have seemed to be a cliché. But in Trevor's hands she became an entirely human figure; she is practical and resourceful. She immediately helps when the baby is due and sits up all night with Mrs. Mallory. She is also unsentimental: "You've got to live no matter what." Despite all that has happened to her, she never loses sight of her essential humanity, and relates to the doctor in that regard. "We're the victims of a foul disease called social prejudice my child," he says to her. "Two of a kind!" the spokeswoman for the Ladies Law and Order League declares. The League is actually inadvertently responsible for another occupant of the stagecoach: It was the prospect of entertaining the ladies at dinner that night which finally decided Gatewood to make a run for it with the bank's money. In addition to Ford's social commentary, some authors have identified a political stance. One wrote, "Running through *Stagecoach* is a pro–Roosevelt pro–New Deal message that glorifies cooperation and ridicules selfishness and prejudice."[9] The same writer noted that Gatewood was the only villain of the piece and that his sentiment of "What this country needs is a businessman for president" was stating the mantra of Coolidge.

Although there were no big romantic scenes in *Stagecoach* but, as Trevor recollected:

> I think Duke and I had chemistry that really came across on film. We liked each other in real life and became great friends, but the on-screen chemistry was all-important. Some people thought we must be having an affair, but that wasn't so. Duke liked dark, Latin types and I was blonde. Not his type at all. And he was in love with Josephine [his wife].[10]

Trevor had difficulty maneuvering the bustle on the dress she wore, and found riding in the stagecoach uncomfortable because of it. The costumes showed great attention to period detail and were suited to each character. There was something remarkably touching about the little purse or bag that Dallas carried. The costumes were designed by the prolific Walter Plunkett, whose career ranged from *King Kong* (1933) to Ford's *7 Women* (1966). He also designed the costumes for *Two Weeks in Another Town* (1962) in which Trevor featured.

Trevor had a narrow escape one time when her dress caught fire in the studio restaurant.[11] It was reported that during lulls in the filming, some of the men tried a spot of Indian wrestling, and which Donald Meek came out the winner. He had been an acrobat in his youth. When Ford and Wayne invited John Carradine for a friendly game of cards, he steadfastly refused; he never played because, he said, he "once lost two dollars at poker."[12]

Trevor's sympathetic portrayal of Dallas contrasted with that of Ann-Margret in the 1966 *Stagecoach* remake. There she was depicted as being as hard as nails, with no softness. It was a one-dimensional approach; *most* of the characters in the remake seemed like cyphers. This altered the whole dynamic and none of them interacted in the same naturalistic way as they had in Ford's masterpiece. It is unlikely that the gallant gentlemanly cowboy Ringo would have been so enchanted by the 1966 version of Dallas.

On his sets, Ford was famously tough on male actors, particularly Wayne, who he often yelled at and belittled. He was different again with women, and Claire thoroughly enjoyed the experience. "Most of the pictures I had made at Fox were pretty dreary," she observed. "I went from one to another, and we always worked long hours. Then to make a picture with Ford! Not only did we quit every day at five or six, John stopped shooting every afternoon so we could have tea."[13] When the film was almost finished, "Ford turned to her and said. 'You are so good, that I doubt if anybody will know how good you are.'"[14] After she went freelance and in the wake of her successful radio series, her stock had risen considerably. So much so that she received the highest salary of the cast, $15,000.[15]

Stagecoach proved to be a critical and popular success and it ushered in a wave of big-scale westerns. Artistically it has influenced many filmmakers including the great Orson Welles, who was so taken with Ford's chiaroscuro lighting and his use of sets with low ceilings that he reputedly watched the film many times when making his magnum opus *Citizen Kane* (1941).

Despite all of Trevor's fine work, new offers did not flood in, and she followed *Stagecoach* with a five-month period of unemployment.[16] Producer Hal Roach and director Lewis Milestone wanted her for the role of Mae in their film of John Steinbeck's *Of Mice and Men*, but the part went to Betty Field.[17] In January 1939, *Variety* reported that Trevor was in discussions with her agent about the offer of a London film project, which she either did not accept, or which never came about.[18] She was in line for a Bing Crosby musical, *East Side of Heaven* (1939), but her role devolved to Joan Blondell.[19] She was sought for the lead in *Pacific Liner* with Victor McLaglen and Chester Morris, but Wendy Barrie ended up playing the girl they fight

The Spanish poster for director John Ford's hugely influential *Stagecoach* (1939), a terrific ensemble piece played by a perfect cast.

Dallas helps a sobered-up Doc Boone (Thomas Mitchell) deliver Mrs. Mallory's baby in a pivotal *Stagecoach* sequence. Orson Welles said he watched this hugely influential film numerous times while making *Citizen Kane* (1941).

over.[20] There was the prospect of *Frontier Marshal* with Randolph Scott, in which she was replaced by Nancy Kelly.[21] RKO planned a modernized version of the romantic tragedy *A Woman Commands* (1932) which had starred Pola Negri as the queen of Serbia. Although Trevor was "seriously considered" for the role, the remake never came about.[22] Cameraman turned producer Lee Garmes wanted Trevor for his directorial debut, the charming Christmas fantasy *And So Good Bye,* later retitled *Beyond Tomorrow* (1940); she was unavailable and the role went to Jean Parker.[23] Trevor was among the many actresses considered for the role of Scarlett O'Hara in *Gone with the Wind,* one of the most coveted roles in film history.[24]

Although Trevor received no nomination for her *Stagecoach* performance, the film raised her profile both nationally and internationally as a result. She was popular in Europe and worldwide; she once said the American movie fans were "frivolous" and compared them unfavorably to Australian fans who, she said, were "intelligent and helpful."[25] She was voted one of the top ten actresses of the year by readers of the popular British film magazines *Picturegoer* and *Film Weekly*.[26] Further proof that she had "arrived" came in the unlikely form of a prisoner on Devil's Island in French Guiana who featured in a newsreel shot by Pierre-Andre Martineau. The convict had tattoos of all the famous film beauties amassed over the 20 years of his incarceration. Beginning with Mary Pickford, he had the others added as they became famous, and Trevor joined Garbo, Dietrich, Miriam Hopkins *et al.* adorning his body (it was not revealed who was where).[27] It was reported that he had "no additional space" for others.[28]

Trevor had some ideas of her own for film projects and bought an option on Steven Gould Fisher's *The Long Straw*, the tale of the wartime romance between an English teacher and a German U–Boat captain. The film was not made.[29] She was almost tempted back to Broadway by the Shuberts, who wanted her to play the lead in *Quiet Please* by F. Hugh Herbert and Hans Kraly, but the role went to Jane Wyatt.[30] Shortly after Trevor's marriage, her husband was employed at Twentieth Century–Fox as a writer and there was speculation that she would appear in his story *The Very Singular Miss Brown*, but this never came to fruition either.[31]

Claire and her husband moved into a Westwood house, described by one commentator as having "a dignified white Georgian-provincial exterior" that contrasted well with its cozy interior, delineated in glowing terms: "The living room [with its] fireplace and low, soft twin-divans which face across the hearth; its oval den, with deep crush-carpet and loungy chairs, and the classic little dining room with its warm gold toned walls and regal blue drapes."[32] The image of cozy domesticity was complete with a "parrot in a grand cage in the bay window."

In the same article, Trevor was shown with "her specialty," a deep dish chicken pie, and the recipe was printed. She once admitted that she was actually a culinary disaster.[33] Her Filipino cook Marcalo Canania was the real magician in the kitchen. He had "been around the world seven times and ... studied the magic of India, China, Japan and Italy" so he was never flummoxed for what to serve.[34] He had worked as a professional magician for 15 years and Claire often took him with her to parties.[35]

Claire and her husband preferred intimate dinner parties of no more than six, and preferably four. They entertained the Brian Ahernes, the Gene Kellys, the Keenan Wynns and Laird Cregar. After dinner they would play bridge, at which she excelled, then hunt the object, play guessing games or listen to records. She loved to argue politics and during the war years was said to be a staunch supporter of Roosevelt, whose portrait hung in her sun room.[36] But she mostly supported the Republican cause, and attended a huge rally at the Los Angeles Coliseum in 1944 for the nomination of Senator Thomas E. Dewey. Most of Hollywood's big names were there including Clark Gable, Cary Grant, Barbara Stanwyck and Gary Cooper. An estimated 93,000 turned out to see their favorite players and hear a speech by David O. Selznick. It was described as "the grandest evening that Republicans had enjoyed in Hollywood since the days of Herbert Hoover."[37]

An avid reader with a large library, Trevor liked to read biographies. Her favorite author was the English writer Beverly Nichols, to whom she sent her one and only fan letter. She once said that his novel *A Village in the Valley* "expressed exactly her ideas of humor and style of expressing it."[38] His was a subtle and refreshingly quaint type of humor which contained unexpected barbs. It was dry and decidedly English in tone; considering her natural use of irony, it was easy to understand why it would appeal to her so strongly.

9

"I'm not the Western type"

> So many of my shady ladies were of the corset period in American life that I actually believe I know more about corsets than anyone else in Hollywood.—Louis Reed, "A Really Good Bad Girl," *Screenland,* June 1950, 72

Right after Trevor's triumph in *Stagecoach*, she was cast mostly in westerns despite her dislike of the genre in general. None of the other films that she and John Wayne made together replicated the magic of Ford's classic. She really needed to branch out into other areas but was seldom given the chance until a couple of years later.

Universal first approached Edward G. Robinson to play the central role in *I Stole a Million* (1939), but when they couldn't agree on terms, the studio offered the part to George Raft. Frances Dee and Joan Blondell were considered for the female lead before it was handed to Trevor.[1] The story saw Raft as a cab driver who goes off the rails when he is done out of money and tries to get it back. He spends most of the film being chased by police. His wife begs him to see sense but he is beyond help. It was a familiar scenario for the phlegmatic Raft, and Trevor did well as his stoic wife. The film performed badly at the box office despite the stars. There was a mixed reaction from critics; one hailed it as a "swell melodrama," adding that it "has emotional power and integrity of viewpoint."[2] Another observed: "Raft plays the unfortunate cabbie competently enough, but he fails to measure to Miss Trevor's splendid performance. She plays a long-suffering role with sympathy and understanding and her parts of the film hold considerable human interest."[3]

During production, cameraman Milton Krasner experimented with a new "transfused light-ray which he said would induce utter relaxation and extreme drowsiness." The device worked only too well while filming a hospital scene with Claire and before long she "lapsed into such a perfect coma that her dialog was inaudible to the most sensitive adjustment of the recording system." After that, she "slept soundly for 30 minutes while they shot another scene."[4] Trevor introduced the director and cast to the notion of daily 15-minute tea breaks at four o'clock, a custom when working with John Ford. "They really give you pep," she said. This being America, Raft, Trevor and director Frank Tuttle opted for ice cream sodas instead of tea.[5] Tuttle was a Yale man known for his noirs, including *This Gun for Hire* (1942), and comedies such as *Don Juan Quilligan* (1945). There was a hiatus in his career in the late 1940s when he named some 36 names for HUAC.

I Stole a Million was based on the exploits of notorious mail train robber Roy Gardner, one of the most infamous gangsters of the 1920s but now largely forgotten. After Gardner committed suicide in a gas-filled room in San Francisco, his widow Dolly Parkes and daughter Mrs. Jan Janofsky filed suit for "$150,000 damages against Universal and Claire Trevor for libel and invasion of privacy."⁶ Mrs. Parkes asked for $100,000 because in the film she was shown in one scene in jail and in another harboring a felon. She contended that this never happened, that she had never been in jail and had never condoned her former husband's crimes. Gardner's daughter asked for $50,000, claiming that she had managed to remain anonymous hitherto but that she had been "shunned ... avoided and held up to ridicule as a result of the film."⁷ In his suicide letter, Gardner had appealed to newspapermen to "give him a break" and not to make the identity of his daughter known.⁸ It was curious that Trevor should have been specifically named in the suit.

RKO was so keen to cash in on the winning team of John Wayne and Trevor from *Stagecoach*, that they cast them in *Allegheny Uprising* (1939). This was despite the fact that there was no woman in Neil H. Swanson's original novel *The First Rebel*. Initially the cast was augmented by Sir Cedric Hardwicke, but he was replaced by George Sanders. Brian Donlevy was added, fresh from his success in *Beau Geste*.

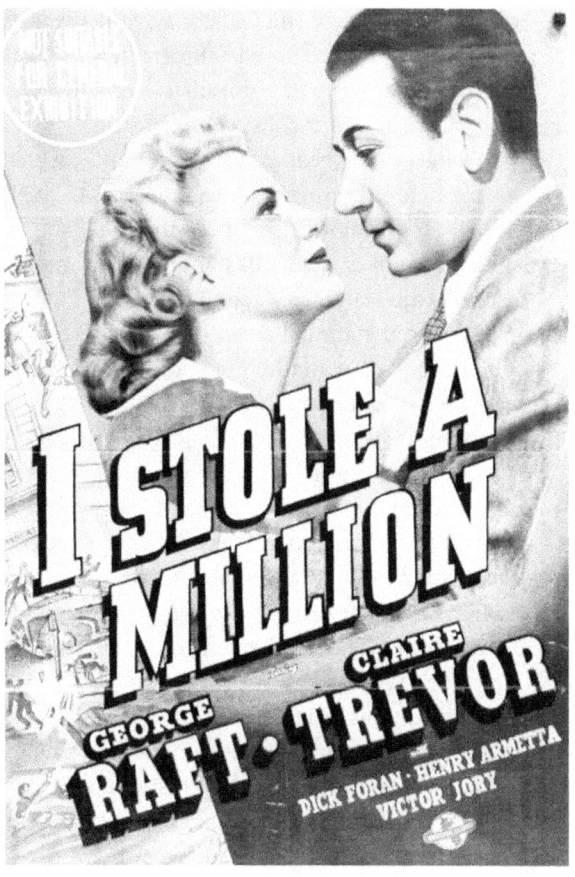

Poster for *I Stole a Million* (1939), based on the life of a mail train robber. His widow and daughter brought a lawsuit against the studio and Trevor, claiming invasion of privacy.

Despite the best efforts of all, *Allegheny Uprising* never really holds the attention. Trevor played the spirited daughter of one of the rebels. Although she was enthusiastic and sprightly, the role was underwritten and the magic of *Stagecoach* was lacking, even in her scenes with Wayne. Still, she looked cute in her coonskin cap. Sanders and Donlevy were both effective in their meatier roles as the villains of the piece. In Britain, the film was banned by the Ministry of Information. War had been declared in September 1939, and unsurprisingly the British government took exception to the portrayal of themselves as cruel colonial masters.⁹ It was not shown for several years in Britain, which further dented its already lackluster box office performance in the U.S. Aside from any controversy, it was just not an inspiring film.

Most of the action scenes were shot at Sherwood Lake in California's Malibu Hills. Trevor commented; "For six weeks we all lived—cast and crew—men and women—on location in tents, and throughout Duke was a delight. Contrary to popular belief, he remained sober while he was actually working."¹⁰ Having been taught how to ride a horse with the help of George O'Brien in her first film, Trevor learned how to shoot for *Allegheny Uprising*. She practiced on the police firing range at Squirrel Hill outside Pittsburgh (as some filming was done in Pennsylvania as well) and proved to be a crack shot, matching the top police marksman Officer Fred G. Simpson.[11] Trevor also took time out to visit Philadelphia's Wilson Humphries art gallery where she picked up several modern water colors to add to her collection.[12]

There was great fanfare surrounding the film's world premiere in Pittsburgh, and Trevor made several personal appearances during a three-day visit. RKO promised a number of stars from the film but in the event she was the only one who turned up. She dressed in the fashion of the 1750s complete with mob cap and corn cob pipe as the official starter of the Sadie Hawkins Race on the city's Duquesne University Campus.[13] Later in the day, she started the annual dances. In addition to numerous radio interviews, she took part in a pioneer parade and held a tea for 200 women at a department store. The following day she "met [the] newspaper gang at a cocktail party"; after the premiere, she was the guest of honor at a supper and ball at the William Penn. She was described as "a big hit" and it was said that she "made a lot of friends."[14] By now firmly established as a western gal, she accepted invitations to such events as the first Intercollegiate Rodeo Festival in which students from 11 western universities competed for the prize of best cowboy and cowgirl. The event was held at a ranch near Victorville where she had made her screen debut six years earlier. She accompanied the two other Hollywood guests, veteran actors Harry Carey and Lewis Stone.[15] She had become quite a celebrity and in October 1939 she was a guest at the New York World's Fair.[16]

Trevor was next offered another western, Republic's *Dark Command* (1940). At first she refused it because she considered the part too bland. Her resolve melted away at a story conference and she agreed.[17] This was her third movie in the space of a year with Wayne, who she said remained one of her "dearest friends."[18] Republic Herbert J. Yates was especially insistent that he wanted Trevor for the role, regarding the young stars as a winning combination.[19]

The Civil War story revolved around Cantrell (Walter Pidgeon) and his love for Mary McCloud (Trevor), who is also loved by Bob Seton (Wayne). A schoolteacher by day, Cantrell leads a double life as the ruthless leader of a gang of mavericks by night. Cantrell was based on Colonel Quantrill, a recurring figure in Civil War films. Brian Donlevy was initially sought for the role and would have been ideally suited; he later played the colonel twice on screen. There was memorable support from Marjorie Main as Cantrell's mother. Another great aspect of this stirring film was its rousing Victor Young score.

In the midst of shooting, Trevor fell ill with strep throat.[20] Director Raoul Walsh shot around her at first but production had to be halted two days before Christmas 1939 and did not resume until February 1, 1940. It was estimated that this delay cost the studio $250,000.[21] Republic had set aside $1,000,000 for two Wayne-Trevor pictures; the other was going to be *Wagons Westwards*. But *Dark Command*'s long delays led to the postponement of the latter, which was recast with Chester Morris and Anita Louise.[22] The press reported that Trevor would take a six-month break after the completion of *Dark Command*, and "if she does not feel better after that she intends to retire."[23] Fortunately, she did feel better.

After three westerns in a row, Trevor was tested for a fourth, Warner Brothers' *Santa Fe Trail*, but the part went to Olivia de Havilland.[24] There was the possibility of a fifth, James Oliver Curwood's *The Hunted Woman* with Randolph Scott. This would have been

Set at the time of the Civil War, director Raoul Walsh's *Dark Command* (1940) focused on the deeds of the renegade Colonel Quantrill (renamed Cantrell). Walter Pidgeon (left) played Cantrell, with John Wayne as his rival for the affections of Claire. It was the third time in the space of a year that Claire and the Duke were teamed.

the third screen version of the tale and the first in sound, but it was not made.[25] She had previously withdrawn from *The Sentence* due to illness and was replaced by Virginia Bruce.[26] Trevor was also sought for a leading role in an adaptation of the Broadway hit play *Separate Rooms* (which starred Glenda Farrell), but the idea did not bear fruit.[27]

Trevor's next was the amiable western *Honky Tonk* (1941) with Clark Gable as a fast-talking con man tired of being chased out of every town. He arrives at Yellow Creek, Nevada, with the aim of running the town himself. In a few short years his achieves his goal, and along the way he marries the daughter (Lana Turner) of a judge (Frank Morgan). The townspeople eventually begin to turn against him, inspired by the judge who denounces

Claire enjoyed playing opposite one of her idols, Clark Gable, in the western *Honky Tonk* (1941).

him. Gable was in top form in the kind of role that could have been written for him, and teamed with Turner it was no surprise that the movie was a "ripsnorter at the box office."[28] Trevor played her usual other woman-bad girl role, straight-talking, sassy, hand on hip, dealing faro dressed to the nines wearing huge picture hats. Her costumes were something to behold: Designer Robert Kalloch outdid himself with some over-the-top gowns and unbelievable hats adorned with ostrich feathers. Although he looked like an academic, he was one of the leading designers at Columbia where he became known for his creative flair as much as his strange phobias. In his 150 films, he dressed many of the leading ladies of the golden era, including Claudette Colbert in *It Happened One Night* (1934) and Irene Dunne in *The Awful Truth* (1937). He died at just 54.

Trevor enjoyed working with Gable, who she said was wonderful. "To me, he was very adolescent," she remembered, "Sweet, sort of naïve in a way."[29] His picture adorned a wall of her home along with her other favorites Tyrone Power and Joan Fontaine.

Believing she had done a good job in her *Honky Tonk* role, Trevor attended a preview and was appalled by the finished result: "I came out in tears and started to cry right in the lobby," she recalled. "I was hysterical. I felt they had massacred my part. I knew it was the death of my career."[30] But director Norman Taurog noticed her in *Honky Tonk,* and on the strength of it she was cast in the comedy *Achilles,* later known as *Design for Living* (1941), starring Rosalind Russell and Walter Pidgeon. But Trevor's character was cut from the released film.[31] It was reported in the press that she would replace Rita Hayworth in *Our Wife,* but the part later went to Ruth Hussey.[32] Trevor and Brian Donlevy were announced as the leads in *Let the Eagle Scream*, a crime drama about a corrupt politician who becomes a banker, but the project was put to one side and then abandoned two years later.[33]

Between film engagements, Trevor returned to the stage in Bella Spewack's comedy *Out West It's Different*. She was joined by the scene-stealer par excellence Sam Levene, and the play began a tryout in Washington in December 1940. But the show seemed to suffer from a pre–Christmas slump. *Variety* reported that it "won strong notices from all critics, most of whom hailed it as the potential equal of *Boy Meets Girl*. Despite the reviews, plus the presence of Claire Trevor for Hollywood and Sam Levene for Broadway, the gross couldn't climb over the estimated $8500."[34] Around the same time, she appeared in the benefit show revue *Tonight at 8.30* in honor of its author Noël Coward, who was in the audience. In the Victorian musical sketch "Family Portrait," she played opposite Joan Fontaine, C. Aubrey Smith and Philip Merivale to great effect and it was reported that between them they "did the numbers proud."[35] The following year, playwright Edward Childs Carpenter, who had written *Whistling in the Dark,* wrote to columnist Jimmie Fidler asking him to help try and help persuade Trevor to return to Broadway for his latest play *Bad Angel*.[36] In the event, the play did not premiere at that time.

George Marshall's *Texas* (1941) was yet another undemanding Columbia western played in roistering style by a familiar cast. It featured rising stars Glenn Ford and William Holden as Confederate soldiers who head to postwar Texas and find themselves on opposing sides and rivals for the same gal (Trevor), a banker's daughter. Notable in the supporting cast

Claire had to rough it as the girl that William Holden and Glenn Ford fought over in *Texas* (1941).

was Edgar Buchanan in his usual avuncular-but-deadly mode, and George Bancroft as a big-talking, larger-than-life character on the make. Trevor was once again the only woman present—by now she was well on her way to becoming what one writer termed a man's star. She worked well with Holden and Ford, and many shared the hope of cast member (and Ford friend) William Gould that she should would be cast again alongside them both in *The Man from Colorado* (1948), but that failed to transpire. "A grand sport she is," said Gould, "and one of the best actresses in town for my money."[37] Trevor was thoroughly bruised and battered by the time *Texas* filming was complete, and did not relish bouncing about on a buckboard over rough terrain or being dragged across the dirt. She reflected that playing a good girl was much harder work than playing a bad girl. One of her admirers left her a huge saddle as a surprise for her one day, and she could barely lift it.[38]

She was next announced for *Mr. Twilight*, which was re-titled *The Gentleman Misbehaves*. This film was shelved for several years and was not made until after the war, then with a completely different cast.[39] Another possible vehicle was *Handle with Care* opposite George Raft and Victor McLaglen but the film also appears not to have been made.[40] She was due to join Cary Grant, Jean Arthur and Ronald Colman in *Three's a Crowd* but dropped out of the film, which was retitled *The Talk of the Town*.[41] Although she never appeared in one of Colman's films, she once described dancing with him as one of her favorite heart-stopping moments: "I almost fainted, I was so in love with him. That's the only time I met him, but he was absolutely handsome—twice as good-looking as on the screen. And his eyes, I'll never forget his eyes—like burning coals—and he was so gentle and sweet."[42]

She was announced for the comedy *Two Yanks in Trinidad* (1942) with Pat O'Brien and Brian Donlevy, but had to be replaced because she had already started work on *The Adventures of Martin Eden* (1942).[43] Based on Jack London's semi-autobiographical 1909 novel, *Martin Eden* was a good movie starring a young and gauche Glenn Ford in the title role. Trevor appeared as his loyal girlfriend, with Evelyn Keyes as the society girl vying for his affections. Eden recounts his life as a sailor under the brutal Captain "Butch" Raglan; before long there is a mutiny, led by Joe Dawson, whose sister Connie (Trevor) is Martin's fiancée. All the time Eden is at sea, he is writing his book which will be a damning indictment of the captain, his barbaric treatment of the crew and the dreadful conditions aboard ship. Once ashore, he tries to defend Joe, but realizes he is up against too many vested interests. He gatecrashes a party and meets a writer who helps him get his work seen and eventually published. In time, Martin's girlfriend Connie Dawson sees a change in him, and not for the better, and tries everything to bring him to his senses.

Unsurprisingly, Hollywood took liberties with London's original. The character of Eden's mentor Brissenden was a socialist in the novel, but appears in the film as a rather bourgeois figure fond of drink. Crucially, the ending was altered; Eden did not commit suicide, but Brissenden did. The movie made some apt observations about the publishing world, and the scene where Martin demands his 15 bucks royalties from his publisher would raise a knowing smile from many small-time authors. Ford possessed the fire of youth but the fight scenes were rather unconvincing and unnecessarily labored the point they were trying to make.

Trevor was a quiet and strong presence as his girl. Eden takes her for granted much of the time, but she proves to be the only character who stays true to herself throughout. Her portrayal was subtle and may have passed some observers by, but she nonetheless

The Adventures of Martin Eden (1942) was a good adaptation of Jack London's semi-autobiographical novel. It contained excellent work by Trevor as the loyal girlfriend of Glenn Ford.

stayed in the mind afterwards. On the set she told an interviewer her feelings about the film and of her career in general. She admitted that she didn't know if the film was right for her or not; "But then—I never know," she reflected. "I can see myself doing things like *Wuthering Heights,* but I'd probably be awful in them. I think I'd be good because they affect me emotionally…" Confessing that she thought she was "terrible" in *Texas* and *Honky Tonk,* she revealed a vulnerability that helped to make her one of the finest actresses of her generation but also one of the most insecure; "I get scared sometimes—thinking, I mean, how I've been in pictures eight years and am no farther along than I am."[44] She was making progress and would soon begin to define the abiding image of the *femme fatale.*

10

The War Years: *Street of Chance*

> She's one of Hollywood's most amiable personalities, has an attractive husky voice and a grand sense of humor. She's mildly intellectual, likes biographies and is good at all sports.—"Life Lines: Claire Trevor," *The World's News*, December 3, 1938, 15

The war years coincided with better roles in more varied fare for Trevor. She could not escape from westerns altogether but made some more interesting forays into noir territory and had her first real *femme fatale* roles. She did her bit for the war effort with many personal appearances and even made a film about life on the home front.

During the war, she took part in a number of morale-boosting events and functions. Shortly after the U.S. entered the war in December 1941, she gave a rousing speech (she co-wrote it with Budd Schulberg) in Boston for the Russian War Relief. "I delivered it with lots of expression and I hope it helped the cause," she remarked.[1] It was delivered before a large crowd and distinguished invited guests including Mrs. Litvinov, wife of the Russian ambassador, who also spoke.

Trevor was one of the stars who contributed to the War Bonds drive. She made several tours with Californian Senator George Murphy.[2] Accompanied by Walter Abel, she toured Iowa, Nebraska, Wyoming, Colorado and Idaho in September 1942.[3] Several events were organized by the Hollywood Victory Committee. Trevor, Jeanette MacDonald, Ruth Hussey and Ann Rutherford toured for "Women at War Week" in November 1942. She spoke in four cities in the course of a week: New Orleans, Memphis, Kansas City, Missouri, and San Antonio.[4] Many actresses were reluctant to make personal appearances because of rowdy audiences and even fear for their safety. For such appearances at a theater for a week, she asked $5000. Claire also took part in various committees that Hollywood organized for servicemen, such as "Shaves for the Boys" which had the aim of obtaining "free minor necessities for the boys in defense camps." Constance Bennett was head of the committee and others included Maureen O'Hara, Linda Darnell and Dorothy Lamour.[5] Along with Phyllis Brooks, Trevor organized Parties Unlimited, a regular entertainment at the Westwood Tennis Club for 150 soldiers.[6] She sometimes entertained at USO Camp shows across the country. During her appearances, she would invite a member of the audience up onto the stage to play Romeo to her Juliet in the famous balcony scene from Shakespeare's play.[7] She frequently danced with servicemen at USO parties and other events. One such was held at the Cheviot Hills Tennis Club, and Trevor was one of the actresses, including Gene

"For 13 years you've lived a lie. You've fooled your wife, your friends, even your country!"

Trevor played one of her first real *femme fatale* roles, a high-class blackmailer of diplomat William Powell, in *Crossroads* (1942).

Tierney, who danced with cadets of the U.S.A.A.F.[8] It was reported that servicemen from "six army regiments, 103 RAF fliers and Annapolis" had asked for a lock of Claire's hair.[9] During the war years, her house was adorned with pictures she had been sent by those in the services.

She never enjoyed being stopped for her autograph, and admitted that she "dies a thousand deaths when people come up to me at the shops and on the street."[10] Years later, when ardent film fan Ray Hagen approached her in a store and asked "Aren't you Claire Trevor?," she turned slowly and said, "Sometimes."[11] At the same time, she once complained that "the only men who whistle after me are truck drivers."[12] Her mailbag was always full from the time of her entry into films; she was still receiving letters from fans just before she died.

Based on the novel *Carrefour* by John H. Kafka, *Crossroads* (1942) was an intriguing crime drama that many have since positioned in the noir canon. Set in 1935 France, the plot concerned ambitious diplomat Talbot (William Powell) and his beautiful wife (Hedy Lamarr). He is suddenly plunged into a court case about an outstanding debt from 15 years before. Talbot claims to know nothing about this, as his memory does not stretch back further than 13 years ago when he was involved in a train accident. The publicity surrounding the case leads Henri Sarrou (Basil Rathbone) and nightclub singer Michelle Allaine (Trevor) to blackmail Talbot into giving them money to keep quiet about his true identity, accusing him of being a murderer.

A well-made drama, the movie maintained a fine atmosphere of mystery and employed an excellent cast to good effect. Rathbone, Trevor and Margaret Wycherly made very plausible blackmailers, and Trevor's role hinted at the femme fatale territory she would inhabit in the following years. She was also required to sing once more, but the actual singer was Connie Russell.[13] It was rumored that Marlene Dietrich was first offered Claire's role.[14] Trevor got on well with co-star Rathbone, having lunch with him and composer Bronislau Kaper most days during the making of the film. "Basil had a great sense of humor and kept us laughing with his 'suave' English stories," she recalled. "Those lunches were about the best thing about doing the picture."[15] Claire was among the many who attended Rathbone's legendary soirees organized by his wife Ouida.

The gowns by Kalloch that the two actresses wore brought real elegance and glamour to proceedings. Jack Conway was a workmanlike director; some of his films proved popular, such as *A Tale of Two Cities* (1935), a Best Picture nominee. *Viva Villa!* (1934) won an award at the Venice Film Festival. *Crossroads'* bathetic ending made the foregoing seem like just another routine crime caper. The original screen version *Carrefour* (1938), directed by Curtis Bernhardt, had many noir elements, some of which were retained in the American version. Bernhardt was a fine director whose films explored psychological depths and if he had been at the helm for *Crossroads* it would have been in a different league.

Street of Chance (1942) was an excellent noir based on a novel by Cornell Woolrich. This lobby card shows a scene in which Burgess Meredith (center) tries to clear himself of a murder charge with the help of invalid Adeline de Walt Reynolds while her nurse looks on.

Trevor's next project was *Street of Chance* (1942), one of the earliest classic American noirs. In it, she began to define the image of the femme fatale. It begins with Frank Thompson (Burgess Meredith) being hit by falling masonry. When he comes to, he is disorientated and does not know what he is doing in that part of town. He goes home to his wife, but finds she has moved, and it transpires that he left his wife over a year ago. He attempts to return to work but believes he is being pursued by someone. When that someone tracks him down, he secretes his wife and determines to retrace his steps in the street where he had the accident. In time he is found by Ruth Dillon (Trevor) and learns that he is wanted for the murder of her employer Diedrich. He goes to the house trying to discover the truth and is aided by Diedrich's invalid mother, who witnessed the murder but is unable to move or speak and communicates with him by blinking.

The curious drama is a slow starter but becomes intriguing once the action switches to the mysterious Diedrich house. The plot had a number of holes in it, and it was especially convenient that Thompson had a wife who had patiently waited a year for him to return. The screenplay was based on a Cornell Woolrich novel, *The Black Curtain*, the first of many screen adaptations of his work. The ploy of amnesia is a natural device in the milieu of noir; Woolrich often utilized it. Perhaps it was used to best effect in *Somewhere in the Night* (1946) with John Hodiak as a returning war veteran. In *Street of Chance*, Thompson's loss of memory was rather selective; he had blotted out the part of his life in which he might have murdered someone and for which he had used an alias. None of this was explained sufficiently well, and from some of the things that were said about his Danny Nearing persona, he was not such an innocent as he appeared. Nor was his use of an alias established satisfactorily.

However, the air of mystery was well-sustained with great use of light and shadows. One senses that the noir universe was beginning to form in some of the passages here, especially in the scenes inside the house and in the summer house. The striking Theodore Sparkuhl photography showed his German expressionist influence. The jazz music score of David Buttolph added to the ambience, lending the film a different feel to others made in the same era. This was allied to the sense of disorientation which the plot engendered. A requisite definition of a film noir seems to involve the use of a plot that few can follow coherently. There was a distinct sense of dread in *Street of Chance* which was at least indirectly linked to the war.

Among the actors, Claire was singled out for praise, one reviewer commenting that she gave "a fine characterization that strikes dramatic depths far beyond any of her previous screen offerings."[16] It was later revealed that her death scene required four takes until she took her shoes off; she just "couldn't die beautifully in closeup because her shoes were pinching."[17] Most of the wardrobe she wore she bought herself after asking the head office; they sent her downtown to get everything she needed.[18]

Director Jack Hively had a varied career that encompassed a Gloria Swanson comedy, *Father Takes a Wife* (1941), a couple of films in the Saint series and *Appointment in Tokyo* (1945), a patriotic documentary about the war in the Pacific. He later found success on television with the series *Lassie* and *The Life and Times of Grizzly Adams*.

The sequence in which Nearing attempts to communicate with the invalid mother was one of the most successful episodes. The veteran actress Adeline de Walt Reynolds, who played the elderly invalid, made it live despite the fact that she had no dialogue to work with and could act only with her eyes. Reynolds had lived a quite remarkable life, raising four children and teaching to support them after the death of her husband. She entered the University of California at Berkeley when in her sixties and then took acting lessons, thus fulfilling her childhood ambition which her father had thwarted. She did not make her film debut until she was approaching 80. While chatting with her on the set one day, Claire asked her why she had waited so long to start acting. "Well, my dear," the old lady replied, "I was preparing myself."[19]

Trevor was announced for a run of westerns in her familiar guise of the saloon girl role, propping up the bar. Firstly in *City Without Men* with Cornel Wilde and Linda Darnell but that time she lost out to Glenda Farrell.[20] Although sought for a long time for *Silver Queen*, set in Alaska, she was replaced by Priscilla Lane. Trevor was tested for a role in *Wherever the Grass Grows* with Rod Cameron and Claudia Drake, but the film was never made.[21] None of these were any great loss, and she instead made *The Desperadoes* (1943), which bore an uncanny resemblance to the other films.[22] Columbia's first color western, it was filmed on location in Kanab, Utah. The good cast is headed by Randolph Scott and Glenn Ford as rivals for Evelyn Keyes. Edgar Buchanan enjoyed himself in support as a seemingly worthy citizen who alternates between his own greed and his daughter's happiness. The film was played at a lively pace and color rendered it more interesting. Trevor had a fairly prominent role, as a dance hall girl The Countess; according to publicity, "Where she got her title, no one knows and wise men don't ask."[23] It was not a role that extended Trevor's range, nor was it ever likely to win her the guy at the end, but as usual she brought verve to the proceedings. She was capable as always and good-hearted. She was equally at home in the romantic and dramatic scenes as she was in the more knockabout routines with Guinn "Big Boy" Williams, who reveled in the unlikely role of a dynamite expert. The leading players made personal appearances at the theater in Kanab which was packed for the occasion.[24] Stuntwoman Ione Reed once again substituted for Trevor in the rugged outdoor scenes, but drew the line at smoking a cigar as was required by the script; Trevor had to smoke her own.[25] She did not mind this, and cited the example of many illustrious cigar-smokers from history such as stage beauty Lillian Russell, Lola Montez, Carmen Sylva, the queen of Romania and Queen Amelie of Portugal. "They were all independent thinkers who refused to be frightened by convention," Trevor observed. "The thing that sticks in my mind is the high mental caliber of these women who made history who are numbered among the world's cigar smokers."[26]

In July 1942, Trevor's marriage to Clark Andrews came to an official end; they had separated five months earlier. At the time of the separation, "mother-in-law trouble" was cited as a contributing cause.[27] However, there had been reports of problems between them for some time. Only 15 months after they married, it was said that they were heading for the divorce courts because of a rumor of her dates with "a lad in the Young & Rubicam offices."[28] They celebrated their third wedding anniversary denying that there was anything to her rendezvous with Victor Mature.[29] Claire instigated the divorce on the grounds of indifference, and accused him of "going out on all-night parties without her."[30] She said that she had "seen him at parties showing amorous attentions to other women, even wrapping his arms all around them."[31] "That sort of destroyed something between us," she remarked.[32] She also said that he "lived extravagantly beyond his means of $250 a week" and in addition "had to borrow money from her to settle his bills."[33] The suit was uncontested and they settled a property agreement out of court.[34]

Afterwards she was often sighted by gossip columnists on dates with Randolph Scott, playwright Marc Connolly and others.[35] She admitted that she had tried to make her private life appear more "colorful" for a brief time during the early war years. She gave out more publicity, wore exotic outfits and was seen more at parties. She found it too trying and soon went back to being herself. She was never a personality in the same way as other stars, and courting publicity was anathema to her.

At the time of her divorce, she had already met the man who was to become her second husband: Lt. Cylos Dunsmoor, a navy pilot, described somewhat erroneously as the "scion of a Los Angeles banking family."[36] He was born five months after the death of his father, a prominent businessman and secretary of Brock's jewelry house. Cylos Sr. died of a stroke at the age of 37, leaving a widow, Marilla, and three daughters, the eldest of whom was ten.[37] Marilla later married banker Charles E. Toll.

Twenty-six years old, six years younger than Claire, Cylos Jr. began his career in the army and worked as an engineer at an aircraft plant before switching to the Navy. He was a cadet at Corpus Christi, Texas, and won his wings in October 1942. He was then posted to the airbase at Alamitos, near Santa Ana.

At the time, Claire was reportedly "worried ill" that the negative publicity surrounding her divorce would harm his standing in the Navy.[38] However, they married on April 17, 1943, in Tijuana, Mexico, with Sally Eilers as a bridesmaid and Lt. Howard Varney as best man. This time, only their immediate families were in on the secret.[39]

In September 1943, he became a flying instructor at Olathe, Kansas; while he was stationed there, Claire visited him, and even tried to cook for him with predictably disastrous results; "I might as well admit it, I'm hopeless in the kitchen," she said.[40] After the breakdown of her first marriage, she was determined to get it right the second time. She even offered to give up her career and become a full-time housewife but her husband said he didn't want her to lose her identity while he was serving.[41] Their son Charles, always known as Chuck, was born in December 1943 and she took about a year off from the screen. Such was the fickleness of fame that the birth of her son went largely unnoticed in the press. When she returned to work, she felt invigorated. "Believe it or not I'm enjoying my movie work more than I ever did before," she declared. "Now that I have somebodies to think about while I'm acting."[42] At the end of 1943, she moved to a house in Beverly Hills with a Victory garden.[43]

Columbia's *Good Luck, Mr. Yates* (1943), originally known as *Right Guy,* was effectively Claire's only film directed entirely towards the war effort. She donned overalls and appeared as a welder, and still managed to look fetching in her dungarees. The story: Oliver Yates (Jess Barker), a military academy instructor, tries to enlist but is told he is 4F and unable to fight because of a perforated eardrum. He consults a German doctor (Albert Bassermann) who tells him that the condition could improve with time. Yates takes a job in a shipyard, but tells his old cadets that he has joined the army. At the shipyard he falls for Ruth (Trevor), which raises the ire of Charlie Edmunds (Tom Neal) who is also sweet on her. Edmunds spreads stories about Yates, impugning his patriotism and willingness to fight. The truth becomes apparent to the young cadets. There is a showdown between Yates and Edmunds, which ends with Yates heroically saving his life when there is a blaze at the shipyard.

Good Luck, Mr. Yates differed from other wartime propaganda films in that it was aimed squarely at the home front, and particularly those who were the right age to take part in the conflict but, through no fault of their own, were unable to do so directly. The shipyard was shown in near-documentary style and looked impressive, emphasizing the scale of the war effort and how every branch of the services and civilians were doing their bit which was just as important as the contribution of those on active service. It is surprising how swiftly Yates goes from being a popular teacher to a hounded turncoat, and it is not long before the lynch mob works itself up into action on the flimsiest of evidence.

Regarding Trevor and Edgar Buchanan, who played her father, a contemporary observer felt that "their hearts just don't seem to be in it."[44] The same critic noted that the film had a comic-strip flavor and declared that some passages had been "lifted whole from *The Adventures of Sam the Ship Builder*."[45]

As entertainment during a lunch break interval at the shipyard, the Three Stooges recorded one of their routines, "Niagara Falls," and Nan Wynn sang a song. This section was deleted entirely from the finished film, although the Stooges' routine later appeared in *Gents Without Cents* (1944).[46] Director Ray Enright was mostly known for comedies and routine westerns. Trevor was due to make another film for the war effort, playing a press agent opposite Janet Blair in Columbia's *Victory Caravan*, but this never came to pass.[47]

Trevor was unimpressed by much of the material she was being offered

Claire donned welding gear as a shipyard riveter in *Good Luck, Mr. Yates* (1943), her only war film. The film was titled *La Injuria* in Mexico, as shown in this poster. The story concerned the problems faced by young men who could not serve in the armed forces, but showed how essential a contribution they could make in civilian occupations.

at Columbia, most of which she called "dog pictures … and I don't mean animal pictures, honey." She felt nauseated by them and finally refused to do one, which she said made her feel physically sick at the prospect. It was practically the first time she had felt compelled to rebel, and studio boss Harry Cohn said he wanted to see her at once. Knowing of her fondness for scent, Cohn tried to bribe her with perfume; "He had a back room full of bribe items," she remarked. Regardless of her love of perfume, she could not be placated and refused to do the film.[48]

The United Artists western *The Woman of the Town* (1943) gave her a chance for only a slight variation on her usual prostitute character, but this was a decent B-picture with a good story. She was paired with Albert Dekker, who often played heels but was elevated here to a lead hero role as Bat Masterson. Western films seem to be continually fascinated with a dozen major characters of history, and Masterson has often cropped up. Here he is introduced as an old man working on a New York newspaper and relates the tale in flashback.

This was one of the better westerns, well-acted by the principals. Once again Claire was a good bad girl, and even had the chance to sing "Jerusalem, the Holy City" in church (Betty Brewer was the real singer[49]), watched by approving reverend Percy Kilbride. The pious local women realize that she was a call girl. The film had good atmosphere and the town had a more authentic frontier feeling than usual. Those newly formed towns must have been a mixture of the sacred and profane, and the juxtaposition was typified by the contrast of the music of the church and that of the saloon. This latter was well represented by the visiting music hall artiste Eddie Foy and the songs "Poor Polly" and "I'm a Heavy Tipper" with their odd combination of schmaltz and double entendre. Dora Hand may represent a composite character of women who actually existed. Although initially shunned for what she does, she eventually wins over the townspeople with her simple faith, her selflessness, benevolent charity and the way she always helps children. She hates all the killing that goes on and wants Masterson to give up his gun and makes him promise to bury it.

The Woman of the Town (1943) was a better-than-average western inspired by the life of Bat Masterson. Left to right: Marian Mains, Trevor and Albert Dekker.

When she is tragically shot, he is true to his word and buries the gun with her and renounces violence. True or not, it made a pleasing story and the sincerity of the actors made it seem believable. Trevor as always eschewed sentimentality in favor of honesty and so made Dora a tragic human figure rather than a make-believe plaster saint. Several of the usual western suspects (Henry Hull, Porter Hall *et al.*) were present and the cast was augmented by a young Barry Sullivan making his film debut in a striking cowboy outfit complete with tassels. The movie was typical of the oeuvre of director George Archainbaud, with whom Trevor had worked on *My Marriage*. In a popular move, producer Harry Sherman initiated hospitality visits to the studios for servicemen. One hundred fifty soldiers were invited to informal festivities at the end of the day's filming. Each day 30 sailors, soldiers and Marines were allowed onto the *Woman of the Town* stages to watch the shooting.[50]

The better-than-average film was well-received; the Miklos Rozsa score won an Academy Award. Trevor was praised but admitted that she hated being the dance hall queen with the heart of gold; "I'm not really the western type," she stated.[51] But casting directors appeared to be deaf.

She was sought to star once more with Sullivan in writer and producer Leslie Fuller's proposed film *Marseilles* for Paramount.[52] The wartime tale, co-written by Leyla Georgie and the renowned French writer Maurice Dekobra, was never made.[53] Hers was one of the names in the frame for the female lead in *Sullivan's Travels*, but director Preston Sturges insisted on casting Veronica Lake.[54] Trevor was also considered for a small role as a gangster's ex-wife in the maudlin melodrama *None But the Lonely Heart* (1944), but the role was given to June Duprez.[55] She was also sought for a starring role in the Broadway farce *Three's a Family* opposite Frank McHugh. This popular show ran at the Longacre Theater for more than a year despite the fact that neither McHugh nor Trevor was able to accept.[56]

The wheel turns, and Claire now entered the most fulfilling years of her career and carved her niche as the screen's definitive femme fatale in a series of films that have become iconic and still seem incredibly modern, delineating the palpable thread of angst in postwar society.

11

Femme Fatale

> Most people are held inside their own personalities, there's no escape from the wishes that can't come true or the things they don't want to remember. But an actor can take on another form, become another personality.—Louis Reid, "A Really Good Bad Girl," *Screenland*, June 1950, 71

One of Claire's ambitions was to play Shakespeare's greatest villainess Lady Macbeth.[1] Unfortunately, although she once played a character with that moniker, she never achieved her goal. But she *was* among the foremost delineators of the inheritors of the Lady Macbeth mantle: the *femme fatale*. It is for these roles that she has latterly been lauded as the "Queen of Film Noir." Her run of peerless '40s portrayals helped shape the image of the genre: alluring beauty that proves fatal. Noir has a powerful hold on the emotions of a world in flux and it was no coincidence that it was born and came into its own during the turbulent war years and their aftermath. In essence, the modern world began then, which helps explain the continued relevance of noir to our own time and beyond. The best of those films seem alive and modern and should continue to feel relevant for all time.

Claire loved murder mysteries and admitted that she had read everything from Edgar Allan Poe to Mickey Spillane, so she was a natural for the terrain of noir.[2] All the same, she was at first reluctant to accept the role of Mrs. Grayle in *Murder, My Sweet* (1944), arguably the best version of the Raymond Chandler novel *Farewell, My Lovely* published four years before. Star Dick Powell was more associated with musical comedies up to that point. The title change was unnecessary because even the most casual observer could tell from seeing the opening credits and hearing the dramatic Roy Webb score that this was not going to be a fluffy musical.

Ex-con "Moose" Molloy (Mike Mazurki) hires private eye Marlowe (Powell) to find "his girl" Velma. Simultaneously Marlowe is asked by Grayle (Miles Mander) to investigate the theft of a jade necklace from his beautiful (and much younger) wife (Trevor). Marlowe's search for the truth leads him into a dangerous world where he is drugged, beaten and deceived.

The cast was well-chosen. Powell proved to be ideal for leading roles in crime films; the tough, cynical and wryly humorous Marlowe was one of his best. Miles Mander was suitably weasel-like as the self-deluding Grayle; his English tones and spare frame gave him a certain bearing that contradicted his complete unreliability. Mander had a full life; he was a sheep farmer and aviation pioneer before becoming an actor and director. Along the way he also married an Indian princess, Prativa Devi of Cooch Behar. On screen he appeared in some of Alfred Hitchcock's silent films and scored as a dope fiend in *The Fake*

"As cute as lace pants": Claire as the ultimate *femme fatale* in *Murder, My Sweet* (1944) with Dick Powell.

(1927). In the 1930s, he settled in Hollywood where he played a wide array of majors, sinister doctors and philandering husbands. He made two good contributions to Universal's Sherlock Holmes series and was especially memorable as the broken-down alcoholic father clinging to his books in *Primrose Path* (1940). His *Murder, My Sweet* role was one of his best. Two years after it was released, he died of a heart attack while dining in the Brown Derby restaurant in Los Angeles at the age of 57. Few others ever made weakness seem such a virtue, and he was ideally suited to the shadowy noir idiom.

The towering (6'5") ex-wrestler Mike Mazurki enjoyed some interesting parts in film but seldom found perfect roles like "Moose" Molloy. Belying his appearance and the way he was typecast, he was by all accounts a rather cultured and well-read man in real life. All the other players, especially Otto Kruger, Anne Shirley and Esther Howard, made telling contributions. One could say it was a perfect screen adaptation of Chandler's universe. The 1975 Robert Mitchum version might be closer to the book in some aspects, but it lacked something intangible—perhaps a real sense of its time—that the earlier film captured.

Director Edward Dmytryk's output ranged from decent horrors such as *The Devil Commands* (1941) to respected war films like *Back to Bataan* (1945). He made his name with a series of noirs which continue to be discussed at length by cineastes, including *Murder, My Sweet*, *Cornered* (1945, which also starred Powell) and *Crossfire* (1947). One of the Hollywood Ten who had been accused of Communist links, he refused to cooperate with HUAC. Threatened with imprisonment for contempt of Congress, he sought exile in Europe.

He made some interesting films in Britain including the curious *Obsession* (1949) aka *The Hidden Room*. On his return to America, he was imprisoned for several months and finally agreed to name others he knew to be party members. He wrote extensively about his experiences in his memoir *Odd Man Out: A Memoir of the Hollywood Ten*.

Murder, My Sweet is now recognized as a noir classic and there has been extensive analysis. One of the best summaries: "There is nothing sweet about *Murder, My Sweet,* a film that remains not only a highly stylized and complex detective thriller but also an uncompromising vision of corruption and decay."[3] There were some particularly memorable scenes that proved hugely influential, such as the narcotic dream sequence when Marlowe is drugged by the mysterious Dr. Sonderborg.

An important aspect of the film was its style and especially the costumes designed by Edward Stevenson, which had a large measure of input from Trevor. The script called for her to wear sexy shorts at one stage, but when she tried them on, they didn't look quite sexy enough; they seemed merely sporty and wholesome, and were not right for the character. Instead she wore a number of outfits including a tantalizing white dress and a split skirt. A reporter quipped that she was typed forever now because of the split skirt; "So my husband tells me," she joked, "He still hasn't gotten over the whistles and stamping that went up when *Murder, My Sweet* was shown at his base."[4] The white dress was almost entirely her own creation; she gave the specifications to Stevenson, who worked on it overnight and added the finishing touches to it as her scene was about to be shot the next morning.[5]

Murder, My Sweet established Claire as one of the leading *femme fatales* of the silver screen. The Belgian version of the film was titled *Adieu, ma Belle!*, as shown in this poster.

Trevor really owed her entrance into noir to producer Charles Koerner, who recognized her worth. He called and offered her the part of Mrs. Grayle in 1943. It was all part of his long-term design for her, with the intention of building her into a bigger star and providing her with better material.[6] Unfortunately, Koerner died in February 1946 and his plans were not followed through by anyone else. But he had started her on the right path, and her RKO films were among the best of her career. Acclaimed director Jean Renoir lauded Koerner as an extraordinary man, and cited the studio during those years as being the "center of real cinema in Hollywood." He commented: "I deeply regretted his death. Had he not died, I believe I would have made 20 films at RKO. I would have worked all my life at RKO. He was a man who knew the business and the exploitation of cinema, but at the same time conceded that one must experiment."[7] Trevor once remarked that she never had an influential director or producer shepherding her career in the way that some actresses had; one thinks of Dietrich and von Sternberg. Koerner was the nearest Claire came to a positive outside influence on the direction of her career at a crucial time and he undoubtedly set her on the right path. Had it not been for the noirs she made at RKO years in the 1940s, it is unlikely she would be remembered in the same way today.

After the gala premiere of *Murder, My Sweet,* Trevor and Powell were guests of honor at a special reception held at the White and Gold Suite of the Plaza Hotel. Also present were officials of RKO along with the usual publicists and journalists.[8]

Her next RKO venture was *Johnny Angel* (1945), a good noir that seemed better than it was due to the presence of Trevor in full bad dame mode. Captain Johnny (George Raft) discovers his father's ship abandoned with the cargo intact, his father dead and the crew missing. His investigation is obfuscated by "Gusty," the head of the line (Marvin Miller), "Gusty"'s overweening secretary Miss Drumm (Margaret Wycherly) and his restless wife Lily (Trevor). Johnny tracks down key witness Paulette (Signe Hasso), who takes refuge at the house of Celestial O'Brien (Hoagy Carmichael). With Paulette's help, he eventually unravels the mystery of who killed his father and why.

Set in a fogbound New Orleans, the underrated noir *Johnny Angel* (1945) had a fine cast which included Hoagy Carmichael (left) singing "Memphis in June."

The film, based on the novel *Mr. Angel Comes Aboard* by Charles Gordon Booth, had a suitably foggy atmosphere, which was apt for the density of the plot. The cast kept things intriguing, and Hoagy Carmichael is always a welcome presence in any film. Here he sings "Memphis in June," which may seem a strange choice for a moody noir but somehow fitted in perfectly. His agreeably sideways humor made a neat counterpoint to the murkiness of the setting and plot. The business with a child's propeller toy was charming and relieved the rather fatalistic feeling that pervaded. At times it was difficult to know what was going on. Often this seems a prerequisite in the noir universe, adding to the sense of unease. This thriller, described as the "year's major surprise package," proved popular at the box office where it recorded profits of over $1,000,000.[9] Director

Edwin L. Marin began his career as an assistant cameraman before moving into directing. He made a plethora of bread-and-butter westerns, but was also responsible for *A Christmas Carol* (1938) and several films in the Maisie series. *Johnny Angel* was one of three films he made with George Raft; the others were *Nocturne* (1946) and *Race Street* (1948).

Trevor was in fine form as the duplicitous Lily, merciless, greedy and cold-hearted, her shifting emotions registering in a flash of her eyes. For the final scene where she had to register horror when she sees her presumed dead husband return, the director was just not satisfied with her reactions. After 12 takes he said "You've got to act scared," but she responded, "It's no use, I'm just too happy today to be frightened." She had received the good news that she was going to see her husband soon because he was on leave. Marin played a cruel joke on her and had a property man in the background of the shot post a sign reading "Telegram posted from the War Department." It did the trick and she acted duly terrified in the scene when she saw it. She had imagined that Cylos' leave had been cancelled. She was less than happy when she found out it was a joke. After that, Marin "hastily made for the door and said 'Take an hour for lunch everybody. Too hot to work now.'"[10]

The other actors filled their roles admirably. Miller played a curiously ambiguous character, at one and the same time menacing and pathetic. The actor showed to great effect here, away from his usual run of limiting roles as Oriental crime bosses and shady generals, and made "Gusty" a memorable personality. He was gracious in his admiration of his co-star: "I learned more about acting from Claire Trevor than anyone else I ever worked with," he remarked. "She's great, just great."[11]

Claire changed her appearance subtly in her noir roles. In *Born to Kill*, she had dark hair in a loose style; in *Murder, My Sweet* it was blonde and highly stylized in curls; in *Johnny Angel* it was similar but piled more on top and intricate. Combined with the style of dress and her differing approach to each role, she made these women distinctive and fascinating in their own right.

Between hard-boiled dame roles in classic noirs, Trevor flitted through *The Bachelor's Daughters* (1946), a fluffy concoction which she once cited as her least favorite film.[12] Four girls who work in a department store pool their resources to rent a Long Island house for a month and pose as sisters. They persuade hard-hearted floorwalker Mr. Moody (Adolphe Menjou) to act as their father, and a faded silent screen actress Molly (Billie Burke) to pose as their mother. Each hopes to snare a wealthy suitor. After a number of misadventures, most of them do so. Gail Russell marries a millionaire, Ann Dvorak's dreams of being a singer come true, and Jane Wyatt is matched with a shipping clerk at the store who actually turns out to be a concert pianist and the son of the store owner. Menjou is paired with Burke. Only Trevor ended up alone; she was the meanest of course and the $8000 asking price of her millionaire's yacht proved to be too much. The music included Beethoven's "Moonlight Sonata" played by pianist Eugene List, who, while he was a U.S. Army sergeant, performed for Truman, Churchill and Stalin at the Potsdam conference in 1945.

What used to be known as "a woman's picture," *The Bachelor's Daughters* was the antithesis of Claire's usual screen roles. She was very much a man's star; it seems strange to see her as part of a mostly female ensemble. Director–co-writer Andrew L. Stone, best-known for hard-boiled crime dramas such as *Highway 301* (1950) and *The Steel Trap* (1952), also dabbled in musicals including *The Great Victor Herbert* (1939) and featherweight

The featherweight romantic comedy *The Bachelor's Daughters* (1946) was a real curiosity for Trevor; she once described it as her least favorite film. Left to right: Gail Russell, Ann Dvorak, Jane Wyatt, Trevor, Billie Burke, Eugene List (playing piano) and Adolphe Menjou.

"comedies" like *Fun on a Weekend* (1947). It is strange that Claire's only film for Stone was one that was least suited to her talents. The movie was shot in black and white when it seemed to cry out for color. *The Bachelor's Daughters* was silly, over-sentimental but entertaining in its own way. "It's one way to keep your mind off the coal strike," observed a contemporary commentator.[13]

Claire returned to her familiar milieu in *Crack-Up* (1946), another intriguing yarn set in the rarefied world of art, a natural background for noir. It begins with George Steele (Pat O'Brien) breaking into the museum where he works as an art expert. He attacks a guard and then knocks over a valuable statue. He recounts a story about being in a train wreck outside New York, and in flashback goes over the events of the previous hours. There is a murder, and while trying to clear his name he uncovers an elaborate plot to steal priceless works of art and replace them with forgeries.

The screenplay was based on the 1943 short story "Madman's Holiday" by Frederic Brown, a prolific author famous for his mystery and science fiction tales. The movie had good atmosphere and a uniformly excellent cast. The suave Herbert Marshall was on hand as a Scotland Yard art expert who keeps his powder dry, with Wallace Ford as a laconic detective and Ray Collins as an urbane villain. Trevor played O'Brien's erstwhile girlfriend, who runs around after him most of the time; for a change, she was not the bad dame. In an excellent scene in a penny arcade, Trevor and O'Brien think they are being watched by a policeman (Ed Gargan). Trevor puts on a broad New York accent to divert suspicion but it makes her seem more suspicious. The policeman walks up to them and passes them and instead goes up to a small individual peering into a "What the Butler Saw" machine, who he believes is a child. "How old are you?" The man turns to look at the cop. "Forty-four, how old are you?" There were numerous other moments of humor, such as one on the train where O'Brien looks at the other people in the carriage and a man notices him staring at him and suddenly becomes suspicious. Whether the humor was intentional or not is a moot point. O'Brien had a deadpan delivery of lines that made his performances seem tongue-in-cheek.

The film was not well-received. One liverish theater manager commented, "These three names (O'Brien, Trevor and Marshall) might have meant something once, but that time has passed. The picture might have meant something in 1929 when people paid to hear sound effects."[14] Now it is possible to view the film in proper perspective. It has many things in its favor, not least a distinct feeling of unease, with some excellent photography by Robert de Grasse. The scenes in the railway carriage were especially successful and the seemingly superfluous characters added to the atmosphere. A number of commentators have mentioned the subject of art and the way surrealism (or modernism) is viewed in the film in a detrimental way. For instance, the man with a heavy "European" accent who speaks

The atmospheric *Crack-Up* (1946) starred (left to right) Pat O'Brien, Claire and Herbert Marshall. An intriguing psychological noir, it raised interesting questions about the use and misuse of technological advances made during the war.

in defense of modernism during a lecture is drowned out by the elitist audience, and carted away as if he is a madman. The connection between modernism and radicalism is strongly evident during an era when any kind of free thinking and deviation from "the norm" was feared. Robert Porffirio, writing in *Film Noir,* makes an interesting point about *Crack-Up*'s use of technological advances made by the war and how they are used for good and ill: "Ironically, both the x-ray and narcosynthesis are means of discovering the 'truth'; and when Lowell (Ray Collins) reminds us that narcosynthesis was a by-product of the war, American concern with the abuse of technology is linked again to the war that culminated with the atomic bomb."[15]

One night there was a break-in at the studio and many of the cast had their property stolen. Claire lost a fur and other items of apparel, Herbert Marshall lost a watch and O'Brien $100. Altogether, thieves stole about $1000 worth of items and cash.[16] The unusual career of director Irving Reis began when he founded CBS Radio's innovative Columbia Workshop in the 1930s. Along with such light comedies as *The Big Street* (1942) and *The Bachelor and the Bobby-Soxer* (1947), he made a successful screen version of Arthur Miller's play *All My Sons* (1948) and even worked on *Hitler's Children* (1943). He died suddenly at the age of 47.

Trevor was touted for the leading role in *Canyon Passage* (1946), when the director Jacques Tourneur hoped to reunite her with John Wayne and Thomas Mitchell, but none of these were available and her role went to Susan Hayward.[17] There was dismay in some quarters when Betty Hutton was cast as Texas Guinan in *Incendiary Blonde* (1945). "The only actress in Hollywood who can bring the one and only Texas to the screen is Claire Trevor," wrote one critic.[18] The film was a musical so it *was* much more suited to Hutton. Trevor had played the same kind of role once too often anyway.

In 1946, she made a long-promised return to the Broadway stage, persuaded by Robert Montgomery to join his production of the light romantic Cold War comedy *The Big Two*, set in Baden Baden. Trevor essayed yet another reporter, with Philip Dorn as a Russian captain. Although the play was judged to have "bright dialog," it was only considered a qualified success; many felt that it lacked sparkle, and others noted that Trevor's part was poorly written and too stereotypical.[19] One reviewer commented: "Claire Trevor does what she can with the hard-boiled and brassy but alert and intelligent newspaper woman. If her performance is at fault, that fault is her overemphasis. But then it's that kind of character."[20] Another critic at least was alive to her art, and wrote that she gave a three-dimensional performance "and gives the lie to those proponents of the idea that Hollywood has a crippling effect upon stage acting."[21] Even so, the play closed after only two weeks.

That did not deter her from doing more stage plays. She often appeared at local performances in California, and played to sold-out houses at the Laguna Beach Playhouse summer theater. Her portrayal of the femme in *Dark Victory* was said to have caused "probably the biggest stir yet" with audiences. A local critic observed, "Miss Trevor's special victory, regardless of all else, is because the role, with its many changes of mood, is exceedingly demanding."[22] In 1947, she starred in *Goodbye Again* opposite Jose Ferrer in summer theater in Detrolt. A romantic comedy of misunderstanding between a once married couple, it proved popular with audiences. Despite the excessive heat that August, it made $8500 in its first week and $7200 in its second.[23] A local playgoer remarked, "Miss Trevor is charmingly sincere, acting quietly, yet able to convey a great deal with a twist of her mouth or a glance of her eyes. Her performance is excellent contrast to Ferrer's [near-burlesque approach]."[24]

In August 1946, Trevor received a default divorce from Cylos Dunsmoor after three years of marriage. When he left the Navy in September 1945, he had not been able to find a job. A court heard that he had become "morose and sulky," and took no interest in their home.[25] Sometimes they would sit down for meals and he would not speak to her the whole time.[26] She said that he "belittled her efforts" when she resumed her screen career. He used profanity and "criticized her friends in their presence."[27] He "finally told her last June [1946] that he could not go on living with her."[28] She was awarded custody of their son Charles, three and a half, and $50 a month alimony from her ex-husband. She received the second and final divorce in August 1947.[29] When reflecting on the marriage shortly afterwards, Claire admitted that it was really a wartime romance which, like many others, did not long survive the conflict. "I think it was the uniform—plus my wish to be patriotic," she said. "It is hard to adjust your life to someone who doesn't understand the demands made upon an actress."[30] She had hoped to keep the divorce a secret but an overzealous fan put paid to that when he exposed the story.[31]

Afterwards she had lots of dates and was reportedly close to marriage with John Shelton. She denied the rumors, saying "there was never anything too it, really."[32] Not long afterwards, she met producer Milton H. Bren and found at last with him the contented family life for which she had always longed.

12

Queen of Noir

> You're the coldest iceberg of a woman I ever saw, and the rottenest inside. I've seen plenty too. I wouldn't trade places with you if they sliced me into little pieces.—Mrs. Kraft to Helen Brent in *Born to Kill* (1947)

The postwar years saw Trevor at her zenith: She was receiving far better roles and had become one of the screen's foremost *femme fatales*. There was something unleashed by the war that was captured by film noir more than any other genre: the propensity for violence and passion, psychosis, a sense of unease and fatalism. Arguably the films she made in this period were the best of her career and culminated in a much-deserved Academy Award.

Born to Kill (1947), originally known as *Deadlier Than the Male*, was to have starred Tallulah Bankhead in the *femme fatale* role.[1] There was also some discussion about the leading man; at one stage it was reported that Lawrence Tierney was still under a cloud with RKO, but then it was decided to give him a second chance. The smaller roles were filled by some expert character players, especially Esther Howard, Elisha Cook, Jr., and Walter Slezak.

Recent divorcee Helen Brent (Trevor) comes across a murder scene at the place where she is staying and, instead of reporting it, leaves immediately for San Francisco to be with her wealthy boyfriend. On the train she meets Sam Wilde, who was responsible for the murders. She is instantly attracted to him. Wilde comes to stay with Helen and her sister, and before long he marries her sister for her money. Helen's jealousy is aroused and she proves deadly to the man she loves.

Tierney was perfectly cast as the murderer: cool, aloof, cynical-looking, with an enigmatic half-smile. Although the script stressed that he was insane, there was something in his demeanor which left the audience wondering. Tierney's tendency to underplay appeared to leave this question open.

The marvelous hardboiled dialogue is full of wisecracks and perfect for noir: "His eyes get me—the way they run you up and down like a searchlight," says Wilde's unfortunate victim, Laury Palmer (Isabel Jewell). Screenwriters Eve Greene and Richard Macaulay adapted the novel by James Gunn, a seldom mentioned writer who later worked on television. Macaulay was well-known for his years at Warner Brothers where he was co-writer of *The Roaring Twenties* (1939), *They Drive By Night* (1940) and others. Mrs. Kraft alone was a great character study; a broken-down dame living vicariously through her young friend Laury. She eagerly asks Laury about her latest boyfriend; "He's this big across the shoulders..." says Laury. "He's the quiet sort. And yet you get the feeling that if you stepped out of line, he'd kick your teeth down your throat." "Why, ain't that wonderful!" replies

Helen Brent (Trevor) has a memorable hotel room encounter with Mrs. Kraft (Esther Howard) in *Born to Kill* (1947).

Kraft admiringly. Even the music seemed to act as a deeply ironic comment on the action; for instance, the dance band playing on the radio in the highly effective murder scene, then the same radio playing "I Don't Have a Thing to Wear" when Helen stumbles across the bodies.

The scenes between Howard and Cook at their remote nighttime rendezvous were full of observation and sardonic humor. "I ain't built for gallivanting on the sand," says the suddenly worried Mrs. Kraft as Marty smilingly guides her towards the beach. Slezak gave a perfectly judged performance as the shabby-genteel private detective; wryly humorous, alert and knowing. His scenes with Trevor were cleverly written and wonderfully realized. The contribution of the supporting actors should never be underestimated; they are part of the warp and weft of a film. The dramatic Paul Sawtell score created a suitably sinister atmosphere. There was a clever scene when Helen and Wilde first encounter one another in a casino. No words pass between them but everything is expressed in a series of glances. The subtle, nuanced scene established their mutual attraction and hinted at the danger for them both.

Born to Kill was an impressive noir with "powerfully candid performances from the two stars."[2] It was considered strong stuff for 1947 and too strong for some: A number of censors demanded changes and the Ohio board rejected it.[3] This reflected the generally hostile view of the contemporary critics, who were largely repulsed by it; Bosley Crowther

Left to right: Trevor, Elisha Cook, Jr., and Lawrence Tierney in a tense scene from *Born to Kill* (1947). Dismissed by critics, it has more recently come to be seen as a noir classic.

labeled it a "smeary tabloid fable."[4] A modern-day critic called it "grim and complicated."[5] It lost a substantial $243,000 at the box office.[6] It was not appreciated at the time and only in recent years has it been acknowledged as one of the best in the noir genre. One reviewer remarked that it "should tempt patrons who like their Tierney tough and ruthless, and their Trevor captivating and calculating."[7] There was a definite chemistry between the two stars.

Stylistically, *Born to Kill* owes a great deal to the distinctive appearance of RKO films and had much in common with the expressionistic Val Lewton horror films which used light and shadow to great effect, conjuring up a sense of foreboding and exploring a more complex psychology than films hitherto examined. A modern critic commented, "*Born to Kill* is an excellent example of the RKO style, not only for its visuals but also for its offhanded depiction of perturbed sexuality and extreme brutality."[8] It's an eminently quotable picture:

> You can't go around killing people when the mood strikes you, it's just not feasible," Marty tells Sam Wilde.
> "Why not?" replies Wilde aggressively.
> "All right then, it is feasible," says Marty, desperate to placate his friend.

Reflecting on her penchant for villainy, Trevor once commented, "I've never known any women as bad as those I've played on screen."[9] Undoubtedly they offered far more scope than the good girls. She was an actress of instinct and imagination. The best actors and actresses are those who are so often required to play the opposite of their own nature.

In Britain, the film was known as *Lady of Deceit,* an apt title emphasizing that although Tierney was the ostensible villain of the piece, he is matched perfectly by Trevor as the most lethal of *femme fatales.* The complex Helen Brent has a moment of self-realization when she is called "an iceberg of a woman" by Mrs. Kraft, a phrase which seems to hit home when Helen later repeats it to Wilde as the reason he doesn't love her.

Eagle-Lion's *Raw Deal* (1948) was a beautifully realized noir infused with a true sense of fatalism. Joe (Dennis O'Keefe) escapes from prison with the help of his girlfriend Pat (Trevor). With the initially unwilling assistance of a prison visitor (Marsha Hunt), they try to reach San Francisco and set up a meeting with the man (Raymond Burr) for whom Joe took the rap. Naturally everything goes wrong.

Raw Deal was wonderfully acted by a well-chosen cast and directed with intent by the peerless Anthony Mann. From the first frame at the prison gates, the tone is set by the eerily effective music of Paul Sawtell cleverly underscoring the perfectly spoken narration by Trevor. "This is the day," she begins. "The last time I shall drive up to these gates. These iron bars that keep the man I love locked away from me. Tonight he breaks out of these walls. It's all set. Eleven thirty. That's the word I'm bringing him…" The use of the Theremin

Left to right, Claire, Marsha Hunt and Dennis O'Keefe hide in the shadows in a lobby card for director Anthony Mann's beautifully realized noir *Raw Deal* (1948). It gave Claire one of her finest roles as a woman who loses everything for the man she loves.

played by Samuel Hoffman was especially telling. Immediately one senses excitement, danger, doom and mystery.

All great art has in it some element that cannot be explained. In this film, it is Trevor who begins and ends the story, and gives voice to her fluctuating feelings throughout. The words seemed to come naturally and the script was well-written. Trevor had an expressive voice, full of emotion; it could be seductive or sensitive, cold or warm. In *Raw Deal*, her narration is a key ingredients that makes the film so successful and memorable. The internal dialogue lends the film the quality of a novel and lodges itself in the mind. The narrated drama has a poignancy and sense of doom because the speaker knows the ending, in the same way that a novelist narrates with hindsight. This gives pause for reflection and a deep sense of irony.

The screenplay offers a stark scenario and no one comes out at the end with anything. Of the two women, Pat loses the most. Essentially she loses everything she ever wanted by doing the right thing. The bleak message of the noir universe is that good doesn't pay any better dividends than bad. This ambiguously bitter ending is entirely in keeping with the ethos of the genre, and seems the natural conclusion. It is perhaps closer to real life in that regard than all the happy endings in Hollywood ever could be. Joe has rightly been designated *un homme fatale*: He causes the good girl to go bad and the bad girl to go good. The consequences are equally disastrous for both.

The music is a key element in the success of the film: perfectly fitting the air of mystery in the fogbound city streets, heightening the feeling of dread. Not only does the Theremin provide an almost ghostly feeling, but it accentuates the sense of claustrophobic horror of the whole scenario. There is no escape from Corkscrew Alley. Theremin player Hoffman provided apt music for other crime dramas including *T-Men* (1947) and *Impact* (1949). His most memorable cinematic contribution was probably to Bernard Herrmann's pioneering score for the science fiction classic *The Day the Earth Stood Still* (1951).

The supporting cast contributed immeasurably. Raymond Burr essayed one of his most chilling psychotic villains and John Ireland was suitably sly and laconic as his wary lieutenant. Even those in smaller roles made an impact. There were some highly effective set pieces such as when, in the taxidermy shop, Joe is met by nervous proprietor Grimshaw (Tom Fadden), who has a nasty surprise waiting for him in the back room. There was great cinematography by the rightfully lauded John Alton, doyen of the genre. All the scenes were beautifully shot and everything seemed perfectly in sync. For instance, the scene when the two cars park on

A pivotal *Raw Deal* scene: Pat (Trevor) finally hears the words she has longed to hear from the love of her life but she knows that time is running out for her rival, who is in peril.

either side of the road at a remote spot and the two women pass each other as Trevor narrates. In one of the most effective sequences, Joe, on the boat to South America, becomes reflective and talks to Pat about their possible future together and settling down to family life. His voice trails off as her thoughts take over: "Why didn't he stop talking, or the clock stop moving?" The room goes dark until all that is seen is Pat in profile and the clock behind her with her reflection. He is saying all the things she has longed to hear, but her conscience takes over: She does the right thing and tells him that Ann is in danger. She loves him so much. Her final words as he lies dying express everything. She is reduced to being a bystander: "There's my Joe in her arms ... this is right for Joe. This is what he wanted."

The screenplay was by Leopold Atlas and John C. Higgins. Atlas worked on *Tomorrow, the World!* (1944) and *My Forbidden Past* (1951); he was among those nominated for an Oscar for *The Story of G.I. Joe* (1945). Higgins was known for his work on murder mysteries including *Kid Glove Killer* (1942) and *Main Street After Dark* (1945). He often paired with director Anthony Mann. The prison sequences in *Raw Deal* were shot at San Quentin.

Marsha Hunt recalled that during the making of the film, Trevor hardly spoke to her—but when they met again years later, Claire greeted her like a long-lost sister. Hunt put her initial aloofness down to being intent on playing her part exactly right and that the intensity of her performance meant she was unaware of everyone around her. "It was something to admire," Hunt said.[10] Despite the probing of eager film buffs, Hunt could remember nothing remarkable about making the movie, only that it was fun to work with such a great cast and that it was completed in three weeks. To the actors at the time, it must have seemed like just another job. It is only with hindsight that the true worth of such films has come to be properly assessed. Other exquisite Mann noirs include *T-Men* (1947), *Border Incident* (1949) and *Side Street* (1950). He made his reputation with a series of superior psychological westerns such as *Winchester '73* (1950), *Bend of the River* (1952) and *The Naked Spur* (1953). Some of his films could be labeled period noirs; one thinks particularly of *The Tall Target* (1951), which is mostly set on a train.

Trevor was originally cast in *Follow Me Quietly* along with Lloyd Nolan. Mann was slated to direct from his own original story about the hunt for a murderer who calls himself "The Judge." But when the film was made, the director was Richard Fleischer and the stars were William Lundigan and Dorothy Patrick.[11] Trevor had the second lead in the minor noir *The Velvet Touch* (1948) starring Rosalind Russell. This time Russell was the femme fatale and Trevor the wronged woman. Broadway producer Michael Morrell (Leon Ames) is murdered by his protégé Valerie Stanton (Russell), but suspicion falls on Marian Webster (Trevor), who discovered the body.

Trevor gave an astute portrayal of a woman who is in love with the man who is dead and who loses the will to live when she is accused of his murder. She enjoyed many a good riposte in the barbed dialogue during the party scene in particular, some of the bitchiness presaging that in *All About Eve*. *The Velvet Touch* was a knowing portrait of theater and its types, from the gossipy newspaper columnist to the blithely unaware backstage staff, and the barely concealed jealousy between those in the same profession, be they writers or actresses. Even the flower sellers and hangers-on who think they know their idols inside out were astutely weighed. Whether anyone could believe that Russell's seemingly worldly character would really fall for such an overarching smoothie as that played by Leo Genn

Trevor (left) did well in *The Velvet Touch* (1948) opposite Rosalind Russell (right). There were some telling insights into stage life and good performances from a marvelous cast.

is another matter. There were some deft touches and some sardonic humor at work—witness the murder of the Broadway producer with his own award used as the murder weapon. The film was rather too slow-paced and took a long time to actually begin, and the constant flashback device initially made it drag. This was the only film directed by Jack Gage, who had previously served as dialogue director on *Double Indemnity* (1944) among others. He later worked on television.

The Velvet Touch was greatly enhanced by the formidable presence of Sydney Greenstreet as a theater-loving detective, and the use of the *Hedda Gabler* motif was cleverly done. In Spain, *Hedda Gabler* was the film's title. All his scenes were done with his trademark subtlety and wit, and the cat-and-mouse detective game he played with Russell was perhaps the chief delight of this minor drama. But a number of reviewers did notice Claire. "Top honors go to Miss Trevor," said one critic. "She projects the right combination of bitter humor, stubborn hope and finally, when her man is dead, complete futility."[12]

Trevor was a friend of Russell and her husband Frederick Brisson, who produced the film. Trevor remarked, "I don't have much to do, but oh, how I pulled for Rosalind Russell and Freddie Brisson in their first picture. Roz is such a darling."[13] She was inspired by Russell to sign as a permanent member of the Independent Artist's Corporation, with the eventual aim of producing films herself.[14] She and Russell were seen in several creations by leading Paramount designer Travis Banton, who designed for many of the leading ladies of the 1930s and '40s and whose work is still referenced by fashion designers. Banton had designed Claire's costumes for *Song and Dance Man* ten years previously. According to some reports, she had a hand in designing her *Velvet Touch* clothes.[15] During filming, Claire made a number of charcoal sketches of her co-stars, including Russell, Greenstreet and Genn. A Philadelphia publisher took an interest in them and intended to publish them as *Claire Trevor's Hollywood Sketch Pad*.[16]

Trevor was disappointed to miss out on several key roles in big dramas. She particularly wanted to play the "other woman" role in Frank Capra's *State of the Union* (1948) starring Spencer Tracy. It was not just the part which appealed to her but the chance to work with the great director. However, the film was made at MGM and the studio chose actors who were under contract there. Angela Lansbury was assigned the role.[17]

13

"Come on, Lady Bountiful!"

> Until I really knew Milton, I had an inferiority complex. I was in a rut. But he brought me out of it. He would say "Would you like me to read your script and help you?" He picked *Key Largo* for me.—Interview with Sheilah Graham, "Claire Trevor Got Her Oscar and with It Leading Lady Roles," *The Milwaukee Journal,* May 30, 1948, 48

The later 1940s was an exciting time for Claire, personally and professionally. She found happiness in her private life when she married in 1948, and after many years of a stop-start career she finally found the recognition she so richly deserved.

Maxwell Anderson's stage play *Key Largo* ran at the Ethel Barrymore Theater in New York during the winter of 1939, starring Paul Muni as a deserter from the Spanish Civil War. When John Huston made a movie version in 1948, he changed the setting to post–World War II and dispensed with most of the characters. Screenwriter Richard Brooks discarded most of the playwright's original blank verse and the fatalistic ending. Neither Brooks nor Huston counted themselves fans of Anderson's political viewpoint, and although retaining his central treatise on the nature of heroism, they constructed a clever and cynically humorous film that made a strong case for the early idealism of FDR.

Huston and Brooks stayed at the Caribbean Club while they were re-writing Anderson's play; this hotel inspired the one seen in the film. The resort of Key Largo was not well-developed at that time, having been devastated by the hurricane of 1935 in which 400 people died. Entrepreneur Carl Fisher began the Caribbean Club in 1939 as a fishing club for men of modest means; it was dubbed "a poor man's retreat."[1] In his memoir *An Open Book,* Huston described the place:

> We arrived out of season and there wasn't any suitable places to stay, but we finally discovered a small hotel which looked attractive, and persuaded the owners to open the place for us before the season started. We had no sooner settled down to work than they moved in a dice table, a roulette wheel and a blackjack table. Thereafter, when Richard and I weren't writing, I was gambling.[2]

Anderson's characters were re-invented for the film. Johnny Rocco was essentially a combination of Al Capone and "Lucky" Luciano. For this role, Huston at first desired Charles Boyer, but Jack Warner would not countenance the idea, remarking that Boyer was not box office enough, and Edward G. Robinson was cast instead. After his experience with Huston's over-budget *The Treasure of the Sierra Madre* (1948), Warner was also adamant that this time there was no chance of filming on location. Apart from a second unit crew sent to Florida for some exterior shots, all filming was done at Warners. The hotel set was based on photographs Huston had taken of the Caribbean Club and surrounding buildings.

The set designers displayed their ingenuity; for instance, the ocean was in fact a huge water tank with miniature boats to help achieve the illusion of depth and scale.

The Gaye Dawn character was not in the original play; she was loosely based on the Russian-born Broadway showgirl Gay Orlova, onetime mistress of "Lucky" Luciano. Claire needed little instruction about how to play the part despite the fact that she had never known a female dipsomaniac. Nor did she need to go downtown and observe the poor unfortunates on Main Street desperate for their first drink of the day as some fellows on the set entreated. Huston gave Trevor an outline of the character as he envisaged her: "You're the kind of dame whose elbows are a little too big. Your voice is a little too loud and you're a little too polite. You're very sad, very resigned."[3] This prompt was enough for her to understand the character in an instant. Her only real concern was singing. "You try singing in front of that group," she remarked. "It's not so much fun. Especially when you can't sing."[4] However, the song was a crucial part of the film's success, and one of the most memorable scenes of her career. Rocco tells her she can have a drink if she sings. Interviewed by Lawrence Grobel for his book *The Hustons: A Hollywood Dynasty*, Claire described the setting-up of the scene:

> I knew I had to sing a song.... The character had been a nightclub singer of sorts and dreamed about becoming a big star, but she got caught up with this gangster. They picked "Moanin' Low," which is a

John Huston's classic *Key Largo* (1948) gave Claire one of her best roles as the broken-down moll of a gangster. Left to right: Humphrey Bogart, Claire, Lauren Bacall.

> difficult song, it goes up and down, and I'm the world's worst singer. I was after John all the time to rehearse this song and he'd always say, "Plenty of time." Then we came back from lunch one day and he said, "We're going to shoot the song." I said, "*What?*" I was furious. I was totally unprepared. And he stood me up in the middle of the room. The piano offstage hit one note. He said, "Go." And that's how I sang it. He knew what he was doing. I was embarrassed. I was *supposed* to be embarrassed. I thought that day would never end. That was torture. But that's what got the effect.[5]

After she finished the song, the cast burst into applause, and Harry Lewis, who played "Toots," turned to Thomas Gomez and said, "She's going to win the Academy Award for that song alone," echoing the thoughts of others there.[6] The scene ends perfectly with Rocco's refusal to give her the drink despite her acute embarrassment and he makes the immortal remark "You were rotten!" She gets her much-deserved drink anyway, thanks to McCloud.

Everyone enjoyed their time on the film. Lauren Bacall recalled the great atmosphere on set:

> *Key Largo* was one of my happiest experiences. I thought how marvelous a medium the movies were, to enable me to meet, befriend and work with such people. What a good time of life that was—the best people at their best. With all those supposed actors' egos, there was not a moment of discomfort or vying for position.[7]

Veteran character actor Lionel Barrymore was suffering badly from arthritis in his legs, which was why he was in a wheelchair. Despite his pain, he never complained, noted Bacall, who said he used to regale them with colorful stories. It was Bacall's last film alongside Bogart, and marked Huston's final picture for Warner Brothers. Trevor remarked, "People always say, 'Didn't you have fun making that picture?' Well you *don't* have fun. It's not a party. It's hard work. But *Key Largo was* fun. And I adored John. I was just enchanted by him."[8] She loved to be working with such a cast, especially Bogart, who she counted as one of her best friends. He shared her and Milton's love of sailing and they all spent a lot of time together. "[Bogart] had great wit, great sophistication," she recalled, "and he was really very sweet. As soft as butter, in fact." When she was Oscar-nominated, he told her, "Listen, kid, when you win I want you to say, 'I'm not going to thank anyone. I did it all myself.'"[9]

The role of Gaye Dawn was one that she really wanted.[10] She did not mind that she had to accept lower billing than Barrymore; billing was something she wasn't concerned about. She made the part live. The pathos was apparent as she clings to the memory of her brief flirtation with minor league stardom. "I had no makeup, just a baby spot ... the gowns I wore were very décolleté..." In the scene in the bar where she shouts encouragement at the radio to a horse she has backed, her cries of "Come on, Lady Bountiful!" sound as much like an exhortation to herself as the horse. Here is a woman who has been taken for granted and used by men, especially her boss, but she shows her true nature when she aids McCloud by getting the gun from Rocco.

They had three weeks of rehearsals and she was paid $5000 a week for the six-week shoot.[11] The film has continued to resonate down the years. The song has appeared on several records and was even sampled by British trip hop band Death in Vegas on their 1996 single "Rocco."[12]

In 1948, the film was not well-received but its reputation has grown in the ensuing years. In a practical way, it helped to create interest in the resort of Key Largo and the Florida Keys in general. So much so that people went looking for the hotel featured in the

"You were rotten!" After putting her through torment, Rocco (Edward G. Robinson, left) refuses Gaye (Trevor) a drink in an unforgettable *Key Largo* scene (Dan Seymour, center). Her performance earned her a Best Supporting Actress Oscar.

film, and in recent years there has even been a Humphrey Bogart Film Festival in Key Largo. The inaugural event in May 2013 was hosted by his son Stephen Bogart with the great film critic Leonard Maltin as the featured guest. Visitors could also take a ride on the boat from *The African Queen* which was moored there. The highlight of the festival was described as the grand Humphrey Bogart Ball at the Hilton.[13] Such events are testament to the enduring allure of the period in Hollywood history and especially of film noir.

Off-screen, Trevor found happiness in her private life when she married film producer Milton H. Bren on November 14, 1948, after what was described as a two-year engagement. The ceremony took place shortly after filming of *Key Largo*. They were married in the Pasadena home of a family friend, Superior Judge Thurmond Clarke. Mrs. Clarke was the sole witness.[14] Claire and Milton honeymooned at Santa Barbara.

Milton's grandfather, a tailor, came from Batavia in Prussia. Moving to the U.S., he settled in Tennessee and during the Civil War he was a captain in the Tennessee Infantry. Born in St. Louis, Milton started his film career as an office boy for Irving Thalberg. He went on to work as a production executive at Hal Roach Studios, MGM and Columbia before striking out on his own as an independent. During the Second World War, he was a Coast Guard lieutenant and later captain of a destroyer in the Pacific theater of war. He had a lifelong love of sailing, and had won the Pacific Coast Starboat Class Championships in the 1920s. He was later captain of two sailboats, *Rhapsody* and *Pursuit*, that won many prizes. He and Claire loved sailing their yacht *The Lady Claire*.[15] Bren's first wife was the socially well-connected Marion Newbert. They married in 1930 when she was 18 and he was 26. They had two sons, Donald H. (born in 1932) and Peter (born in '34). Milton and Marion divorced in 1948.

Claire said that when she and Milton married, they were an instant family, and she made certain to treat all three children alike; for instance, she never called Donald or Peter her stepsons, nor did she regard them as such. She found her greatest happiness with Milton who, she said, was everything she had ever wanted: "He was intelligent, humorous, caring, soft, deep—a wonderful father and husband."[16] Their happiness was apparent to outsiders who remarked that Bren's sincerity was evident on meeting him for the first time. Observers talked of their "boy and girl–like devotion" to each other."[17]

The "Queen of Film Noir" admitted that she was disappointed to miss out on two big roles in the genre, in *Double Indemnity* and *Sorry, Wrong Number*, both of which went to Barbara Stanwyck.[18] At the same time, Trevor was weary of the type of roles she was being offered and her wider public perception. "Even my family is getting ashamed of me," she quipped. "A gun factory wanted to name a new pocket pistol after me."[19] Another time she observed wryly, "You can't play a social outcast as many times as I have without beginning to feel a little reprehensible yourself. It's enough to get a girl down."[20] Apart from her mother, Claire's family had never warmed to the idea of her being an actress, and especially disdained the kind of bad girl roles she played.

The Academy Award for *Key Largo* raised Trevor's profile, and she began to be besieged by offers. Immediately there was the prospect of reteaming with Bogart in Lynn Riggs' *Domino Parlor*.[21] Later she had yet another chance to make a film with him, *The Harder They Fall*, a boxing drama.[22] However the first was dropped and her role in the second went to Jan Sterling. She was considered for a co-starring role in Clark Gable's *Any Number Can Play* but was superseded by Alexis Smith.[23] She was sought by director Michael Curtiz to join Joan Crawford in *Flamingo Road* but lost out to Gladys George.[24] There was the prospect of the starring role in Jerry Wald's *Storm Center* for Warner Brothers, which did not happen.[25] She was announced as the star of the James S. Burkett production *Barbed Wire*, playing the part of a cattle rustler, but that film was shelved.[26] It was reported that her asking price had shot up by $20,000 per film, purely on account of the Oscar.[27] She reportedly turned down Sam Goldwyn's offer to pay "her usual salary" of $50,000 for two scenes in *Beloved Over All*, which was later released as *Our Very Own* (1950).[28] She was among the actresses seriously considered for the female lead in *The Set-Up* (1949).[29] Although she was announced for the western *New Mexico* with Franchot Tone, neither of them appeared in the film, which was not made for another two years.[30] Nor did she star in *South of St. Louis*; that role too went to Alexis Smith.[31] She turned down a role in the sprightly Betty Grable musical *Burlesque*, which became *When My Baby Smiles at Me* (1948).[32]

After the high watermark *Key Largo*, Trevor went from the sublime to the faintly ridiculous as the wife of William Bendix in *The Babe Ruth Story* (1948), often cited as the worst sports movie of all time.

Trevor had none of the high-handedness of some stars. Which other actress could have played with such unconscious ease as the love interest of both John Wayne and William Bendix? Some actresses would have bristled at the very idea of being paired with Bendix, or even with the likes of Pat O'Brien and Luther Adler. But again, Trevor's lack of ego made her a far more natural and believable actress whoever her screen partner might be. Interviewed at the time, she related how thrilled she was to play the part of a living person: "I have been stuck in such a series of grim, hard-boiled parts ... that I was tickled silly when the Babe's life gave me the chance to play a successful normal human being at last."[33] She met Ruth and had dinner with his wife, with whom she got on well. In her portrayal, Trevor said that she made no effort to imitate her. This was in contrast to the approach of Bendix, who tried to emulate Ruth's mannerisms, and was fitted with a sponge rubber nose in an attempt to make him look more like the baseball legend.

The film's reputation goes before it, but taken as a work of pure fiction it is surprisingly entertaining. Bendix attacks the role, and to his credit does a reasonable job. The screenplay described the rough arc of his career from hopeful debutant to oldtimer. The physical and emotional toll of season after season on players was made apparent. After all his years of service, he is effectively fired, after which one of the boys in the dressing room tells him that he should sue his employers. "Sue baseball?" he replies incredulously. "That would be like suing the church!" This typified the over-reverent approach which the film's makers adopted. Undoubtedly there were glaring inaccuracies in the script, and the Babe comes across as a saint who can make lame children walk again by merely saying, "Hiya kid." This is not to disparage Ruth himself, who may well have spent a lot of time in children's hospitals, and was no doubt popular with the young. Also, the power of sport is not to be underestimated: It can be a unifying force for good.

Critics cried "Foul!" upon the release of the much-derided biopic *The Babe Ruth Story* (1948). But Claire managed to emerge with her reputation enhanced and even received offers of work as a result. Pictured: sheet music from the film shows singer Gertrude Niesen (top left), with William Bendix and Trevor (bottom right).

Trevor contributed a living portrait as his wife. Ruth's energetic womanizing was glossed over with only a few chance remarks, such as when he is invited to judge an Atlantic City beauty contest, an idea his wife vetoes at once. The supporting actors hold the film together when it becomes too saccharine for its own good. At times, particularly in the first half, Bendix's comic approach and even the portentous narration at the beginning while surveying the baseball Hall of Fame make the whole thing sound like a parody. This feeling is enhanced by some of the music such as the opening song, "Take Me Out to the

Ball Game" delivered in rollicking barber shop quartet style, and "Wait Till the Sun Shines, Nellie" sung in the tavern. The tune "I'll Get By" underscored the more tender scenes with his wife and recurred during the hospital interludes. Hospitals featured rather a lot throughout, an unusual aspect to a film about a great sporting hero. Charles Bickford and the reliable Sam Levene were on hand to reassure the public that the film was worthwhile, and there was an effective turn by the virtually unknown Fred Lightner as Ruth's nemesis Miller Huggins. The film has been vilified since its release, and may stand for all time as the blueprint for how not to make a biopic. According to one critic, "Hollywood has alas hit a foul ball for a fabled fence-buster. ... [The screenwriters] have permitted their reverence to run away with them, and in doing so, what comes out is a tasteless fiction compounded of juvenile drivel.... Protecting a legend is one thing; suffocating it is another."[34] Few had anything good to say about it; one reviewer commented that Bendix was "straight from the smokehouse."[35]

For the role of Babe Ruth, Paul Douglas was the choice of Mrs. Ruth. Others considered included Jack Carson, Brian Donlevy and Broderick Crawford. Bendix was chosen for financial reasons; the studio knew they were guaranteed to make money because of the way his contract was arranged. "Bendix was nice, he was willing," commented Mrs. Ruth. "But the baseball swing was a mystery he never conquered."[36] Stung by the criticism that he and the film got, Bendix remarked, "The director ordered things you knew were wrong. It was a turkey and I wonder that it didn't kill me in the business."[37] In theory, Ruth was an advisor on the film, but had practically no input; most of the time he was kept at the hotel and did interviews. With his wife, he toured the country for a grueling month promoting it. He was already suffering from cancer, and the makers were keen to finish the film before he died. "I feel that the picture lost whatever little quality it had because it was rushed to the public," commented Mrs. Ruth.[38]

The premiere was attended by Ruth, members of the New York Yankees and Baseball Commissioner Albert B. "Happy" Chandler. The "Babe" was ill and left halfway through. He had been allowed out of hospital for the first time in a while, but returned to the hospital that day and remained there until he died a few weeks later.

One critic astutely noted that Bendix's performance "throws the whole cast, excepting Claire Trevor, off-balance."[39] Trevor showed fine judgment in her honest and sensitive portrayal. Against the odds, she emerged with her reputation enhanced. Producer Milton Sperling was so impressed with her work that he signed her almost immediately for *Distant Drums*.[40] Originally Joel McCrea and Lilli Palmer were penciled in as the other stars. However the film was not made until two years later and instead starred Gary Cooper with two far less famous actresses. Incidentally, the leading actors from *The Babe Ruth Story* also appeared on some collectable cards for Swell Bubble Gum that are now quite rare and sought-after. Trevor sold the rights to *Win-Drift*, a novel by Lester McCullough, to *Babe Ruth Story* director Roy Del Ruth, with the hope of starring in it herself. Before long, Bendix and Trevor were announced for the director's next project *Bright Shines the Sun*; but both these ideas came to naught.[41]

Trevor was offered a role in the noir *A Dangerous Profession* (1949) opposite George Raft, but the part was given to Ella Raines. Yet another potential Raft project, *The Syndicate*, appears not to have seen the light of day.[42] *Handle with Care* was about the use and misuse of sleeping pills, adapted from an original play by Irwin Gielgud. The film was designed by Universal especially for Claire but for some reason never got beyond the planning stage.[43] She was also sought for the role of the minister's wife in director Jacques Tourneur's unusual western *Stars in My Crown* (1950) but the part went to Ellen Drew.[44]

The Lucky Stiff (1949) sounded like a promising tongue-in-cheek noir and boasted a fine cast of Trevor, Brian Donlevy and Dorothy Lamour. The screenplay was based on a story by Craig Rice about an incompetent lawyer, Malone (Donlevy), besotted with nightclub singer (Lamour), and loved by his ever-loyal secretary (Trevor). The needlessly complex plot got in the way and spoiled what could have been a minor classic of the genre. Nevertheless, the movie had its moments and the three appealing leads worked well together. Donlevy and Trevor made a natural comedy team, both having great timing and by now being used to working together. Lamour was a suitably languid femme fatale. The film felt like a missed opportunity to parody the noir genre when it was beginning to appear too predictable. The major problem was the over-complicated plot which meant that attention drifted.

The director was the multi-talented Lewis R. Foster, a prolific composer, writer and one-time newspaperman. His most famous writing credit was *Mr. Smith Goes to Washington*'s (1939) original story. Early in his directing career, he helmed Laurel and Hardy shorts; later he made the odd crime drama such as *Crashout* (1955), before moving almost exclusively into television. *The Lucky Stiff* had some elements in common with the films of Laurel and Hardy, a similar whimsical humor and some sight gags almost worthy of the two great clowns. In one sequence, Trevor and Donlevy are slowly driving along in a rickety old car which gets stuck in the tramlines with a fire engine trying to get past. This was well handled by the two, who displayed their comedic side; both had a natural aptitude for the lighter side of things even though they became associated almost exclusively with the dark side of life.

During filming, Trevor had a minor car crash which left her bruised but determined to continue working. In the supporting cast, Marjorie Rambeau contributed a suitably quaint vignette as an eccentric widow. The drollery of the piece seemed to jive with Trevor's own appealing sense of humor.

Trevor was considered for several other interesting roles. Screenwriter-producer Martin Mooney, a former crime reporter, owned the rights to controversial Pentecostal preacher Aimee Semple Macpherson's life story and wanted Trevor to play her in a biopic. Macpherson was immortalized in popular culture as the female faith healer in Sinclair Lewis' *Elmer Gantry* and she was believed to have inspired the movie *The Miracle Woman* (1931). This was the kind of part which would have been a welcome change for Trevor at this stage of her career, but nothing came of the idea.[45] She was offered a role in *Women Without Men*, Virginia Kellogg's powerful drama set in a women's prison; it was later retitled *Caged* (1950). Although tempted, Trevor declined because she wanted a rest.[46] When Fritz Lang was set to direct *Winchester '73* (1950), he sought John Payne and Trevor as the leads. However, Universal objected to Lang using his own production company, Diana, and instead assigned director Anthony Mann, who opted for James Stewart and Shelley Winters.[47] Trevor was assigned the second feminine lead in *I Married a Communist*, later released as *The Woman on Pier 13*, but withdrew, which caused a delay on that film.[48] After much discussion, she switched to her husband's project *Borderline* instead.[49]

14

Hard, Fast and Beautiful

> When I'm working, then everything is given to the task in hand, but in the larger sense, I let things happen.—Grace Wilcox "Gift of Laughter: Subject: Claire Trevor; Reason for Inquiry: She's Contented," *Long Island Sunday Press: Screen & Radio Weekly*, September 12, 1937, 7

Entering her forties at the start of the 1950s Claire's star was at its highest. Respected throughout the acting profession and beloved by audiences, she had also found happiness in her personal life. The early part of the decade saw her in some highly effective offbeat roles and by 1955 she was once more nominated for an Academy Award.

James Hilton, who had written about a heaven on earth called Shangri-La in his famous novel *Lost Horizon,* named Claire Trevor as one of those who he would like to take there if he could. It was a measure of how much she had entered the collective consciousness. She was in good company with, among others, Ingrid Bergman, Deborah Kerr, Eleanor Roosevelt and Jo Stafford.[1]

Produced by her husband Milton and directed by William A. Seiter, *Borderline* (1950) was an entertaining noir that mildly sent up the genre. Claire played a Los Angeles policewoman sent to Mexico to investigate the activities of a narcotics ring. Unbeknownst to her another undercover policeman (Fred MacMurray) has also been sent there to ferret out the leaders of the gang. Both suspect each other of being involved with the real criminals which leads to many comic misunderstandings. She and MacMurray had a good rapport and the film had charm and was well-paced. Some of the funniest scenes were at the beginning when Trevor, in a song and dance line-up, tries everything to catch the eye of the gang's boss (the implacable Raymond Burr) in the nightclub. It worked well because Burr was so deadpan throughout. Another successful scene was when she feigned drunkenness and chatted up one of Burr's henchmen, Deusek (Don Diamond). Despite the Mexican backgrounds most of the location work took place in California at Chatsworth. Trevor got to wear a number of stylish costumes including a fetching black lace bathing suit designed by Lilli. Reportedly, some scenes had to be re-shot when "the censors decided her sighs were too amorous."[2] According to one observer her aviation phobia asserted itself when she refused to do a scene in which she had to sit in the cabin of a light aircraft or even allow herself to be taxied to the airport.[3] However she must have got around this problem somehow because the scene is in the film.

At one stage she slipped and fell during eight-hour rehearsals, badly hurting her foot which became swollen. Although in great pain she insisted on completing the dance routines so as not to delay the filming. It was reported that a "first aid attendant massaged her foot

The comedy-noir *Borderline* (1950) was produced by Claire's husband Milton Bren. Left to right: Roy Roberts, Trevor, Jose Torvay and Fred MacMurray.

and kept ice packs on the swollen area" at regular intervals.[4] Husband Milton was full of praise for her; "It's a tour-de-force for Claire," he remarked, "It's got everything, comedy, heavy drama—everything Claire does so well."[5] Seiter brought a whimsical touch to his films. He was a long-time friend and collaborator of Bren. Seiter started as a bit player in Mack Sennett comedies and was the director of the wonderful Laurel and Hardy feature *Sons of the Desert* (1933). He had also been at the helm for *Allegheny Uprising*, but was more remembered for such appealing light-hearted comedies as *One Touch of Venus* (1948).

The two stars, as well as the producers, Milton and Seiter, took no salary for working on the film but instead agreed to share the profits.[6] Both stars embarked on personal tours to promote the film. Trevor toured the mid-west and the east in a one-woman routine based on a one-act play by the humorist Corey Ford. This was essentially a monologue in which she played a New York shop girl talking to her fiancé long distance on the telephone and relating the goings-on of her life and the working day.[7] The two-month tour of theaters and small venues was described as "rugged."[8] She appeared at out-of-the way movie theaters such as that at Aldine, Pennsylvania.[9] Despite any discomfort she was at her scintillating best and husband Milton was amazed how she managed to have such emotional impact each day. She was a sensation everywhere and "the audience loved it."[10]

Interviewed during the making of *Borderline* she expressed an interest in another project with her husband, *Three for Bedroom C,* a comedy by Goddard Lieberson.[11] Initially

Bren and William Seiter pursued Robert Donat to play the part of the university professor opposite Trevor.[12] However, Donat could not be secured and Trevor also bowed out. She believed the film required a star name and suggested Gloria Swanson for the role, who agreed. Trevor decided to do *Hoodlum Empire* instead. Bren had a number of vehicles in mind for her including another western, *Snow Covered Wagons*, but as it transpired she never made any more films with him.[13] Once shooting of *Borderline* was complete she expressed a desire to play in summer stock in New England.

Trevor was one of the choices for the lead in *Paid in Full* (1950), the other was Joan Blondell, but in the event the part was given to Lizabeth Scott.[14] An intriguing project was the role of the Queen in a proposed English language film version of Jean Cocteau's play *The Eagle Has Two Heads*. Cocteau's film was released in 1947 and shortly afterwards a rough translation played on the London stage. This transferred to New York with Tallulah Bankhead in the role, but according to Cocteau, Bankhead made a number of significant alterations to the play to its great detriment.[15] Filming was due to start in Paris but the project would appear to have been abandoned.[16] Among other ideas proposed was *The Life of Rafael Sabatini*, one of British producer Alexander Korda's projects for which the makers hoped to engage George Sanders in the lead role as the adventure writer, with Claire as his wife. Although R. C. Sherriff was suggested as the writer, nothing came of the idea.[17] Veteran director William Dieterle wanted Claire and Joan Fontaine to star in a big screen version of Jack London's sometimes controversial love triangle novel *The Little Lady in the Big House*. This too was never realized.[18]

Trevor had a great sense of humor, often ironic and with a decided penchant for satire. At a Screen Writer's Guild banquet in February 1951 she wholeheartedly joined in the fun with other actors. The evening entertainment showed Hollywood laughing at itself. The show was emceed by Van Heflin and included turns by most of the famous actors and actresses of the day. Trevor appeared in a skit called "All About Fairfax Ave" in which she "played a combination of Bette Davis and Gloria Swanson with overtones of Tallulah Bankhead."[19] The sketch was written by George Oppenheimer and also featured Nancy Davis and Edmond O'Brien; the latter played an intolerant author who hates talkies. It was described as "screamingly funny" and proved to be one the most popular sketches of the night.[20]

Hard, Fast and Beautiful (1951) was an ideal project for Trevor who always loved tennis, and she jumped at the chance. The screenplay was based on the novel *American Girl* by John R. Tunis, first published in 1930. Tunis' story was reputedly inspired by the life of Helen Wills Moody, one of the greatest tennis players of the 1920s and 1930s. Sally Forrest starred as the talented girl whose mother is determined will go places. The rest of the cast consisted of less well-known names drawn from the ranks of radio performers. Lupino liked to employ new faces and was a strong believer in the medium of radio as a training ground for good actors. "Radio personalities must have voice training as part of their equipment," she remarked, "Too many newcomers in Hollywood don't at all know how to use their voices, a pre-requisite of dramatic expression."[21]

Ex-player Eleanor "Teach" Tennant was credited with helping to coach Sally Forrest who played the role of the young girl at the center of the story. Tennant had coached many leading players including Bobby Riggs, Alice Marble and Maureen Connolly. The coach was quite tough on Forrest who had never previously held a tennis racquet and at the beginning could barely hit four barn doors. However after three weeks of eight hours practice a day she put in a tremendous effort and was commended by Miss Tennant who said she showed "surprising agility and fair accuracy."[22] Much of the action was filmed at the Beechwood Tennis Club, with shots of Forrest Hills and Wimbledon interwoven. Originally the story was called *Loving Cup* or *Mother of a Champion* before the title was suggested by RKO studio boss Howard Hughes. The film did well at the box office but any profits "disappeared in RKO's lavish promotion," done at the behest of Hughes.[23]

Curiously, tennis has seldom been the subject of cinema, which is surprising in a way considering the drama, suspense and plot twists in some matches. The only other memorable tennis match was in *Strangers on a Train* (1951), in the course of which director Alfred Hitchcock evoked the sense of anticipation and the build-up of tension and suspense. He cleverly used the game as an integral part of the plot during a crucial stage to establish an alibi. *Hard, Fast and Beautiful* was considered a successful tennis film, but was first and foremost a drama with a tennis background. Some contended that it would be of limited appeal to those who didn't like the sport but actually it is not essential to be a sports fan to appreciate the film. As an actress, Lupino was one of the best, and she proved equally impressive as a director. Her subject-matter was wide-ranging and challenging; rape, bigamy, arbitrary murder—but all her films reflected the same qualities of intelligence and sensitivity which she possessed. There was no sensationalism in her work, she delved deeper into the emotional side of her characters and displayed remarkable balance and fidelity. Every film she made is worth seeking out, even those less talked about such as *Not Wanted*

Trevor (right) gave an incisive portrait as the ambitious mother of a gifted tennis player (Sally Forrest) in director Ida Lupino's telling drama *Hard, Fast and Beautiful* (1951).

(1949), *Never Fear* (1949) and *Outrage* (1950). Her maturity of treatment ensures that her films retain their relevance and power to move.

Trevor gave a devastating portrait of Millie, a woman who lives vicariously through her daughter who fulfills all her own thwarted ambition. The daughter also undergoes a major transformation, turning from wide-eyed innocent to a calculating and mercenary character, but then does a volte-face and returns to being naïve once again. Such are the pitfalls of fiction. Although Millie is shown to be cold, selfish and ruthless, the actress makes her oddly sympathetic. The film begins and ends in a tennis stadium. From watching the opening credits and judging by the title and the dramatic, mysterious score by Roy Webb, the viewer could be forgiven for thinking that this was another noir. This impression is almost confirmed by the opening scenes, with the use of sound especially telling. Here Lupino's instinctive radio sensibility came into its own. The first sound heard is that of a tennis ball being hit against the garage door by Florence (Forrest), while her mother Millie (Trevor) is inside working on her dress. It is the voice of Trevor with its distinctive timbre that provides the early narration: "From the very moment you were born, I knew you were different…" she intones, "I could see things in you that no-one else could…" The combination of the sound, image and narration makes for an effective introduction. The use of narration, as mentioned previously, can be most intriguing, easily drawing the viewer into the narrative. "Listening to you driving that ball against the garage door used to drive me mad. That's because I always wanted something better for you. And I made up my mind to get it, no matter what the cost." From there the action progressed naturally, and flowed with the minimum of fuss. Trevor's narration was also used to effect during the tennis matches, neatly encapsulating Florence's advance and her own growing pride and ambition. Millie is so bound up with Florence's success that her husband recedes into the background and his health breaks down. The marriage, which has been decaying for some time, finally disintegrates. There appears to be a moment of self-realization at the hospital as her husband lies ill in bed, by which time it is too late for them to salvage anything from their marriage. Her lack of words says everything. The final shot of her sitting alone in the darkened empty stadium holding the winner's cup, with only the echoing sound of a ghostly tennis ball on racquet was both eerie and sad. Interestingly, the sound that began the film is the same that is heard at the end; but whereas the sound was full of promise when first heard, it is heard in the light of bitter realization at the end and sounds merely empty and mocking. Trevor succeeds in making a seemingly heartless woman understandable and investing her with an elusive pathos.

Lupino took pains with all parts of the film, and especially so with her use of sound. Engineers tried various ideas to capture the sound of the tennis ball after discovering that the real thing was just not coming across. They experimented with all kinds of different balls and in the end they used "a kid's marble shooter projected from a slingshot against a treated stiffened mosquito net."[24] An important aspect of the film was the eerily atmospheric score by Roy Webb. Seven times Oscar nominated, Webb provided the music for over 250 movies in a thirty year career. He composed for many horrors and noirs at RKO including the *bone fide* classics *Curse of the Cat People* (1943), *The Seventh Victim* (1943), *Blood on the Moon* (1948) and *The Set-Up* (1949). With a touch of the Hitchcocks, Lupino put in a cameo appearance; she can be seen in the crowd at the tennis match alongside Robert Ryan.

The two women clashed somewhat temperamentally during the making of the film.

"Ida is intense and emotional," Trevor commented, "I don't react to that type of person. In the test for a picture, she kept draping me all over the set. I couldn't give. I baulked. I went home and told my husband that Ida was going to drive me crazy with all the dramatic talk."[25] For her part Lupino felt a degree of trepidation about working with Trevor. "I was never so nervous in my life," she said, "Going up to her and asking if she'd mind doing this or that. I'll say this, though. She's going to be the most sex appealing mother on the screen."[26] They had "strong disagreements but no fights," said Trevor. The disagreements were about the portrayal of her character. Trevor saw the mother as the kind who loves too much and smothers her daughter, whereas the script called for the type who merely browbeats.[27] Although some observers noted that the two women were "scrupulously polite" to each other, Claire admired Lupino greatly, saying she was "a very warm, very sensitive and intelligent lady."[28] She added that she "knows more about directing than a lot of men."[29] She further commented "I never fight with directors. Ida has a lot of talent and she's more alive to everything that pertains to women than anyone in the industry."[30]

Any slight difficulties they had encountered did not put them off wanting to collaborate again. Lupino hoped to work once more with Trevor and sought her out for *Pier's End*, a modernized reworking of an old story written by her beloved father Stanley Lupino, an English Music Hall comedian and actor.[31] They also discussed another idea, *The World Within* or *The World Inside*, a drama about "a war veteran whose battlefield service rendered him sterile and who adopts a little girl to brighten his life."[32] Yet another idea they discussed

In *Best of the Badmen* (1951), Claire showed to excellent effect in a sympathetic role with an otherwise all-male cast led by Robert Ryan. Despite their obvious potential as a noir couple, it was the only film they made together.

was a film version of Leland Laurence's play about a female alcoholic, *Halfway to Nowhere*, the rights to which Claire had previously bought.[33] Unfortunately, none of these projects were realized. However Lupino did direct Trevor again in an episode of *Alfred Hitchcock Presents* on television some years later called "A Crime for Mothers."

Each day on the set, Trevor made sure everybody was happy, and if not, spent time talking with them about their worries. This was something she did on most films by all accounts and rendered her a popular figure.[34] On the last day of filming the two actresses were talking about the many problems of acting and directing. "You've given me an idea," announced Trevor, "I wish to direct." "The field's wide open," Lupino answered, "Besides, I need you. Have you ever attended a Screen Director's Guild meeting—alone?"[35] Unfortunately Trevor was not serious and never tried her hand at directing.

Trevor was put forward for a number of roles in a range of genres, but usually as the wife of prominent men. When casting a proposed film of the life of the great but tortured ballet dancer Vaslav Nijinsky, producer Alexander Paal wanted Gene Kelly to play the title role, with Claire as his wife.[36] Another intended biopic was about the life of Hollywood showman Max Reinhardt, for which the makers sought Edward G. Robinson with Claire as his spouse, who was also an actress.[37] Neither film was made.

After her welcome change of pace, Trevor returned to well-worn territory in RKO's *Best of the Badmen* (1951). This was an entertaining western which featured many of the familiar names from western folklore such as the James and Younger brothers, all one-time Quantrill men caught in the aftermath of the Civil War. A fine cast was headed by Robert Ryan, with Trevor the only woman present. Still, she proved before that she could easily hold her own in such tough company as Lawrence Tierney, Barton Maclane, Bruce Cabot, Jack Beutel et al. A good-looking film in pure fifties color it suffered from a rather contrived plot but no western fan would have left the cinema disappointed. Trevor played the estranged wife of Robert Preston, a duplicitous detective. Her role gave her more room for maneuver than she was often allowed in westerns; this time she was not the stock prostitute character but a genuine lady, albeit a robust one trying to escape a loveless marriage. During filming at Kanab, Utah, a flash-flood turned a shallow creek into a raging stream seven feet deep, which left Ryan, Trevor and sixty four members of the cast and crew stranded for eight hours before they could ford it safely.[38] Her six-year-old son Chuck accompanied her on set and during one of her key romantic scenes with Bob Ryan as everyone fell silent the boy "threaded his way through the equipment and personnel and blurted out 'Here, Mommy, hold my hat!'" much to the merriment of cast and crew.[39]

Having decided against appearing in *Three for Bedroom C*, Trevor next appeared in *Hoodlum Empire*, based on the Kefauver hearings into organized crime. Ostensibly another noir drama she said that she was attracted to the project for a number of reasons including the excellent cast and the documentary-like combination of fact and fiction. "It's not only hard-hitting but a very colorful picture," she observed.[40]

Hoodlum Empire was the story of Joe Gray (John Russell), one time hoodlum for his "uncle" Nick Mancani (Luther Adler). On his return from war service Gray wants to set himself up in legitimate business, but he is unwittingly drawn back into his previous life. He eventually decides to testify against his former mentor before a grand jury run by Senator Bill Stevens (Brian Donlevy), who does not believe he is a changed man. The film relied a lot on flashbacks, but rather than advance the narrative, this tended to slow it down.

Trevor fares badly at the hands of gangster Luther Adler in *Hoodlum Empire* (1952), a crime drama based on the real-life Kefauver Senate hearings into organized crime.

However the presence of such stalwarts as Adler, Donlevy, Trevor, Gene Lockhart and Forrest Tucker made up for any faults in direction. A series of large interior apartment sets paradoxically enhanced the sense of claustrophobia, which was heightened by the painted background view of skyscrapers. Trevor was one of the standouts and invested her character with a life of her own. At one point she sashayed in to the committee room and injected some dry wit into the proceedings. Essentially the moll of Nick Mancani, she has loyalty to him—up to a point—but really loves Joe Gray, which proves to be her undoing. Her changing allegiances reflect her conflict of emotions, which she gets across in a glance when she is not speaking at all. She described her character Connie Williams as "a tough southern girl with no honey-chile stuff about her. She's a snappy Dixie babe."[41] Although it seemed like a familiar role to her she recognized some leeway; "I could do something new with the part—namely, play it with a southern accent. Not just a soft southern accent but hard, brash and brittle. It meant an excellent chance for characterization,"[42] she noted. Connie was based on Virginia Hill who had testified before the actual committee. The Kefauver hearings were televised live and provided compelling viewing at the time. It was one of the first cases of television setting the pace for Hollywood. The movies had a hard time keeping up and the hearings engendered a number of films including *The Captive City* (1952) and *The Turning Point* (1952), but all lacked the immediacy and unexpected drama of the original televised showings.

Director Joseph Kane spent much of his career at Republic and made a mountain of westerns. However he did make occasional forays into other territory with adventures such as *Fair Wind to Java* (1953), along with unheralded but intriguing crime dramas *The Crooked Circle* (1957) and *The Notorious Mr. Monks* (1958). He began in the film business as a writer and editor after abandoning a career as a professional cellist.

Trevor often expressed a desire to return to the stage, and wanted to play in *The Country Girl* at the La Jolla Playhouse. However, the New York sponsors insisted on a ten week countrywide tour and she was reluctant to leave her family for such a length of time, and especially her young son who was then at school.[43] There was also the prospect of starring on Broadway with Robert Ryan in *We're Late the Sweet Birds Sang*.[44] The play had a western theme and was written by Irving Ravetch who later found fame as a scriptwriter; his most notable contribution was *Hud* (1963). Although he was on the verge of seeing his plays on Broadway several times none of them ever came to fruition, despite the backing of producer Danny Mann.[45] Trevor was to have played Blanche Dubois in a summer theater version of Tennessee Williams' *A Streetcar Named Desire* with John Hodiak. Unfortunately her young son was ill at the time and she was unable to rehearse.[46]

When Kim Hunter dropped out of *A Lion Is in the Streets* starring James Cagney, Trevor was one of two names considered for the role. The other was Nina Foch, but after disappointing screen tests neither appeared in the film and the role went to Barbara Hale.[47] Trevor was also sought by the author Richard Llewellyn, famous for *How Green Was My Valley*, who wanted her for his *Poison Pen Letter*, which was never made.[48] She was mooted to play a prominent role in Lloyd Bacon's project *Cabin on the Hill*, set in the cotton fields of the deep south, which was adapted from a story by Douglas Fremont, but although the film was discussed at length it never came about.[49]

Trevor also expressed an ambition to make a film abroad, something she had not done hitherto; perhaps it was due to her reported fear of flying; "I've never been outside this country," she remarked, "I'd like to make a picture in Paris with my husband."[50] However she must have overcome her fear in the later 1950s when she began to attend a number of film festivals in South America and Italy, and travelled to the French Alps to make *The Mountain*.

When Jean Hagen became pregnant, Trevor replaced her in *Letter from the President* which later became *My Man and I* (1952). Although it was only a supporting role, it attracted her, and she gave up other projects in order to do it.[51] Set in southern California, this was a curiously compelling drama that told the tale of a Mexican immigrant Chu Chu Ramirez (Ricardo Montalban) with big dreams of a great new life in America. His most treasured possession is a letter from the president welcoming him as an American citizen. Chu Chu works for local small landowner Ames (Wendell Corey) for a month. The Mexican's presence complicates the life of Ames' emotionally disturbed wife Anson (Trevor). Chu Chu finds romance with disillusioned alcoholic waitress Nancy (Shelley Winters). When it comes time to pay, Ames presents him with a dud check, but Chu Chu is determined to find redress. He confronts the couple a number of times, and after the last encounter, Ames attacks his wife and is accidentally shot. He contends that Chu Chu shot him and the case comes to trial. However Chu Chu's friends come to his assistance and in the end right prevails. Even Ames and his wife find reconciliation of a kind.

My Man and I was a thoughtful, well observed drama which contained moments of

14. Hard, Fast and Beautiful

William Wellman's vastly underrated *My Man and I* (1951) was an offbeat tale about an idealistic Mexican immigrant in Southern California, with Trevor (left) outstanding as the embittered wife of Wendell Corey (right). The film contains some of her finest screen work. Shelley Winters is at center.

comedy and pathos. The central relationships, between Chu Chu and Nancy, and between the Ames, described an intriguing dynamic; the one uncertain but loving, the other bitter through experience in which love has long since turned to hate. Anson Ames was one of Trevor's most interesting but least acclaimed roles in which she gave voice to a particular kind of longing for love which is never met. She is drawn to Ramirez but rejected by him. Perhaps there are lots of marriages and relationships that resemble that of the Ames— defined by bitterness and resentment but somehow the couple remains together, almost held together by hate. The background characters were well seen and believable; Chu Chu's friends, the understanding sheriff, even the bartender and the concerned landlady at Nancy's digs. Jack Elam seldom enjoyed such a good role despite his lack of Mexican looks. The narrative moved along in a straightforward manner, and the screenplay's lack of sensationalism allied to its humane treatment of its subjects made a refreshing change. On screen Mexicans have largely been viewed in a negative way, and too often treated as either comedy relief or heavy menace. *My Man and I* was a human drama first and foremost which spoke in a quietly profound way for the human predicament regardless of race.

Wellman astutely delineated the marriage of Anson and Andrew Ames. Even the land on which they attempt to subsist seems barren, mirroring their marital situation. In one scene Ames sits in his room polishing his gun, while Anson is in her room at the window.

Both are watching Chu Chu at work; both with their own thoughts. Anson regards him with a desperate longing. Knowing what she is thinking, Corey goes to the door adjoining their rooms and makes a loud noise. Anson almost jumps out of her skin, rudely woken from her reverie, Ames smiles maliciously. Such a simple scene with only a few words, but so cleverly seen and acted, said volumes about the psychology of both characters and the terrible state of their relationship.

The film was shot at locations in the San Joaquin Valley in Southern California and Calabasas. Monterrey, Sacramento and downtown Los Angeles were also mentioned as filming locations.[52] The screenplay was written by John Fante and Jack Leonard. Fante was a neglected writer until recently but was a major influence on Charles Bukowski who called him his god. Fante's most famous book was the semi-autobiographical *Ask the Dust* published in 1939, which, like many of his novels took place in Los Angeles. The recurring themes of his work centered on poverty and labor problems and his genre of fiction became known as the "dirty realist" school. Leonard was co-writer of a number of interesting noirs including *His Kind of Woman* (1951) and *The Narrow Margin* (1952), the latter of which was completed just prior to *My Man and I*. He died at the age of only 41.

Seeking different projects, Trevor played opposite Broderick Crawford in the musical comedy *Stop, You're Killing Me* (1952). The leading roles had first been offered to Lauren Bacall and Danny Kaye, who turned them down.[53] In a story set after the repeal of Prohi-

Claire displayed her range in the noisy but whimsical comedy musical *Stop, You're Killing Me* (1952) with Broderick Crawford (left).

bition, Crawford played an ex-bootlegger who starts his own legal brewery. He hopes to attract a better social clientele and leases a big house where he throws a party to impress his prospective in-laws. His past catches up with him and his life is complicated by the corpses of his previous business rivals.

The basis of the screenplay was Damon Runyon's stage play *A Slight Case of Murder*, with the addition of a few songs. It was a half-hearted musical; the songs were not especially memorable and uncertainly delivered at times by the principals. The director was Roy Del Ruth, whom Trevor knew from *The Babe Ruth Story*. She joined Crawford for a wayward rendition of "You're My Ever-Loving" with some much-needed help from a vocal group on a record in the background. This was one instance when they must both have been singing for real! Many of the era's famous songs put in appearances, including "Baby Face," and there was a curiously surreal moment when a visitor sang "Let the Rest of the World Go By" over the telephone to a dying man in a hospital. An amiably noisy film, it was fairly standard but was played with gusto by a good cast even though they all seemed somewhat out of their element. The sublime Margaret Dumont, the veteran Marx Brothers stooge, appeared as the potential society mother-in-law, who was required to scream and faint at regular intervals at the sight of corpses. There was excellent support from ex-vaudevillian Charles Carter, and the redoubtable Sheldon Leonard, with his great New York brogue, was always a welcome presence. *Stop, You're Killing Me* was poorly received then and gets no plaudits now, but many worse films have been committed to celluloid. Trevor was singled out for some of the only praise for the way she alternated "beautifully between natural stridency and artificial refinement."[54] The two leads played with charm, lifting the whole venture, and it was something different for Trevor. While making the picture, she was sent a 30-pound salmon by a devoted fan in Oregon, and it provided a great luncheon for the cast and crew.[55]

During filming, a fire on the set began and someone shouted "Fire!" just as Crawford was getting ready to sing; thinking it was a gag, he said, "Quit kidding." But everyone soon realized the danger and the set was hastily evacuated. There were two films in production that day on the affected sets; the other was *The Desert Song* with Gordon MacRae and Kathryn Grayson. All the actors and crew from both films watched the conflagration from a safe distance. In total, 12 sets were destroyed, in addition to two storage buildings containing numerous props from 30-plus years of productions: mummy cases, roulette wheels, horsehair sofas and even Robin Hood's arrows. Eighteen studio workmen were treated for minor burns but no one was seriously hurt. Investigators suspected arson; two fires had been started almost simultaneously. This was the second fire on the Warner lot in less than two months. The film vaults were in the direct line of the fire, but quick thinking ensured that valuable cans of film were rescued. The estimated cost of the damage was over $1,000,000.[56]

Trevor was offered the script for another comedy, *I'm Going to Maxeme's*, a project by British director Victor Saville. The film was due to be shot in Paris. Her role as Freddi was described as "a svelte darling of the Place de la Opera."[57] Saville hoped to interest French actress Hugette Oligny in the venture. Nothing came of it.

In the world of westerns, it would come as no surprise that *The Stranger Wore a Gun*; the real surprise would be if no one wore a gun. This routine 1953 horse opera was made at the height of the 3-D craze. Trevor once more essayed a variation on her by now entrenched bad girl persona. This time she was a female gambler who falls for ex–Quantrill spy Randolph Scott. It was directed with typical vigor by Andre de Toth and employed a remarkably similar style and look to his earlier *Springfield Rifle* (1952). This was de Toth's second 3-D film, his first, *House of Wax* (1953), caused a sensation on its debut. *The Stranger Wore a Gun* caused no such sensation and was repetitive, consisting mostly of one set of men on horseback chasing another set. It was a poorly conceived enterprise and squandered the talents of a good cast, which included Ernest Borgnine, Lee Marvin and Alfonso Bedoya. Claire was given no material to work with although she invested some scenes with her trademark humor, particularly when trying to make her love-rival jealous. Trevor was offered plenty of other similar projects including another spot as a wronged woman in producer Hal Makelim's *Desperate Men*, which would appear never to have got off the ground.[58]

One of the most curious offers she received around the same time was the lead in a national touring production of *The King and I* which she unsurprisingly did not accept.[59] She was disappointed to miss out on several roles including those in the film versions of *The Country Girl* and *Come Back, Little Sheba*. A part she especially coveted was that of the United Nations worker in the Korean War drama *One Minute to Zero* (1952) starring Robert Mitchum. That time she lost out to Ann Blyth.[60]

15

The High and the Mighty

> I have some aunts and other relatives in the East. Very dignified people. They often write to me and say, "Why can't they let you play nice girls in pictures, dear?"—Bob Thomas, "Claire Trevor's Kin Dislikes Bad Girl Roles: Conservative Father Feels the Same Way But in Strong Vein," *The Gloversville Leader-Republican* (Johnston, New York), April 30, 1953, 23

By 1954, Trevor's film career was beginning to wind down, and by 1958 she considered herself to be semi-retired. Her attention switched to television like many actresses of her generation. She was well loved and valued by the cinema-going public and everyone in the acting profession. She had nothing to prove as an actress and did not feel the compelling need to perform. Unexpectedly she received an Oscar nomination—her third—for *The High and the Mighty*. It was a measure of the regard and affection she had accrued in her twenty year career.

William A. Wellman's *The High and the Mighty* (1954), one of the earliest disaster films, enjoyed both critical and popular acclaim. The story concerned several passengers and crew of a Honolulu to San Francisco flight, during which one of the fuel tanks catches fire. The plane may need to make a forced landing. While awaiting their fate, all those aboard think back over their lives and experiences. This provided several unheralded pros of the era, such as Paul Kelly, Jan Sterling and Sidney Blackmer, a chance in the spotlight.

John Wayne was the star but was cast effectively against type as the troubled co-pilot with Robert Stack as the jittery pilot and the all-too-human Wally Brown as a confused navigator. Between them, they manage to reach San Francisco with all the clichés intact. Wayne was subdued as the co-pilot; it was a curiously wistful role for him. One critic noted that he was "as lonely at the end as at the beginning."[1] The normally over-exuberant Robert Newton gave one of his most understated and effective performances. Some episodes were rather tiresome, and the flashback scenes were obviously played out against a pantomime-style painted backdrop that only emphasized the feeling of artificiality. Trevor played May Holst, a variation on the familiar game dame of a certain age, the kind who has never been short of male company but who "never quite managed to make it legal." She invested her few short scenes with humor and pathos. Despite high billing she was rather underused, and her story was not so fleshed out as much as some of the other characters. Nor did she enjoy the experience working in the confined set: "Everybody whose ear was in camera range had to sit there, it was a dreary picture to make," she observed.[2] Nevertheless the touching scene she played with David Brian, during which she tries to comfort the surprisingly vulnerable big man, was spontaneously applauded by the rest of the cast; "Beautiful. Just beautiful," director Wellman reverently whispered.[3] He hailed Trevor as "one of the greatest actresses, if not the greatest actress."[4]

When Wellman began working on the picture, he could not persuade Bette Davis, Barbara Stanwyck, Ida Lupino, Ginger Rogers and a host of others to accept because of the size of the roles offered. Joan Crawford refused the role of May Holst. Wellman was turned down flat by Spencer Tracy who "thought it was lousy."[5] Nor could he get financial backing until Wayne, one of the producers, agreed to star. Wellman's faith in his own enterprise was vindicated by the film's warm reception.

Despite the brevity of her role, Trevor was Oscar-nominated as Best Supporting Actress, one of the film's six nominations. Dimitri Tiompkin deservedly won for his plaintive and captivating score. The film's tremendous box office success ensured that it became the blueprint for the many disaster movies that followed, notably the *Airport* series which began 15 years later even though the whole scenario seemed ripe for parody even at the time.

The Oscar nomination seemed to renew interest in Trevor; it was as though casting directors suddenly remembered she still existed. And yet her film career waned from the mid–1950s as she moved increasingly into television. In the handful of movies she made in the latter half of the decade, she gave a good account of herself but usually in smallish roles.

In spite of all the adulation that came her way she was seldom satisfied with her performances.

One of the earliest disaster films, *The High and the Mighty* (1954) concerned passengers in peril on a flight from Honolulu to San Francisco. Dimitri Tiomkin won an Academy Award for his plaintive score. Claire was among those nominated in a fine cast. Clockwise from top: John Wayne, Trevor, Robert Stack, David Brian, Robert Newton, Phil Harris, Jan Sterling and Laraine Day.

"You think you're doing something in a scene," she once reflected. "Then you see the rushes and you think, 'That isn't what I meant to do.' You keep talking to yourself. You look back at the mistakes you've made. You say to yourself, 'Anybody could make those. A lot have made worse mistakes. I did fairly well with the equipment I have.'"[6]

In March 1954, she was one of 16 leading Hollywood stars attending the first film festival in Argentina. Held at Mar del Plata, it attracted many famous names of international cinema. Mary Pickford was among the guests.[7] Trevor enjoyed her time there and later recalled, "Peron was in power then and I met him. He ran the country like a woman. The film festival was a national observance and it was really something to see."[8] The U.S. State Department was somewhat affronted that the Argentine press praised Soviet cinema at the expense of Hollywood, and considered stopping any future American participation in the festival, but wiser counsel prevailed.[9] The festival did not become a regular event until 1959 and was held most years up until 1970 when it was discontinued. It resumed in 1996 and has become an annual event once more.

Among Trevor's abandoned projects was a big-screen version of F. Scott Fitzgerald's *The Last Tycoon*; the producers approached her to play a key role as a bootlegger.[10] She was *Johnny Guitar* (1954) Joan Crawford's preferred choice to play the other female protagonist, Emma Small, in that ambiguous western fable. According to Michael Schlesinger, Crawford later changed her mind because she thought Claire was "too pretty."[11] The role was famously given to Mercedes McCambridge. Coincidentally, McCambridge also got the role of Luz in George Stevens' *Giant* which Trevor had hoped might come her way.[12] Although there was speculation that Trevor would be offered the lead in *The Search for Bridey Murphy* (1956), the role of an ordinary American housewife who regresses to a past life in Ireland went to Teresa Wright.[13]

Trevor's next was yet another western, *Man Without a Star* (1955). This time the subject was range wars and the fencing-off of the land. Kirk Douglas played the title role, a wanderer with a hatred of barbed wire. Trevor appeared as the chief prostitute of the town where Douglas hitches up for a spell. She has known him previously and becomes jealous when he begins working for (and falling for) new landowner Reed Bowman (Jeanne Crain). Some of the best scenes were at the beginning when Douglas and young William Campbell hitch a ride on a freight train and strike up a tentative friendship. They soon find themselves on opposite sides but come together at the end to thwart nasty range boss Steve Miles (Richard Boone in excellent form, as usual). The film contained fine performances from an interesting cast and was enhanced considerably by the cinematography of Russell Metty, who worked for most of the great directors over the course of his long career. The rousing opening theme sung by '50s favorite Frankie Laine set the right tone. A generally good-humored western, *Man Without a Star* had its serious moments, but it was not especially memorable. Trevor was good, as always, but she was hardly stretched and for her many fans she just wasn't in it enough.

Set in Texas, *Lucy Gallant* (1955) was an amiable film about the romance between dress shop owner Jane Wyman and cattleman Charlton Heston. Trevor was featured as brothel-keeper turned wise counsel Lady Macbeth, another local businesswoman of a kind—this was a modern reworking of her all-too-familiar saloon gal persona. Thelma Ritter, William Demarest and Wallace Ford stood out among the supporting cast amid the full glory of VistaVision. It could well have been subtitled "Fashion from Mud," such was the stark contrast of the setting and Gallant's ambitions. One hundred fifty-four costumes were seen, designed by Edith Head who also made a rare on screen appearance. It was a polished affair, much of the action taking place during the World War II years, but the whole of the war itself was reduced to a few short scenes showing Heston getting his kit and sending postcards to Wyman.

The look of the oil boom town was well-realized by director Robert Parrish, who started in Hollywood as a teenage extra. When Wyman first arrives in town in the rain, the streets are a sea of mud; after oil is discovered, the place seems even messier. In a few short years, the town becomes gentrified and she has a thriving fashion business, despite the incongruity of high fashion and oil wells. Although the movie was pleasant enough, Heston seemed miscast and there was none of the pulsating undercurrent of social and sexual tension that characterized Wyman's other screen appearances such as in her recent *Magnificent Obsession*. The question posed here was a familiar one: "Can a career woman live without love?" The 1950s answer was a qualified "No." However, although she is bought out of her

Fashion hewn from mud: Trevor had a good supporting role in *Lucy Gallant* (1955), a colorful romantic drama set in a Texas oil boom town. Charlton Heston is shown with her.

own company by an ambitious board member ("Little Boy Blue wants to sit at the head of the table," says Claire pithily), the end leaves the future open to big new business opportunities, so maybe the answer to the question is "She can have both—kind of."

At the beginning, the rummage sale scene in the hastily opened store was cleverly realized. The director was dissatisfied at first, and did not get the effect he wanted until he told the women extras that they could keep whatever clothes they were able to grab. After that it was a free-for-all which gave the scene its sense of reality.[14] The opening song "How Can I Tell Her?" was composed for the picture by veterans Jay Evans and Jay Livingston, and delivered with typical '50s panache by the Four Freshmen, whose close harmonies and lush arrangements epitomized the pre–rock'n'roll era and were infused with all the distinctive romantic nostalgia of their era.

Claire was easily persuaded to return to the stage at intervals. She was especially impressed by Arthur Laurents' bittersweet romance *The Time of the Cuckoo,* for which Shirley Booth had won a Tony on Broadway. Claire appeared in a version at the summer theater at the La Jolla Playhouse in August 1955. Gilbert Roland was approached to play the male lead but he had two film commitments and the role went to Jacques Bergerac, the husband of Ginger Rogers.[15] After five days of rehearsals, Bergerac was told he was ineligible because he was not a member of Equity[16]; Stephen Bekassy took his place. Benay Venuta was also featured in the cast. Claire played a spinster desperate for love who, on vacation in Venice, meets a man only to find disillusionment with him. The play was described as "one of the most memorable in the Playhouse's history, playing to packed houses since its opening."[17] Trevor gave a memorable performance and the production was met with a "remarkably hearty response from its audience."[18] Among the stars who saw it: Lucille Ball, Desi Arnaz, Gregory Peck and Dorothy McGuire.[19]

Claire relished the role: "Playing that woman was a revelation in all that I've missed," she reflected. "It was exciting to play her because it gave full extension to whatever characterizing talent I possess."[20] She noted that playwrights were far better at writing good women's parts than screenwriters, and lamented the paucity of good female roles during all her Hollywood years. The roles she rated best were Scarlett O'Hara, Mildred Pierce, the protagonist in *The Letter* and Gaye in *Key Largo*. But such well-rounded roles were few and far between and too often she had been called on to play what she called "half a woman"— a part so sketchy that characterization was hard to make interesting. "You don't get a good purchase on those one-dimensional ladies," she observed. "It's like wrestling with a ghost." She maintained that writers didn't know how to write for women and never penetrated beyond surface appearance or showed a woman as she really is. "Only occasionally [do you come across] a 'whole woman' ... a complete motivated female, with all the emotional subtleties and byplay that is women." She feared that the comic strip and the soap opera had been the ruin of good characterization.[21]

Trevor was one of a group of players, including Anthony Quinn, Robert Ryan and Jack Palance, involved with a stage project under the direction of Daniel Mann. They had ambitious plans for producing Las Palmas Theater plays in the mid–1950s including an attempt at the works of Shakespeare. Most of these plans did not come to fruition, often because of busy filming schedules.[22]

Claire's next screen assignment was in *The Mountain* (1956), set in the Swiss Alps, where an airplane has crashed atop the highest mountain in the area. Oldtimer Zachary (Spencer Tracy) has climbed the mountain many times but refuses to help the expedition investigate the wreck. The search party returns after their guide is killed. Zachary's workshy brother Chris (Robert Wagner) is determined to reach the wreck to take all the money and valuables from the dead passengers. Zachary is appalled at this but goes with him, knowing that Chris cannot scale the mountain alone. After an arduous climb, the two reach the plane and find a woman is still alive. Chris tries to strangle her but Zachary is determined to save her. Chris loses his life on the way down. Zachary returns with the woman and tells the story in reverse, that it was Chris who saved the woman, but no one believes him. Trevor played a robust widow sweet on confirmed bachelor Zachary but unable to get him to marry her. The director Edward Dmytryk had been at the helm for *Murder, My Sweet*. The scenery was impressive; it was filmed in Chamonix in the French Alps.

The film was dogged by problems. To begin with, the mercurial Tracy objected to the supporting cast which, apart from Trevor, included such other familiar faces as William Demarest, who popped up as a priest.[23] *The Mountain* was scuppered from the outset by the ridiculous casting of Tracy and Wagner as brothers. Tracy was a magnificent actor, but not only did he seem old, he looked far too out-of-shape to go climbing. Their unsuitability was further underlined by the choice of costume: Tracy, wearing a bright red shirt, appeared even wider, and Wagner in baby blue with a bobble hat pushed back on his head looked incredibly boyish. Perhaps the makers were inspired by their successful pairing in *Broken*

Lance (1954), but the scenario this time had little to commend it. Trevor was underused but livened up her few scenes. The assessment of the critics was damning. One wrote: "An indeterminate production in which one believes neither the setting, the plot, nor the characters; especially not with VistaVision making everything sharply unreal and the brothers seemingly two generations apart."[24] Asked about the film, Trevor exclaimed, "Oh God, that was a terrible picture!" she said. "It goes on forever and it's really bad."[25]

At this stage in Trevor's career, the interesting parts were just not coming along. It was always much harder in Hollywood for actresses, and once they reached a certain age many tended to vanish from the screen. The exceptions were the character actresses, but even they were not getting the good material they needed. At the same time, the studio system was breaking down and the cinema had lost much of its glamour in the television age.

Claire never entered the mad social whirl of the '50s Hollywood and Riviera set, but she knew Grace Kelly and managed to live down that she had once advised her against becoming an actress. "I told her to stay out of the profession," she said, "as there are too many heartaches and the life would be unbearable."[26] She made some trenchant observations about the decline in fashion she had noticed in the film capital in recent times: "You see the most awful freaks on Hollywood Boulevard," she remarked. "Women in shorts, women in bathing suits looking sloppy and fat. This is a city. The women should look like they were in one."[27]

Trevor took part in a number of charity fundraising events such as a Ribbons Ball to aid of Bide-a-Wee Homes. Other actresses involved included Irene Dunne and Ava Gardner.[28] Bide-a-Wee Homes is dedicated to finding homes for abandoned pets, especially dogs and cats. Claire modeled gowns designed by Don Loper for the third annual Damon Runyon Cancer Fund Dinner held at Hollywood's Ambassador Hotel.[29] She attended a bazaar, buffet and square dance at the Bud Abbott estate in aid of the 12–30 Club for disabled war veterans.[30] She was also a member of a group that raised money for the Vista Del Mar Children's Home.[31] And in 1953 she was guest of honor at the International Mother's Day celebration, where she was voted Mother of the Year.[32]

She was very much affected by the death of her good friend Humphrey Bogart in January 1957 at the age of 57. His funeral was well-attended by most of the leading stars in Hollywood. Even many years later, she felt emotional when talking about him.

By this stage of her career, cinema seemed to be diminishing in importance while television was on the rise. While the studio system was crumbling, the small screen was attracting some of the best talent and often had the most innovative ideas. It was not surprising that TV's success led to many of its plays and shows being given big-screen treatment. One such was *The Unholy Wife* (1957); in the original TV version, Claire had played the leading female role.

At the same time, she talked more frequently about retirement. "What's all this about anyway?" she asked. "The fame is nonsense—I've found that out—and I've been to all the parties I want to go to and had the social chi-chi. I can't take it any more." She expressed concern over some young actresses such as Marilyn Monroe and Elizabeth Taylor and the physical and emotional effects the filmmaking business was having on them. She wondered why Monroe became ill whenever she made a film. "Is it exhausted nerves or a bronchial condition?"[33]

By now, Claire's screen persona was so established that some parts were designated as "a Claire Trevor role." She took this as a great compliment. "I really feel that I have put my name to something in Hollywood and am recognized for a definite kind of role," she averred. She also spoke of her career as a positive example for up-and-coming actresses: "If some of these young stars would think about it, they would realize that there is a successful future in my type of role. They don't have to be beautiful or make themselves over as they approach 40. It's a good thing—being bad."[34] She was already admired by many of those young stars, including Barbara Nichols, a blonde who hoped to emulate her and eschew the usual "dumb blonde" stereotype. Nichols commented, "[I] hope one day to meet her and tell her how much I think of her. She's a real versatile professional. And I have hopes with my current role ... in *The Sweet Smell of Success* ... of getting going on the Trevor dream."[35]

It was another three years before Claire returned to the big screen for a decent role in *Marjorie Morningstar* (1958) as the shrewd Jewish mother of Natalie Wood. Based on the Herman Wouk bestseller, the story centered on a star-struck girl who falls for an aging lothario she meets when acting in a summer theater. Lee J. Cobb was cast as the father but Everett Sloane was later given the part. Wood was excellent in the title role, playing with great sensitivity and awareness. Gene Kelly did well as the all-too-human object of her affection, with great support from a good cast and a finely judged performance from the underrated Martin Balsam as a rejected suitor. Trevor was never close to caricature, and had some especially good scenes with Wood, Kelly and Sloane. One memorable sequence

Trevor (left) enjoyed one of her better later roles as the shrewd mother of Natalie Wood in the bittersweet *Marjorie Morningstar* (1958).

when she turns up unexpectedly at the summer theater showed her to great effect. She sounds out putative son-in-law Kelly, continually probing him with acutely embarrassing questions about his income, age and prospects. It is so embarrassing that the audience squirms with him.

Working with Natalie and watching her rush to prepare for another film gave Claire the shudders. "She reminds me of me when I rushed from picture to picture, and I wonder 'How can you do it?' Then I remember that Shirley Temple is almost 30 and I played her mother in *Baby, Take a Bow* and that answers my question. Natalie is me 25 years ago."[36] She had nothing but praise for the young star, saying she was one of the finest talents with whom she had ever worked. "If she wants, she can grow up to be anything," she commented. Claire was also concerned that Wood had missed out on a childhood and spent too much time with older people. "She's been acting since she was four. She's 19 now. She's reaching out for understanding and love," she observed. "I love Natalie and hope she'll allow me to remain a close friend."[37] The director Irving Rapper had made some memorable Bette Davis films including *Now, Voyager* (1942), *The Corn Is Green* (1945) and *Deception* (1946).

In September 1958, Trevor's father, three months short of his ninetieth birthday, died at an Orange County rest home. He had been in good health for most of his life, something he attributed to long daily walks and a diet that consisted mostly of raw vegetables and lots of fruit. He stayed active well into old age, had good eyesight and still had his own teeth.[38] His wife had settled in California and they eventually divorced at Pasco, Florida, in 1945. Claire was the sole beneficiary of her father's estate, valued at well over $10,000, with an estimated annual income of $2000.[39]

By the time Claire made *Marjorie Morningstar*, she considered herself to be semi-retired. She would occasionally appear in teleplays, but it would be another four years before she could be persuaded to make another movie.

16

The Small Screen

> Really, I think it's too late for me to become a star.—Trevor quoted in Erskine Johnson, "Johnson in Hollywood: Substitutes for Abbott and Costello Use Own Routines," *Long Beach Independent,* January 18, 1954, 18

As her film career went into decline after the mid–1950s, Trevor was seen increasingly on television. Like many of her generation, she came late to the medium. She was in her forties when she started and appeared infrequently. Her career lasted a mere nine years in the main, ending in 1962; it would not resume until 1983. Although she felt that she had little chance to make a big impression, she underestimated herself. She was allowed to display her range more so than she had ever been able to do on the big screen and created some memorable character studies, winning the ultimate television accolade, an Emmy, for her performance in *Dodsworth*.

She made her debut on the medium in October 1948 in a historic broadcast on KFI-TV in California. This was the first television transmission from the West Coast on a show that went out live from 7 p.m. to 10 p.m. She was among dignitaries and invited guests who included Adolphe Menjou, retired football star Tom Harmon and Los Angeles Mayor Fletcher D. Buron.[1] The station had begun experimenting in August with six hours a week on air, and from October transmitted programs for 12 hours a week.

After that entry into the medium, she had several false starts to her actual TV career. As early as 1950 she had planned to star in her own detective series, *Miss Private Eyeful*. She had first proposed the idea to radio producers but was unable to get the necessary backing in either medium.[2] She was slated to appear opposite Lew Parker in a television run of a popular radio comedy, *The Bickersons*, but the part was played again by the original actress, Frances Langford.[3] The following year she was reportedly set to sign for her own series, *Claire Calls*, but this too failed to get off the ground.[4] Although she was in talks with NBC to appear with Vincent Price in what was described as "a new type of panel show," that also never transpired.[5] She was one of many stars who expressed an interest in *The National Repertory Theater* program in the early 1950s, but only one was filmed, "The Victim," and the series did not materialize until four years later in 1956 when it reappeared as *The Ethel Barrymore Theater*.[6] Claire's only early appearances on the small screen were confined to a commercial for watches and a brief spot as a guest on Hollywood columnist Sheilah Graham's talk show.[7] During that interview, she talked about having her own TV series which was due to start "in the fall" (of 1951), and mentioned a pilot film she had made for the medium, but neither of these has come to light.[8]

Trevor made her dramatic debut in 1953 in a short drama, "Alias Nora Hale," for NBC's

Ford Television Theater. She played the part of a woman who was once wrongfully imprisoned, and now sets about taking revenge on those responsible: a judge (Warren Anderson) and his wife (Rosemary de Camp). In "The Summer Memory," also for *Ford Theater*, a selfish, drink-sodden old man uses his age to bind his children to him. When his daughter (Trevor) receives an unexpected offer of marriage, she must decide whether to sacrifice her own chance at happiness and stay with her dissolute father. Veteran character actor James Barton played the father with Richard Kiley as his son. Its director Fred F. Sears started as an actor and later directed the science fiction opus *Earth vs. the Flying Saucers* (1956) as well as such minor league crime dramas as *Escape from San Quentin* (1957). He died at the age of 44. "The Summer Memory," a colorcast written by Rod Serling, was described as "morose but compelling with a liberal amount of extra fine acting."[9]

For *General Electric Theater*, Claire appeared in "Foggy Night" (1954) as a woman who becomes embroiled in a murder case when she stumbles upon the body of a woman in a parked car and has difficulty proving her innocence. The teleplay was adapted from a tale by Robert Patterson, who had written the story on which the powerful prison-bound noir *Brute Force* (1947) was based. Director Alfred E. Green's career stretched back to 1910; among the highlights were the films *Baby Face* (1933) and *The Fabulous Dorseys* (1947).

At first Claire found the pace of the medium rather too fast in comparison to that of cinema. Nonetheless she enjoyed working in live television. "You get to be a nervous wreck," she remarked. "But you know it's that very nervousness that makes TV more fresh than the movies. The nervousness keeps you 'up.' And that makes each scene more exciting—that is, as long as you have a good script."[10] She had not been impressed with the standard of writing she had generally encountered on the small screen, which was one reason why she had not been tempted by many of the numerous scripts she had been offered. She also noted that because she was not afraid of live television, she got to do roles other actresses were reluctant to try.[11] Despite her success, she also admitted, "Really, I think it's too late for me to become a star," saying that she wanted to appear infrequently "just to keep the ham in me happy."[12] She certainly had no desire to become tied down to a series, explaining that "an occasional play or a good story is all right, but not a series. At least not any that have been suggested to me—lady district attorney, lady judge, visiting nurse…"[13]

Her television work had the same hallmark of quality that characterized her films. In some ways it extended her scope, and gave her a chance to show her range in roles that had been denied her on the big screen. For instance, she was effective in "No Sad Songs for Me" as a selfless woman dying of cancer and given only ten months to live, a part originally essayed by Margaret Sullavan. She got to do lots of character work and was marvelous in a version of *Ladies in Retirement* with Elsa Lanchester and Edith Barrett. This popular murder mystery had first played on the London stage and had been made into a successful film starring Ida Lupino, Lanchester and Barrett. The eerie atmosphere of the eastern marches of England made a suitably sinister backdrop to the curious tale and eccentric characters. Trevor and the other actresses brought the characters vividly to life in a well-realized version of the play which measures up to the film. She was nominated for an Emmy for her portrayal.

Claire achieved her greatest TV success in a dramatization of "Dodsworth," for which she received an Emmy. This was also a live colorcast, one of the first color broadcasts long before it was the norm. Most people did not have a color television set until the 1960s or

1970s. The adaptation was faithful to the Sidney Howard play which was based on the novel by Sinclair Lewis. The story concerned a Midwest businessman (Fredric March) with a younger wife who persuades him to sell his business so they can take a grand tour of Europe. Once there, she begins to pursue shallow Continental lovers but eventually returns to her husband, who finally rejects her in favor of his secretary (Geraldine Fitzgerald).

Critics hailed the teleplay as "richly satisfying theater, 90 minutes of adult drama beautifully and faithfully produced." The acting was warmly applauded as "brilliantly incisive and sensitive."[14] Despite the fact that the play was set in 1933, and might seem to contain easily stereotyped characters, the actors made it live. Trevor played a seemingly unsympathetic, flighty woman but managed to convey layers of emotion that transcended any limitations imposed on her. She was mature and yet immature, railing against the coming of age and the loss of part of herself. The actress made her into a curiously pitiable and human figure. She actually wore a memento of the original film, a wrap that Ruth Chatterton had sported and which Claire had bought at auction.[15]

Trevor never played the diva, either on the big or small screen, and was considered "extremely cooperative and easy to work with" by ATV's wardrobe mistress Claire Fournier.[16]

For an episode of the popular anthology series *Climax!*, Trevor appeared with a stellar cast in "The Prowler," sometimes known as "The Prowler and the Lady." Phyllis, bored wife of a rancher, shoots her husband in order to inherit his money. She tells police that she thought he was a prowler. Actually the man she shot was not her husband, but another man, and at the ensuing trial she attempts to pin the blame for his murder on her husband, and is acquitted. Family friend Carl (Wallace Ford) discovers that Phyllis' invalid mother-in-law was a witness to the killing and her sudden unexpected death leads to Phyllis' conviction for a murder she did not commit. The production employed a fine cast including Pat O'Brien and Cameron Mitchell plus a "well-paced and tightly scripted" screenplay.[17] It was roundly lauded by critics who especially hailed Trevor's strong portrayal of the femme fatale. There was much speculation that the tale had been based on William Woodward's murder, a *cause celebre* in the fall of 1955. Woodward, an affluent New Yorker and heir to a banking fortune, was shot by his wife, who said she thought he was a prowler. At the trial, she was exonerated. The makers of the drama took pains to explain that any resemblance was purely coincidental. Host William Lundigan even wrote a letter to the press stating, "There have been a number of items recently in syndicated columns to the effect that ... 'The Prowler' is patterned after the sensational 'Woodward Case.' This is just not so. 'The Prowler,' an original by F.W. Durkee, Jr, was purchased more than six months ago—and we have been holding it until we could convince Claire Trevor to do it."[18] Nevertheless, the old adage stood that any publicity was good publicity. RKO bought the rights to Durkee's teleplay, and although it was hoped that the same players could be employed, the director assigned to the project, John Farrow, chose an entirely different cast. *The Unholy Wife* (1957) was shot in Technicolor with Diana Dors and Rod Steiger in the leads.[19] It was a measure of the rise of television that it was influencing the big screen to such a degree by then.

For the *Schlitz Playhouse of Stars,* Trevor next appeared in "Fool Proof" as a teacher in a school for the blind who, after an accident, wakes up with her head and eyes bandaged. She is made to believe that she is in a hospital, but in truth she has been kidnapped by a gang who demand $50,000 for her release. Thanks to her shrewdness and ability with the blind, she is able to outwit her captors.[20] The episode was well directed by veteran Robert Florey, who had been at the helm of *King of Gamblers* almost 20 years earlier.

Trevor appeared twice on the fondly recalled suspense series *Alfred Hitchcock Presents*. In "Safe Conduct" (1955), she played an American journalist on a trans-continental train. She is constantly interrupted by Eastern Bloc secret police and befriended by a smooth-talking captain (Jacques Bergerac) of the national soccer team whose allegiance is hard to pin down. Although Trevor did well, the story was not the strongest; it fit in with the times when the Cold War was at its height and mistrust was the watchword. In 1961, "A Crime for Mothers" saw her to far better advantage. She played Mrs. Meade, a slatternly drunk who visits the Birdwells, adoptive parents of her daughter Eileen, and demands either the child's return or money from them. A belligerent man claiming to be a private detective persuades her to kidnap the child and ask for $25,000 reward. But not everything is as it seems. The role was first offered to Ida Lupino, who turned it down because she didn't think it was right for her, but she was keen to direct it.[21] It provided a good role for Trevor who, against the odds, made the seemingly monstrous Mrs. Meade into a troubled, naïve "lost soul" who is ultimately more the victim of the wiles of others than willfully evil. Her voice sounded different, slightly higher pitched, but her trademark penchant for sly humor was intact. The "detective" tells her to pass herself off as a cleaning woman when she meets the girl for the first time; "Cleaning woman!" she exclaims, affronted. When pressed by the child, she tells her she is a governess, but then later forgets herself when the girl asks what time her parents will arrive. "How should I know?" she retorts. "I'm just the cleaning woman."

Bette Davis and Anne Baxter were struck down by illness and could not appear in the lead role of the *Playhouse 90* drama "If You Knew Elizabeth" (1957). Davis pleaded "exhaustion" and Baxter was hit by a virus, so Claire entered the breach.[22] Davis' husband Gary Merrill appeared as a professor who proposes marriage to his assistant Elizabeth (Trevor). She discovers that he wants to marry her because he wants to become a college proxy, and runs away. As the professor tries to track her down, he gains a different perspective on her from everyone he meets, and begins to realize he doesn't know her at all. The scenario gave Trevor a chance to show her range: She appeared as seven different versions of the same woman. She was seen as "a nice girl, a gold-digger, model of efficiency, drill sergeant, soap opera alcoholic, little old lady and lively teenager."[23] This was an interesting vehicle for her, and reviewers called her admirable. Among the cast was Ernest Truex with whom Trevor had played in *Whistling in the Dark* on Broadway 25 years before. Another familiar face was Joseph Sweeney, who achieved immortality as elderly Juror No. Nine in the movie *12 Angry Men* the same year. The distinguished director was John Frankenheimer, who gave the episode a polish it might otherwise have lacked. Frankenheimer often directed on television and later went on to acclaim for his political dramas including *The Manchurian Candidate* (1962).

In the *Westinghouse Desilu Playhouse* presentation "Happy Hill," she played the wife of an escaped convict (Gene Evans), and, through her concern for her husband and young son, inadvertently becomes the bait in a police trap. Set in the swamplands near New Orleans, the hour-long tale featured such stalwarts as Edith Barrett and John Qualen. Royal Dano appeared as a taciturn character who helps the family in their time of greatest need. Despite the promising-sounding premise, the drama was dismissed by one critic as "vapid."[24]

The popular anthology *The United States Steel Hour* attracted many of the big names of the acting fraternity. In 1960, Trevor played the title role in "The Revolt of Judge Lloyd," a juvenile court judge in Cuyahoga County, Ohio. Presiding over a case of vandalism, she is pressured by her politically ambitious fiancé (Jeff Morrow) and local vested interests not to prosecute the case of an influential citizen or his children in open court. Trevor gave a strong performance as a judge who stands by her principles. The story was reportedly inspired by "a little-known statute in Ohio which permits a judge to jail the parents of a juvenile."[25]

Claire guest-starred on an enjoyable episode of *Wagon Train*, "The C.L. Harding Story." Portraying a feisty reporter, she joins the wagon train and annoys wagon master Seth (Ward Bond) with her continual espousal of women's rights and stirs up the other women to rebel until they are allowed to vote for a new judge. She even leads the women in a rousing chorus of the old hymn "The Hand That Rocks the Cradle Rules the World," which brings Bond to the boiling point (not a difficult thing to do!). Theirs was a curious kind of romance which mostly consisted of them yelling at each other. Bond frequently played volatile characters and even when seemingly calm he could appear to be on the verge of exploding. Trevor's excellent narration seemed surprisingly wistful and almost poetic at times when describing the journey. Johnny Cash made his acting debut in a small role as a newly married trail hand.

In 1959, Trevor was in searing form as Ma Barker in an episode of *The Untouchables*, "Ma Barker and Her Boys," about the notorious brothers who robbed banks and kidnapped millionaires in the 1930s Midwest. Their daring and sensational raids held the country spellbound and led to a nationwide manhunt. After being tracked down to a Florida hideout, they were all killed during a six-hour gun battle with the FBI. In real life, Eliot Ness had nothing to do with the case, and there is some conjecture about the true character of Ma Barker. Be that as it may, Trevor presented a powerful depiction of intense mother love that leads to the destruction of all her sons and herself. The story had a strangely epic quality that seemed almost akin to a Greek tragedy in its themes. She held the whole thing together and made the transition from hymn-singing churchgoer to criminal mastermind seem not only believable but natural. Ma Barker was one of her most memorable TV roles and makes one realize just what she could have achieved on the big screen if she had been given such chances to explore her range.

The Investigators, a short-lived CBS series which aired between October and December 1961, was intended to capitalize on the success of *77 Sunset Strip*. Starring James Franciscus as Russ Andrews, it revolved around a group of insurance agents at a top New York firm. The series attracted some star names including Rhonda Fleming and Mickey Rooney. In "New Sound for the Blues," the third of the 13 episodes, Trevor played a nightclub pianist and singer, Kitty Harper, whose athlete son is accidentally killed by Andrews. She refuses to believe that her son was ever involved in any nefarious activity or that he was carrying a gun, as Andrews describes. Trevor came in on extremely short notice for the role but managed to learn the script in a day. In addition, she learned five songs but in the event her singing voice was dubbed by Jo Ann Greer.[26] Despite her lack of preparation, she was judged to be "outstanding" in the role.[27] The episode's director Joseph H. Lewis always lent true noir style to all his work.

In December 1962, Trevor and her son appeared in an episode of *Dr. Kildare* entitled

"The Bed I've Made." She played a nurse, Veronica Johnson, who falls for Dr. Gillespie (Raymond Massey). Charles appeared as a medical student. Charles had previously worked as a MGM studio tour guide but had ambitions to act and studied with Jeff Corey.[28] As it transpired, he did not make a career of acting. Trevor's character was considered as a possibly recurring one, but she never appeared again on the show.

During the 1960s and '70s, she popped up occasionally on television in brief interviews and star tributes to other performers such as her friend John Wayne. But by 1962 her small-screen career was effectively over. It would be another 21 years before she would appear again. This was a big loss for television culture in general and for her in particular, because she missed the glory years of the medium, which really came into its own during that time. Surely she would have continued to add to her laurels, and, crucially, become known to a whole new generation.

Trevor's TV work had fine quality if not quantity and along the way she won an Emmy, something which others who spent a lifetime in the medium never achieved.

17

The Sixties

> I like to get in a car and drive. I like books. And I like to see a lot of my family.—Interview with Sheilah Graham, "Claire Trevor Got Her Oscar and with It Leading Lady Roles," *The Milwaukee Journal,* May 30, 1948, 48

In the mid–1950s, Trevor slowed down considerably, and she was seen far less on the big screen. She said that she classed herself as semi-retired. But she was not forgotten by the public and was still in demand. She only accepted a role if she was attracted or inspired by a particular project. As a result, she made only four films during the 1960s but had lost none of her quality and, tellingly, she was nominated for an award for one of them.

In 1958, Trevor was almost tempted to return to Broadway in Tennessee Williams' *Sweet Bird of Youth,* staged and directed by Elia Kazan.[1] Two years later, Frank Capra called to offer her the central role in his screen dramatization of the play *Lady for a Day.* In this new film, *Pocketful of Miracles,* the part went to Bette Davis instead, but even then the film was not judged to be a success.[2] Also in 1960, she turned down an offer of a summer theater tour of William Inge's *The Dark at the Top of the Stairs.*[3]

When her TV career wound down in the early 1960s, she made a tentative return to the cinema. After four years' absence, she said yes to a script for Vincente Minnelli's *Two Weeks in Another Town* (1962). The film seemed to owe a great deal to Minnelli's own *The Bad and the Beautiful* (1952): It had the same star, Kirk Douglas, and was a similarly caustic look at the world of moviemaking. It even included some scenes from the earlier film which the stars watch in a projection room. Douglas played Jack Andrus, a washed-up actor with psychological problems. He is invited to make a picture in Italy by once great director Maurice Kruger (Edward G. Robinson); when Andrus arrives there, he finds that he is not wanted as an actor but only to work on dubbing the other actors. He reluctantly agrees, and although still troubled, he begins to regain confidence. When Kruger falls ill, he is asked to take over as director.

A clever and well-made film, *Two Weeks in Another Town* had a good old-time cast that was well-chosen for its subject matter. Robinson, Douglas and Trevor were three big names from the classic era, and in Minnelli's hands the film became a wry homage to film-making and a sly comment on the whole process. The bright, clear color tended to highlight the very artificiality of the camera eye. Trevor's thankless role as Clara, the harridan wife of Kruger, was a familiar one at this point in her career, and she made the most of her opportunities, imbuing her character with an elusive and unexpected pathos. This was especially apparent in the scene where she tries to commit suicide. Here is a woman carried along by her own deep-seated unhappiness, sustained only by bitterness, but intensely vul-

139

nerable. An effective scene depicted one of the bitterest wedding anniversary dinners ever; the rendition of "The Anniversary Waltz" seems embarrassing and ironic. The role had first been offered to Jo Van Fleet, who rejected it because she said she was tired of playing embittered dipsomaniacs.[4] It has been suggested that Clara was based on Darryl F. Zanuck's wife Virginia. The film was highly regarded in Europe (Europeans have always appreciated Minnelli). In *Cahiers du Cinema*, Jean-Luc Godard called it one of the ten best of the year.[5]

Minnelli's films are always infused with life and light. His acute sense of observation renders each scene remarkably piquant. The backgrounds, the lighting, the vases of flowers, the spacious hotel rooms, the balconies at night, the streets, all resonate. Nothing happens in a void. His characters are vivid and it is clear that he understands those in the film business inside and out. Everything he does seemed casual but that is deceptive.

Trevor said she enjoyed making the movie, commenting: "It's like the days of old-time moviemaking. Everyone is treated like a star, not like in television or B-pictures."[6] She was the only member of the cast not required to fly to Italy. "That's why I took the role," she said. "Getting myself to drive into Hollywood is a chore enough."[7] She spoke warmly of working with Minnelli, and admitted being more than a little in awe of him. She admired

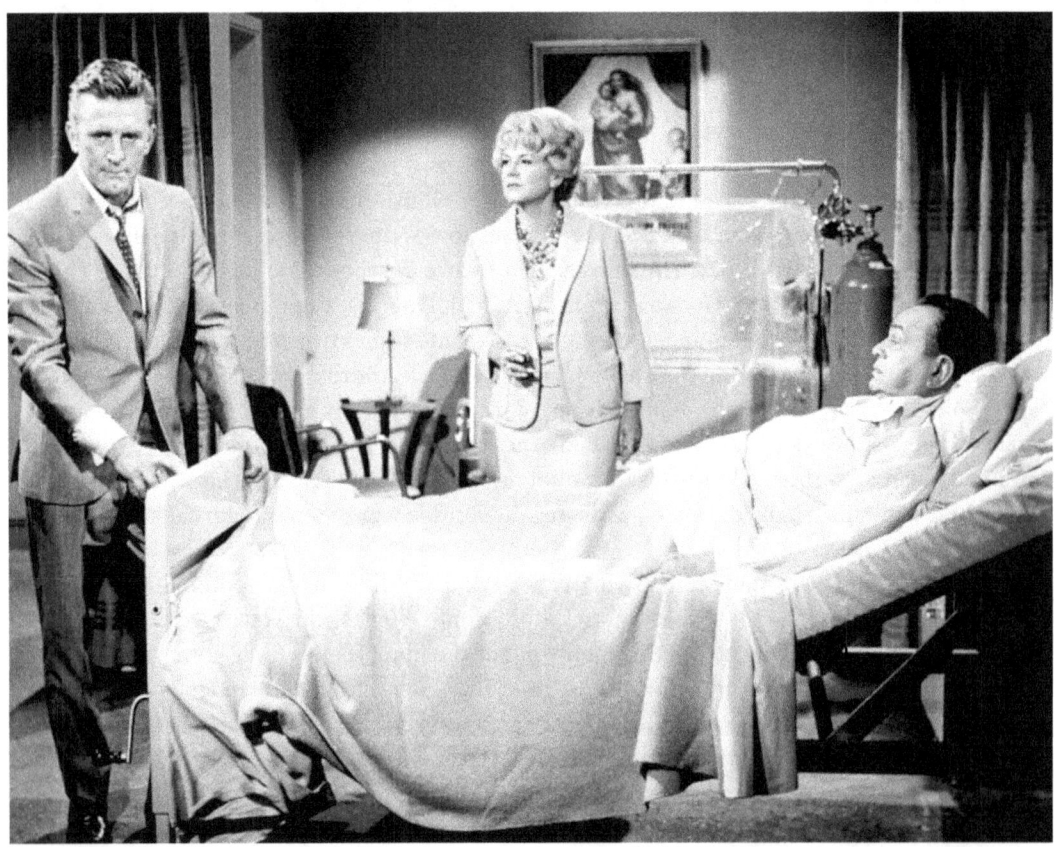

"You stab your benefactor in the back on his death bed!" Trevor was memorable as the harridan wife of one-time big-shot director Edward G. Robinson (right) in Vincente Minnelli's *Two Weeks in Another Town* (1962). Kirk Douglas is at left.

him enormously and said that making the film was "a revelation." She spoke of his "taste, talent [and] sophistication," and lauded his "great desire to bring beauty to people. And, God knows, he did."[8]

The misleadingly titled drama *The Stripper* (1963) was originally known as *The Loss of Roses*, a far more apt description of a slow-moving, rather mawkish tale. Struggling actress Lila (Joanne Woodward) is abandoned by one of her stage partners, Rick (Robert Webber), while touring the Midwest; he absconds with all the money. She takes refuge at the home of widow and one-time neighbor Helen Baird (Claire Trevor) and her son Kenny (Richard Beymer). Lila's presence worsens the already frayed relationship between mother and son, and between him and his on-off girlfriend Miriam (Carol Lynley). Before long, Kenny proposes marriage to Lila, but then Rick unexpectedly returns with the offer of a lucrative job for her—as a stripper in a seedy club. In the end, she leaves Kenny, the job and the abusive Rick and goes off on her own.

William Inge's play was not successful on Broadway, and the big-screen treatment added little to the original. Inge went over much of the same ground he had already covered in *Picnic, The Dark at the Top of the Stairs* and *Splendor in the Grass,* and once again his favored setting was a small town in the Midwest. The focus of the film was shifted from the mother-son relationship of the play to concentrate on Lila. Joanne Woodward is a marvelous actress who did well wearing a platinum blonde wig looking for all the world like Marilyn Monroe. It was no surprise that the part was intended for Monroe, which would have put the film in a different league. Monroe would have been a natural to convey the little girl lost at the center of the piece, but died a short time before filming began. The male lead was first offered to singer Pat Boone, who turned it down on moral grounds.[9] Warren Beatty was also offered the role and he too declined.[10] The part of the mother was first offered to Jo Van Fleet, who turned it down, after which it was given to Trevor.[11]

Some of the action took place in Chino, California, and on the first day of filming, the actors and crew were on a bus traveling to Chino Prison. The story goes that Beymer sat next to Trevor, but apparently did not recognize her and presumed she was an extra. The young actor had his greatest success in *West Side Story,* and proceeded to give her the benefit of his wisdom about how to act in movies, with tips on makeup and wardrobe, which assistant directors to avoid and numerous other tricks he had learned over the course of his brief career. When he had finished, she replied with a wry smile; "Thank you ever so much for your suggestions. I shall try to follow them in the future—just as I have in my last 84 pictures."[12] It seems curious he did not know who she was when he had spent seven years in acting and declared himself to be steeped in Hollywood history.

Trevor's part was somewhat limited by the emphasis of the screenplay, but she was noticeable and thoroughly convincing as the knowing, acutely disappointed mother. It was a great piece of observational and instinctive acting; her naturalism belied just how effective she was. Helen Baird hasn't moved on since the death of her husband and still wears the watch he gave her even though it doesn't work properly. The watch is a symbol of her inability to accept that any man could take his place or even live up to him. Her reaction when she received the present of a wristwatch from her son for her birthday was priceless. Ellsworth Fredericks' moody black-and-white cinematography and the slightly jazzy soundtrack of Jerry Goldsmith enhanced the somber mood and sense of place.

But the critics had little good to say, and several commented on the rather sterile feeling that pervaded the film. Those who went to the cinema expecting a sleazefest must have been disappointed, although the striptease scene was actually well executed: Lila dancing with balloons covering her modesty singing "Something's Gotta Give" while a room of boozy ugly patrons leered, jeered and popped the balloons—this was indeed a hellish vision. In another successful scene, Kenny and Lila visit an empty school and she recounts her life as a child. *The Stripper* was the first feature film directed by Franklin J. Schaffner, who went on to great success with *Planet of the Apes* (1968), *Patton* (1970), *Nicholas and Alexandra* (1971) and *The Boys from Brazil* (1978).

The tiresome comedy *How to Murder Your Wife* (1965) starred Jack Lemmon as a carefree bachelor and cartoonist who gets drunk at a party and wakes up married to a nubile Italian girl (Virna Lisi). Believing that marriage is a fate worse than death, he concocts ways to kill her which he enacts and then draws in his cartoon strip. When she disappears, he is charged with her murder on the evidence of the cartoons but acquitted by a sympathetic all-male jury.

The titles and opening scenes seemed promising and the jaunty Neal Hefti score was a great asset. Viewed now, it seems very much of its time, but Lemmon was nominated for awards, and Terry-Thomas, who played his valet, described the film as his favorite, and described how much he enjoyed the experience. Many reviewers didn't find much to laugh at. One summarized it thus: "Amusing preliminaries give way to dreary plot complications and an overlong courtroom scene. Leave after the first hour."[13] Even so, despite yet another dead-end role as a termagant wife, Trevor managed to rise above the caricatured confines imposed on her and rendered her character curiously human. The whole thing felt like a cartoon approach to life and the characters had a similarly two-dimensional feel. However she made the most of the humorous early exchanges with her put-upon husband (Eddie Mayehoff) and only narrowly missed out on a Golden Laurel Award at the Cannes Film Festival as Best Supporting Actress. Former actor Richard Quine was the modish director whose films seem trapped in their era like a fly in amber. Among others, he was responsible for *The World of Suzie Wong* (1960), *Paris When It Sizzles* (1964) and *Synanon* (1965), a dramatized account about the work of a hostel for drug addicts. He was at the helm for Arthur L. Kopit's *Oh Dad, Poor Dad, Mama's Hung You in the Closet and I'm Feeling So Sad* (1967), which also benefited greatly from a Neal Hefti score.

The Cape Town Affair (1967), also known as *Escape Route Cape Town,* was an ill-advised venture which was an unashamed reworking of *Pick-Up on South Street,* transposed to a South African setting. Jacqueline Bisset and James Brolin were the ostensible stars, but Trevor was top-billed. She had the old Thelma Ritter role of a police informer, and gave it a good try. She livened things up as soon as she appeared, delivering her lines with spirit to two rather deadpan agents. There was the memorable sight of her dancing, or rather drifting, around the room while the radio played an old song. But the movie failed to hold the attention, particularly when she was absent from the screen, which was most of the time. After she was killed, there was really no reason to continue watching. Her final scene with the memorable line "Go ahead and kill me, you'd be doing me a favor" was so derivative that it had a hollow feeling to it, like evoking the ghosts of an era of classic filmmaking that was long dead. Trevor was accompanied to South Africa by her husband and they took the opportunity to tour of the country and make it into an extended vacation trip.[14] Director Robert D. Webb spent much of his early career as an assistant; he won an Academy Award for his work on *In Old Chicago* (1937). He branched out on his own and made Saturday-afternoon style adventures such as *Seven Cities of Gold* (1955), the Elvis Presley film *Love Me Tender* (1956) and the semi-documentary *A Little of What You Fancy* (1968), an affectionate tribute to the stars of British Music Hall.

Wisely perhaps, Trevor practically retired from the screen after *Cape Town Affair*. Her last TV appearance had been five years earlier. In 1967, she was persuaded by her husband to accept the leading role in Frank Marcus' once controversial play *The Killing of Sister George*. A surprise hit in London and on Broadway, the story concerned an aging actress, June Buckridge, who is being written out of a radio soap opera, and embarks on an affair with a much younger and rather dimwitted actress, "Childie." In time the woman in charge of the show takes "Childie" away from June. It was a deeply ironic comedy that contrasted the homely Sister George character that the actress played, beloved by millions of viewers, with the erratic, insecure woman she was in reality. English character actress Beryl Reid had created the role on stage and her replacement was Hermione Baddeley. After its long New York run, a tour seemed like a potentially good idea. According to press reports, Trevor "added a British accent and dropped to a basso profundo" in her portrayal.[15] In addition, she was taught how to do a North Country accent by Anthony Newley, who made a recording for her.[16] She appeared with a Sassoon haircut and miniskirt, and was once again required to smoke cigars. Speaking about the play, she observed: "I don't think the subject should shock anybody. There is discussion of homosexuality on television all the time and I think it is a good thing to have such matters out in the open."[17]

The play had not been a great success on its initial run in the English provinces, but in London it picked up momentum and found its audience. Away from the metropolitan areas, it was never likely to do well, and so it proved in America. The Midwest was hardly the place to pitch a play about lesbianism with an all-female cast, even in the 1960s. Nevertheless, Claire relished the challenge: "I was getting too damned comfortable," she remarked, "and decided to stir myself up."[18] The play had sardonic humor and undoubtedly many bright spots, one of which was when Trevor dressed as Oliver Hardy with her co-star, Patricia Sinnott, as Stan Laurel at a fancy dress party. There were some changes made from the original, and the cigar-eating and dirty-bathwater scenes were omitted.[19]

Claire's experience was not a positive one. From the beginning, she had found problems during rehearsals; "You're memory gets lazy in movies," she reflected.[20] She felt daunted as soon as she was handed the hefty script and told to learn it in three weeks. This was in contrast to the way she was used to working in movies where it was a case of learning a couple of pages a day. It was over ten years since she had played on any stage and over 20 since she had last appeared in a major production on Broadway. An early reviewer complimented her on how "wildly young and attractive" she looked, and said that she handled the role "with style and sympathy."[21] Another commented that she "does her professional best to arouse our sympathy for Sister George."[22] But most of the critics were scathing; many vented much of their bile on the play itself, which some did not seem to understand. It was a difficult play that seemed almost doomed to failure away from New York. Not only was its background subject matter controversial at that time, but it was decidedly British in its references and humor. Even in San Francisco it did not find favor; a local critic began his review in a mordant tone which continued throughout his piece:

> Sister George died last night and Warren Clarke is directing a funeral celebration at the Geary Theater through March 9. The casket opens at 8:30 p.m. ... Rarely did the principals seem comfortable with each other or the author's comic byplay.... Miss Trevor's reactions were barely discernable through her android-like gestures and movements.[23]

The tour stuttered on to Chicago, where after four weeks Claire finally decided she had had enough. She found the part strenuous and was understandably brought low by some of the worst notices of her career. In addition it had been hard for her to spend so much time away from her husband and family. The William Morris Office contacted Hermione Baddeley to ask her if she would take over. She agreed, but felt bad for Claire. They had not met at that point but she had long been an admirer of Claire's films. Baddeley was always alive to the feelings of others and, although it was usually the case that actresses in that situation would tend to avoid meeting each other, she wanted to meet Claire. Hermione was staying at the Blackstone Hotel in Chicago with her friend Joan Assheton-Smith. They met two businessmen at the bar and Hermione happened to mention that she was taking over the part of Sister George from Claire. "'Claire Trevor!' cried the man. 'Oh what a doll! My favorite screen actress. Oh, I'd just love to meet her.'" Baddeley described the episode in her entertaining and warm-hearted memoir *The Unsinkable Hermione Baddeley*:

> I knew that Claire Trevor would be feeling depressed and that her self-confidence would need bolstering so I telephoned the theater and asked if Miss Trevor could possibly come to my room at the Blackstone after the show that night. I had friends with me who would love to meet her. A message came back saying that she would be happy to come.
>
> Our two new friends turned out to be quite rich business men. They insisted on setting up hors d'oeuvres and a table of drinks in my room—they quite took our breath away. Then this pretty little thing, looking exactly as she used to in all those films, walks in and immediately took their breath away. "I saw you in *Stagecoach*," said one. "Oh boy! What a film!" Claire absolutely bloomed. It was exactly what she needed. We'd all got so much to say to each other that the time flew by and we talked to the early hours. At the end of the evening she said she wished she had been on the tour with them from the beginning. "But darling," I said. "you know I couldn't have done—I'm taking your place!" We both laughed happily. Claire had clean forgotten the circumstances of our meeting.
>
> She stayed and watched me play the part of Sister George and then she came backstage and wanted to know why she hadn't been told to do all the little things I did. Just as I thought, Claire, with her film background, was used to getting a lot of direction. She went off to her lovely home in Palm Beach quite happily, knowing that she wasn't to blame, and leaving us all invitations to stay with her.[24]

Claire deserved great credit for tackling a role that was so far out of her element at that stage of her career. When it came to casting the film version, both Bette Davis and Angela Lansbury turned it down, and the part reverted to Beryl Reid. After her experience, Trevor never felt tempted to take on such a demanding part again, and it was only the coaxing of her friend Rock Hudson that persuaded her to emerge briefly from retirement to appear once more on stage some eight years later. She moved into a more contented phase when she did not feel the need to perform and enjoyed her life and family to the full, far away from the glare of the spotlight.

18

Swansong

> After the skies opened up and fell on me, I tried to eliminate a lot of memories that were painful. The result is that I can't remember anything. My doctor tells me that it is only natural, and I will start remembering again. I guess it's nature's way of helping people recover from tragedies.—Bob Thomas, "Trevor Comfortable in Career," *The Victoria Advocate,* June 26, 1982, 80

Since Trevor effectively retired from stage and screen in 1968, she lived a contented life at Newport Beach and made a short-lived return to the stage in 1976. After the double blow of losing her son and her husband within a year of each other, she moved to New York and briefly resumed her acting career. In her final years she returned to California, much supported by her sons and their families.

After abandoning his initial idea of pursuing an acting career, Claire's son Charles became a construction engineer and built her house in Newport Beach, which incorporated an indoor swimming pool.[1] He married twice, first on May 22, 1971, to Katharin A. Nauss in Orange County, California. That ended in divorce and he married Betty J. Jefson in Clark, Nevada, on October 6, 1974.[2]

Claire became a skilled artist and was in demand to paint portraits of her friends and colleagues. She tended to work from photographs. Claire painted a large portrait of actress Diana Lynn which Lynn hung over the fireplace of her home.[3] Others including Arlene Francis, Lauren Bacall and Barbra Streisand had her work in their houses, and she once painted an expressive portrait of Tyrone Power. After her semi-retirement from acting, she rekindled her interest in art and took classes. "I worked hard," she said. "I forged ahead in painting and outgrew our class which became more of a social thing. I wanted to go into color, so went to work with Japanese artist Serisawa when I realized I was in earnest."[4] She contributed a painting to the Sunset Strip arts festival as early as June 1958 at the request of Paramount head Y. Frank Freeman, in a show that was in aid of the Variety Boys Club.[5] She had several exhibitions of her oils beginning with a September 1962 show in New York.[6]

A lifelong knitter, she had often brought her knitting to the studio during her career. She found it kept her occupied during the long hours of filming, especially in the times spent waiting around, and it helped to her keep calm. In later years she used to crochet while watching TV in her study. Her last house contained few mementos of her cinema career. She was critical of the way in which *Stagecoach* and her other films were edited when shown on TV. She hated watching herself and once remarked, "I'd rather remember *Stagecoach* than watch it."[7]

A well-known and much-loved denizen of Newport Beach, Trevor took part in a number of campaigns over the years to keep the beach environment clean and prevent the spread of disease. In the early 1950s, she received a letter from Leonard Roach, the Los Angeles County Supervisor, thanking her for her efforts. According to figures, she had been at least partially responsible for a 20 percent drop in cases of polio in the vicinity.[8] Not a natural committee woman, she nonetheless served as chairwoman of the Orange County Arthritis Foundation in the 1970s.[9] She suffered from the affliction herself in her later years.

A committed Republican, she supported the candidates for every election from Dewey to Reagan. She felt that actors were well-suited to politics and that the way they dealt with probing TV interviews was telling. She followed her friend Ronald Reagan's progress with interest. When he was running for governor of California, she stood in for him at a luncheon organized by the Fullerton Federation of Republican Women and made a speech on his behalf.[10] When he became governor, she remarked, "He's a dedicated man. He has a good brain, a good education, and was an excellent head of the Screen Actors Guild."[11] She was one of many actors invited to both his inauguration parties. In the 1960s, she was also recruited, along with her friend John Wayne, to mobilize the vote in their county.[12] Together they handed out prizes at Santa Ana High School to winners of a competition to find a slogan urging people to use their vote.[13]

She and Milton first got to know Rock Hudson in 1956, shortly after they moved to Newport Beach. She helped him out with furniture when he was setting up home not far from her house. She gave him a large silver chest that he used as a coffee table along with carpets and other items. He had a player piano and on Saturday nights they used to have a good time dancing at his house. The three became good friends and Milton also taught him how to sail.[14]

In 1976, Claire was persuaded to return to the stage after eight years away. This time there was to be no repeat of the difficulties she had faced with *The Killing of Sister George*. She was sure of her material and was happy to appear in a touring production of *John Brown's Body*, a revival of an acclaimed Civil War verse play by Stephen Vincent Benét written in 1929. The most famous production had starred Tyrone Power, Raymond Massey and Judith Anderson; it successfully toured the country in 1952–53, ending on Broadway. On the second tour in 1953, Anne Baxter replaced Anderson. Brooks Atkinson called it "a work of art not only in print but on the stage. It refreshes the whole conception of theatre."[15]

For the revival, Rock Hudson had the role that Power had played, and the other main role was filled by Leif Erickson. They were backed by a 15-strong vocal chorus. The director was the renowned John Houseman. The 20-week tour was timed to coincide with bicentennial celebrations across the U.S. It began in April and was due to finish in September 1976, crossing the country east to west. A challenging play, it was generally well-received, and the actors all got glowing notices. Each had to take on a number of different personas to tell the epic story. One observer described Trevor as "a bundle of energy" during the press conference prior to the opening, reflecting excitedly about how she and Hudson had asked Power to get them tickets for the original show in 1952. The same witness noticed how young she still looked and marveled at how she was able to transform herself "from a love-sick teenager to the belle of the ball to a steely-eyed old woman" in the course of the play.[16] As the only woman present, she drew much of the attention; one reviewer noted that "the classic drape of [her] decorous lady white chiffon and her arrogantly erect shoulder corsage mock her ride through battle and ruin and her sooted night before the flames of Wingate Hall."[17] Another reviewer commented, "Claire Trevor, looking like Joan of Arc or a young Jean Arthur, is assertive, wary, immensely self-contained.... The timbre of the pewter voice rings clear and true. The years and the Newport sun have been kind."[18] She had been drawn back to the stage by the enthusiasm of Hudson and the material. "It's the dignity and beauty of it," she remarked.[19] The play was her final work on stage.

Despite the positive response of the critics, the tour was cancelled "because of poor management. They were booked at college campuses, but most of the campuses were deserted in the summer, and they played to empty houses."[20] The last venue they played was Denver on June 5, less than halfway through the tour.

In September 1978, tragedy struck when her son Chuck, 34, was one of 144 people killed in the crash of PSA Flight 182 over San Diego. The disaster was caused by the head-on collision of the Boeing 727 jetliner with a Cessna 172 light aircraft. All those on board were killed, along with the student pilot of the Cessna and his instructor. Additionally, seven people on the ground were killed, some by falling bodies from the wreck.[21] An investigation into the crash concluded that the crew of the jetliner "must bear prime responsibility" for the disaster.[22] Afterwards, procedures were tightened to try and prevent any such future situation.

Devastated, Claire got great support from her family and friends. She received a heartfelt letter of sympathy from John Wayne, who was then suffering himself with cancer. While Chuck was growing up, Wayne had lived a few minutes away and saw a great deal of Claire and her family. They were often guests on board Wayne's yacht *Wild Goose*. He spent time with Chuck and often played chess with him. She treasured the letter ever afterwards. "He was a man of deep feelings," she reflected, "much deeper than you would expect of John Wayne."[23] She further recalled, "What I can say for certainty about Duke is that he had a great capacity to love. He loved his friends and if you were a friend of his, you could do no wrong and he'd do anything for you."[24] His last years were extremely difficult as he had to undergo extensive surgery. Claire and Milton visited him one Sunday and he could barely walk. "It just killed me to see him like that," she recalled. "I knew I would never see him again."[25] He died in April 1979 at age 72. In December of that year, Claire lost her beloved husband Milton: at the Hoag Memorial Hospital in Irving near Newport Beach, he died of a brain tumor after a long illness at the age of 75. The funeral service took place at the Pacific View Memorial Park and his ashes were scattered at sea according to his wishes.[26]

To cope with the acute pain of her double loss, Trevor moved to New York in 1980. There she entered into the social life of the city and renewed old acquaintances. She also made new friends, including actresses Claudette Colbert and Arlene Francis, who she had not known well during her career. She took trips abroad and even spent one Christmas in Egypt with friends. During her time in New York, her interest in acting was rekindled. Encouraged by friends to return to acting, she commented, "I'd love to, but I don't have an agent and I don't know many people in the business any more."[27] She eventually found an agent, Paul Kohner, and in 1982 was finally enticed back to the big screen. The project was *Kiss Me Goodbye*, and she was at least partially encouraged to accept the role by her friend Rock Hudson. She stayed at Hudson's Beverly Hills house during filming.

She had been sent other scripts over the years, including an offer for *Agnes of God* on Broadway. While she admired the play, she preferred something lighter. *Kiss Me Goodbye* director Robert Mulligan was delighted to succeed where others had failed to entice her back into movies. "I wanted a real sense of style for the role of [Sally Field's] mother," he remarked, "and no one has that sense the way Claire does."[28]

Trevor was invigorated by the prospect of her return, but wanted to come back on her own terms; "I didn't want to come back as a bag lady—or looking like somebody dug me up," she commented dryly.[29] Once she had started filming, an interviewer asked her how long it took her to get back in to the groove after so many years away from making films: "About two minutes," she replied swiftly, "If you learn your craft and know it—and God knows I should know it after 50 years—it all comes back and seems easy."[30]

The story concerned a widow (Field) who begins to be visited by her first husband Jolly (James Caan), a Broadway showman intent on driving away her fiancé Rupert (Jeff Bridges). Trevor appeared as the acerbic mother of Field who is equally disparaging about her future son-in-law. The film was not a classic and seemed to lose everything in translation from its Brazilian original, *Dona Flor and Her Two Husbands* (1976). Whereas the earlier film had verve and playfulness, the remake was merely tiresome. Few critics had any positive comments about it but those who did mentioned Trevor. One said, "[T]he primary pleasure is the catty line readings of Claire Trevor as Ms. Field's sharp-tongued mother."[31] Many lamented that she was not a prominent enough character; she only had a handful of scenes. However, on a personal level, she enjoyed making the film and working with all the cast, especially Sally Field who she rated highly as an actress and got to know quite well. Trevor found it fun to be the center of attention once more after so long away, and commented on how attentive everybody was to her on set and off. Although she later made a television film, *Kiss Me Goodbye* was her final big-screen feature. She was not enamored of the changes wrought in cinema or society since her heyday and strongly disapproved of the trend towards excessive violence and profanity. "The big trick is to make it work *without* using those words," she observed.[32]

Thereafter she appeared sporadically on the small screen. In an episode of the romantic comedy series *The Love Boat*, she played a retired actress who tries to reconcile with her estranged daughter (Morgan Brittany) through her son-in-law (James Houghton). One of her last TV appearances was in an episode of the popular mystery series *Murder, She Wrote* starring Angela Lansbury. In "Witness for the Defense," Trevor appeared as the devoted mother of a writer accused of murdering his wife by arson. Patrick McGoohan featured as a voluble defense attorney with Juliet Mills for the prosecution. Trevor was recognizable and had retained her acting verve. She was also striking in some of her fashions and had lost none of her unique style of dress. It felt as though the costume ideas were entirely her own.

It was obvious she could have gone on acting but in the event she made only one more feature for television, *Breaking Home Ties* (1987). This was a warm-hearted coming-of-age story set in the 1950s, based on a famous painting by iconic artist Norman Rockwell which depicts a father saying goodbye to his son as he goes off to university and the big wide world. It was also known as *Norman Rockwell's Breaking Home Ties*. The film begins with the painting and brings the drama and poignancy of the situation to life. Doug McEwan starred as the son, with Jason Robards Jr, and Eva Marie Saint as his parents. An added burden for McEwan: His mother is dying of leukemia. Claire appeared as his old schoolteacher and created a vivid and touching portrait of a warm person who never stops caring about her pupils. With such a cast, it could never have been less than an excellent and touching drama. It had an old-fashioned feel to it, not just because it was set in the 1950s but because its story was told simply and seemed heartfelt.

After several years in New York, Claire began to miss her old friends and her growing grandchildren and in 1993 she settled once more in Newport Beach. During the following years, she was much supported by her stepsons Peter and Donald. Although never recovering from her losses, she appeared to discover a kind of serenity and enjoyed spending time with her many grandchildren.

Trevor invested her money wisely and also bought and sold real estate for many years, beginning with property on the Sunset Strip.[33] In 1998, she donated $500,000 to the University of California at Irvine towards the renovation of the Performing Arts Theater.[34] The college was later named the Claire Trevor School of the Arts so that in a very real way her legacy lives on. The following year she was in good form at an Academy Award Winners party. "At 89," one observer noted, "the classic Trevor attitude is still visible; simultaneously earthy and aloof, haughty but brazen, offering some cocksure Joe a delicious put-down."[35]

Longtime friend Robert Wagner admired her for many reasons, and said that not only did she have a very happy marriage but "also had the complete respect of everybody in show business." He added, "Claire was very much her own woman, and I came to admire her honesty and directness. She was a straightforward, creative human being who became a good painter. She was also terribly underrated as an actress."[36]

After a brief illness, Claire Trevor Bren died of respiratory failure on April 8, 2000, a month after her 90th birthday. As she had requested, she was cremated and her ashes scattered in the Pacific where she had enjoyed so many hours sailing with her husband. Her stepson Donald Bren commented: "Claire was a special woman whose lifelong passion was to bring joy to others. Her legacy will be the many ways she touched people. We will all miss her. She was a great lady."[37]

Epilogue

> She is one of the most sincere, natural and warm human beings I have ever known.—Norma Mayer quoted in Dennis McLellan, "Claire Trevor: A Hollywood Reputation," *The Los Angeles Times*, May 28, 1995

Claire Trevor never became a big star in the way she might have done, but she is far from forgotten. In fact, her popularity seems to increase with the passing years. It is unlikely that many people will be digging out her early Fox pictures in the years to come, but if they did they would be rewarded because, against all odds, she brightened them all. By any yardstick, the best of her work should live for all time. *Stagecoach* is a timeless picture which has arguably never been bettered in its genre and, indeed, transcends genre. Her significant contribution to noir films ensures that she will be remembered. Noir is a genre which retains its relevance and sense of modernity, encapsulating the psychological dislocation ushered in by the war. *Murder, My Sweet, Born to Kill, Raw Deal* and *Key Largo* are superlative examples of her work as are the non-noirs *Hard, Fast and Beautiful* and *My Man and I. Street of Chance, Dead End, Johnny Angel, The Woman of the Town* and many others feature excellent Trevor performances. She never gave a bad performance even in the most unworthy enterprise.

Looking back on her career, Claire once said that she wouldn't have changed many things, but that maybe she would have "promoted herself a little more, given more interviews and be seen in more places—maybe."[1] Any perceived failure in her career was offset by the happiness of her personal life, and she was clear that she lived first and thought about films after. "I'd rather do my work

A studio publicity still of Claire among the flowers, circa 1937.

the best way I can, and live my life the best way I can, and if I can't do both, the work will suffer first," she asserted.[2] She was self-aware and yet sometimes too self-critical; "I never pushed myself," she once said. "Maybe I was afraid."[3] She didn't like her appearance and even hated her voice, which she said made her sound like she was weeping all the time. Ironically, many obituary writers described her as beautiful and specifically lauded her distinctive and seductive voice. This underestimation of her own qualities sometimes led her to acquiesce when called on to take lesser roles. She even wondered herself why she was so obliging. She readily acknowledged her lack of searing drive and ambition which prevented her from becoming a major star. She identified another crucial factor: "Some people have it, that flair for the spectacular, but I'm not one of them. It would be ridiculous for me to try it. So I'll never be 'good copy,' will I?"[4]

If she had done all those things and possessed those attributes, then perhaps she would be as feted today as others. But then perhaps she wouldn't have been the great actress she was. For much of that same vulnerability and warmth—her humanity—was arguably why she was so touching and remains so loved. There was no artifice in her art. Claire acted with her heart, and as a consequence her work still speaks to us today and maybe always will.

Appendix: Appearances

Film

The Meal Ticket. (short) 1931. Director: Roy Mack. The Vitaphone Corporation–Warner Brothers. Trevor as the baron's wife.

The Imperfect Lover. (short) 1931. Director: Roy Mack. The Vitaphone Corporation–Warner Brothers. Trevor as the doctor.

Good Times. (short) 1931. Director: Arthur Hurley. The Vitaphone Corporation–Warner Brothers.

Angel Cake. (short) 1931. Director: Roy Mack. The Vitaphone Corporation–Warner Brothers.

Life in the Raw. 1933. Director: Louis King. Fox. Trevor as Judy Halloway.

The Last Trail. 1933. Director: James Tinling. Fox. Trevor as Patricia Carter.

The Mad Game. 1933. Director: Irving Cummings. Fox. Trevor as Jane Lee.

Jimmy and Sally. 1933. Director: James Tinling. Fox. Trevor as Sally Johnson.

Hold That Girl. 1934. Director: Hamilton MacFadden. Trevor as Tonie Bellamy.

Wild Gold. 1934. Director: George Marshall. Fox. Trevor as Jerry Jordan.

Baby, Take a Bow. 1934. Director: Harry Lachman. Fox. Trevor as Kay Ellison. (DVD)

Elinor Norton. 1934. Director: Hamilton MacFadden. Fox. Trevor as Elinor Norton.

Black Sheep. 1935. Director: Allan Dwan. Fox. Trevor as Janette Foster. (DVD)

Spring Tonic. 1935. Director: Clyde Bruckman. Fox. Trevor as Bertha "Betty" Ingals.

Dante's Inferno. 1935. Director: Harry Lachman. Fox. Trevor as Betty McWade. (DVD)

Navy Wife. 1935. Director: Allan Dwan. Twentieth Century–Fox. Trevor as Vicky Blake.

My Marriage. 1936. Director: George Archainbaud. Twentieth Century–Fox. Trevor as Carol Barton.

Song and Dance Man. 1936. Director: Allan Dwan. Twentieth Century–Fox. Trevor as Julia Carroll.

Twentieth Century-Fox Promotional Film. 1936. (documentary short) Twentieth Century–Fox. Trevor as herself.

Sunkist Stars at Palm Springs. (musical short) 1936. Director: Roy Rowland. MGM. Trevor as herself.

Human Cargo. 1936. Director: Allan Dwan. Twentieth Century–Fox. Trevor as Bonnie Brewster.

Fox publicity still (1935).

To Mary—With Love. 1936. Director: John Cromwell. Twentieth Century–Fox. Trevor as Kitty Brant.

Star for a Night. 1936. Director: Lewis Seiler. Twentieth Century–Fox. Trevor as Nina Lind.

15 Maiden Lane. 1936. Director: Allan Dwan. Twentieth Century–Fox. Trevor as Jane Martin.

Career Woman. 1936. Director: Lewis Seiler. Twentieth Century–Fox. Trevor as Carroll Aiken. (DVD)

Time Out for Romance. 1937. Director: Malcolm St. Clair. Twentieth Century–Fox. Trevor as Barbara Blanchard.

King of Gamblers. 1937. Director: Robert Florey. Paramount. Trevor as Dixie Moore.

One Mile from Heaven. 1937. Director: Allan Dwan. Twentieth Century–Fox. Trevor as Lucy "Tex" Warren.

Dead End. 1937. Director: William Wyler. United Artists. Trevor as Francey. (DVD)

Second Honeymoon. 1937. Director: Walter Lang. Twentieth Century–Fox. Trevor as Marcia. (DVD)

Screen Snapshots Series 16 No. 10. (documentary short involving a beauty contest) 1937. Director: Ralph Staub. Columbia. Trevor as herself.

Big Town Girl. 1937. Director: Alfred A. Werker. Twentieth Century–Fox. Trevor as Fay Loring.

Walking Down Broadway. 1938. Director: Norman Foster. Twentieth Century–Fox. Trevor as Joan Bradley.

The Amazing Dr. Clitterhouse. 1938. Director: Anatole Litvak. Warner Brothers. Trevor as Jo Keller. (DVD)

Valley of the Giants. 1938. Director: William Keighley. Warner Brothers. Trevor as Lee Roberts.

Five of a Kind. 1938. Director: Herbert I. Leeds. Twentieth Century–Fox. Trevor as Christine Nelson. (DVD)

Stagecoach. 1939. Director: John Ford. United Artists. Trevor as Dallas (DVD)

Screen Snapshots Series 18 No. 10 (documentary short about a Basil Rathbone party) 1939. Director: Ralph Staub. Columbia. Trevor as herself.

I Stole a Million. 1939. Director: Frank Tuttle. Universal. Trevor as Laura Benson.

Allegheny Uprising. 1939. Director: William A. Seiter. RKO. Trevor as Janie. (DVD)

Dark Command. 1940. Director: Raoul Walsh. Republic. Trevor as Mary McCloud. (DVD)

Screen Snapshots Series 19 No. 5: Art and Artists. (documentary short) 1940. Director: Ralph Staub. Columbia. Trevor as herself.

Picture People No. 2 Hollywood Sports. (documentary short) 1941. Director: Clay Adams. RKO. Trevor as herself.

Picture People: Hobbies of the Stars. (documentary short) 1941. Director: Clay Adams. RKO. Trevor as herself.

Texas. 1941. Director: George Marshall. Columbia. Trevor as "Mike" King. (DVD)

Honky Tonk. 1941. Director: Jack Conway. MGM. Trevor as "Gold Dust" Nelson. (DVD)

The Adventures of Martin Eden. 1942. Director: Sidney Salkow. Columbia. Trevor as Connie Dawson.

Crossroads. 1942. Director: Jack Conway. MGM. Trevor as Michelle Allain. (DVD)

Street of Chance. 1942. Director: Jack Hively. Paramount. Trevor as Ruth Dillon.

The Desperadoes. 1943. Director: Charles Vidor. Columbia. Trevor as Countess Maletta. (DVD)

Claire in a languid publicity pose circa 1938 looking not unlike one of her avowed favorites, Joan Fontaine.

Good Luck, Mr. Yates. 1943. Director: Ray Enright. Columbia. Trevor as Ruth Jones.

Murder, My Sweet. 1944. Director: Edward Dmytryk. RKO. Trevor as Helen Grayle/Velma. (DVD)

Johnny Angel. 1945. Director: Edwin L. Marin. RKO. Trevor as Lilah "Lily" Gustafson. (DVD)

The Bachelor's Daughters. 1946. Director: Andrew L. Stone. United Artists. Trevor as Cynthia Davis.

Crack-Up. 1946. Director: Irving Reis. RKO. Trevor as Terry Cordell. (DVD)

Born to Kill. 1947. Director: Robert Wise. RKO. Trevor as Helen Brent. (DVD)

Raw Deal. 1948. Director: Anthony Mann. Eagle-Lion Films. Trevor as Pat Cameron. (DVD)

The Velvet Touch. 1948. Director: Jack Gage. RKO. Trevor as Marian Webster. (DVD)

Key Largo. 1948. Director: John Huston. Warner Brothers. Trevor as Gaye Dawn. (DVD)

The Babe Ruth Story. 1948. Director: Roy Del Ruth. Allied Artists. Trevor as Claire Hodgson Ruth. (DVD)

The Lucky Stiff. 1949. Director: Lewis R. Foster. United Artists. Trevor as Marguerite "Maggie" Seaton.

Borderline. 1950. Director: William A. Seiler. Universal. Trevor as Madeleine Haley aka Gladys La Rue.

Best of the Badmen. 1951. Director: William D. Russell. RKO. Trevor as Lily. (DVD)

Hard, Fast and Beautiful. 1951. Director: Ida Lupino. RKO. Trevor as Millie Farley. (DVD)

Stop, You're Killing Me. 1952. Director: Roy Del Ruth. Warner Brothers. Trevor as Nora Marko. (DVD)

My Man and I. 1952. Director: William Wellman. MGM. Trevor as Mrs. Ansel Adams. (DVD)

Hoodlum Empire. 1952. Director: Joseph Kane. Republic. Trevor as Connie Williams. (DVD)

The Stranger Wore a Gun. 1953. Director: Andre de Toth. Columbia. Trevor as Josie Sullivan. (DVD)

The High and the Mighty. 1954. Director: William Wellman. Warner Brothers. Trevor as May Holst. (DVD)

Man Without a Star. 1955. Director: King Vidor. Universal. Trevor as Idonee. (DVD)

Lucy Gallant. 1955. Director: Robert Parrish. Paramount. Trevor as Lady Macbeth.

The Mountain. 1956. Director: Edward Dmytryk. Paramount. Trevor as Marie. (DVD)

Marjorie Morningstar. 1958. Director: Irving Rapper. Warner Brothers. Trevor as Rose Morgenstein. (DVD)

Two Weeks in Another Town. 1962. Director: Vincente Minnelli. MGM. Trevor as Clara Kruger. (DVD)

The Stripper. 1963. Director: Franklin J. Schaffner. Twentieth Century–Fox. Trevor as Helen Baird.

How to Murder Your Wife. 1965. Director: Richard Quine. United Artists. Trevor as Edna. (DVD)

The Cape Town Affair. 1967. Director: Robert D. Webb. Twentieth Century–Fox. Trevor as Sam Williams. (DVD)

Kiss Me Goodbye. 1983. Director: Robert Mulligan. Twentieth Century–Fox. Trevor as Charlotte. (DVD)

Theater

AS CLAIRE ST. CLAIRE

Six plays with the Robert Henderson Repertory Players, Ann Arbor, MI, May 23 to circa July 1930:

Antigone. Tragedy by Sophocles, May 23, 1930, Central High School Auditorium, Kalamazoo, MI; May 26, 1930, Lydia Mendelson Theater, Ann Arbor, MI; May 29 to June 3, 1930, Michigan League Building, Ann Arbor, MI. Trevor was in the chorus.

Salome. Tragedy by Oscar Wilde, Michigan League Building, Ann Arbor, MI, June 4 to June 8, 1930.

Serena Blandish. Comedy by S.N. Behrman, Michigan League Building, Ann Arbor, MI, June 11 to June 14, 1930.

The Seagull. Drama by Anton Chekhov, Michigan League Building, Ann Arbor, MI, June 16 to June 20, 1930. Trevor as Nina.

Excess Baggage. Musical comedy by Jack McGowan, Michigan League Buidling, Ann Arbor, MI, June 22 to June 25, 1930. Trevor as Mabel Ford.

The Royal Family. Comedy drama by George S. Kaufman and Edna Ferber, Michigan League Building, Ann Arbor, MI, June 26 to June 29, 1930.

Lady Windermere's Fan. Comedy by Oscar

Wilde, Michigan League Building, Ann Arbor, MI, June 30 to July 3, 1930.

As Claire Trevor

The Stork Is Dead. Satiric drama by Hans Kottow, October 2, Lyceum Theater, Paterson, New Jersey; October 6 to October 11, 1930, Opera House, Bayonne, New Jersey.[1]

It's a Wise Child. Drama by Laurence E. Johnson, December 25, 1930, to January 2, 1931, Skowas-Warner Grand Central Theater, St. Louis, MO.

As Good as New. Comedy drama by Thompson Buchanan, January 8 to January 12, 1931, Skowas-Warner Grand Central Theater, St. Louis, MO. Trevor as Mary Banning.

Broken Dishes. Comedy by Martin Flavin, January 17 to January 20, 1931, Skowas-Warner Grand Central Theater, St. Louis, MO. Trevor as Elaine.

Strictly Dishonorable. Comedy by Preston Sturges, January 31, to February 4, 1931, Skowas-Warner Grand Central Theater, St. Louis, MO. Trevor as Isabelle Parry.

Broadway. Drama by Phillip Dunning and George Abbott, February 9 to February 12, 1931, Skowas-Warner Grand Central Theater, St. Louis, MO. Trevor as "Billie" Moore.

Jonesy. Farce by Anne Morrison and John Peter Toohey, February 16 to February 20, 1931, Skowas-Warner Grand Central Theater, St. Louis, MO. Trevor as Mildred Ellis.

Gold Diggers. Farce by Avery Hopwood, February 23 to February 28, 1931, Skowas-Warner Grand Central Theater, St. Louis, MO. Trevor as Violet Dayne.

Too Young to Love. Comedy by Harry Selby, Parrish Memorial Hall, Southampton, Long Island.

Rhapsody in Black. Comedy by Alice Brady, July 1931, Parrish Memorial Hall, Southampton, Long Island.

No Money to Guide Her. Comedy by Leslie Squires, Masonic Temple, Easthampton, July 21, 1931. Parrish Memorial Hall, Southampton, Long Island, July 24 to July 27, 1931.[2]

Phantom Footsteps. Mystery drama by Walter Livingston, Parish Memorial Hall, Southampton, Long Island, August 5 to August 8, 1931. Trevor as Caretaker's Daughter.[3]

Immodest Violet. Comedy drama by David Carb, August 25 to August 30, 1931, Parrish Memorial Hall, Southampton, Long Island. Trevor as Violet Rose.

Whistling in the Dark. Farce by Laurence Gross and Edward Childs Carpenter. Ethel Barrymore Theater, New York, January 19, 1932, to September 1932; Waldorf Theater, New York, November 3, 1932, to February 1933; tour: Belasco Theater, Los Angeles, June to July 1932; Geary Theater, San Francisco, July 7 to August 1932; Erlinger Theater, Chicago, October 1932; American Theater, St. Louis, MO, October 24 to October 30, 1932; Shubert Theater, Cincinnati, Ohio, November 7 to November 14, 1932, *et al.* Trevor as Toby Van Bruten.

The Party's Over. Comedy by Daniel Kusell. Vanderbilt Theater, New York, March 27, 1933, to circa April 23, 1933. Trevor as Betty Decker.

Tonight at 8:30. Variety revue by Noël Coward, performed by the Theater Guild of Southern California; in sketch "Family Album," El Capitan Theater, Hollywood, CA, August 12, 1940.[4]

Out West It's Different. Comedy by Bella Spewack. National Theater, Washington, D.C., December 5, 1940, to December 18, 1940.

Dark Victory. Drama by George Brewer and Bertram Bloch. Laguna Beach Playhouse, Orange County, CA, July 25 to August 1, 1946. Trevor as Judith Traherne.

The Big Two. Comedy by Ladislaus Bush Fekete and Mary Helen Fay. Booth Theater, New York, January 8, 1947, to January 25, 1947, and tour. Trevor as Danielle Forbes.

Goodbye Again. Comedy by Allan Scott and George Haight. Denver, Colorado, and tour, August 7 to 12, 1947. Trevor as Anne Rogers.

Cross Examination. Drama by Byron Haskin. Lobero Theater, Santa Barbara, March 1948. Trevor in the leading role.

Detective Story. Drama by Sidney Kingsley. El Capitan Theater, Hollywood, CA, February 1 to March 15, 1951, and tour to Denver and Salt Lake City. Trevor as Mary McLeod.

The Time of the Cuckoo. Drama by Arthur Laurents. The Playhouse, La Jolla, CA, August 9 to August 21, 1955. Trevor as Leona Samish.

The Killing of Sister George. Drama by Frank Marcus. National Tour organized by the Theater Guild and the American Theater Society, December 1967 to April 1968: Including Hanna Theater, Cleveland, Ohio, January 1968; Geary Theater, San Francisco, CA, March 1 to March 9, 1968; Studebaker Theater, Chicago, Illinois,

March 10 to April 13, 1968. Trevor as June "George" Buckridge.

John Brown's Body. Drama by Stephen Vincent Benét. Tour from April to June 5, 1976; including Civic Auditorium, Bakersfield, CA, April 20 to April 26, 1976; California Theater of the Performing Arts, San Bernardino, CA, April 30 to May 8, 1976; Paramount Theater, Portland, Oregon, May 12 to May 18, 1976; Sioux City, South Dakota, June 2, 1976; Denver, Colorado, June 5, 1976. Trevor played a principal role.

Radio

Hollywood Hotel. CBS syndicated broadcast. *To Mary, with Love* with Myrna Loy, Warner Baxter, Ian Hunter, May 22, 1936. *Career Woman* with Dick Powell, Isabel Jewell, January 1, 1937. *One Mile from Heaven* with Sally Blane, Douglas Fowley, August 13, 1937.

Claire Trevor. WHN (New York) broadcast interview by Radie Harris, November 6, 1936. Trevor guested.

Dead End. CBS syndicated broadcast. Humphrey Bogart, Joel McCrea, Sylvia Sidney, Allen Jenkins, 1937. Trevor as Francey.

Review Program. NBC Blue Network review program. Interview with Elza Schallert, November 15, 1937. Trevor guested.

Big Town. CBS drama series. With Edward G. Robinson, Hanley Stafford, Carlton KaDell (announcer), Phil Ohman's Orchestra, October 19, 1937, to June 30, 1939. Trevor as Lorelei Kilbourne. Known episodes: "Wilson Is Shot," October 19, 1937; "The Harding Factory Fire Trap," October 26, 1937; "The Gambling Pool Expose," November 2, 1937; "Slot Machine Racket," November 9, 1937; "Breach of Promise Frame," November 16, 1937; "Fake Accident Racket," November 23, 1937; "Parole Board," November 30, 1937; "Race Track Pay-Off," December 7, 1937; "Christmas Charities Racket," December 21, 1937; "Case of the Missing Milk," May 2, 1938; "By-Line," May 17, 1938; an episode involving a C.C.C. Camp, June 25, 1938; "Scoop Davis Retired," October 4, 1938; "Poultry Dealers Protection Racket," October 18, 1938; "Remote Control," November 2, 1938; December 8, 1938; December 23, 1938; February 7, 1939; "Gold Star Mothers" May 28, 1939; June 19, 1939; "Reform Town" June 30, 1939.[1]

Lifebuoy Soap. Syndicated commercial, CBM Montreal, January 2, 1938. Trevor as narrator.

Salute to Columbia Square. CBS variety all-day broadcast, with CBS president William S. Paley, Eddie Cantor, Al Jolson, Deanna Durbin *et al.*, May 1, 1938. Trevor guested.

The Kate Smith Hour. CBS variety interview show, including the playlet "The Story of Ruth Taylor" by Clark Andrews, with Johnnie Williams & His Swingsmiths, January 18, 1939. Trevor as Nurse Ruth Taylor.

Big Sister. CBS soap opera broadcast over KRNT, January 28, 1939. Trevor guested.[2]

Lux Radio Theater. CBS drama. "Bordertown" by Carroll Graham. The story of a poor Mexican lawyer determined to raise himself, with Don Ameche, Joan Bennett, Cecil B. DeMille, July 3, 1939. Trevor as Marie Roark. "Dust Be My Destiny" by Jerome Odlum. A Depression-era romance, with John Garfield, Adelaide Irving, Arthur Q. Bryan. Mabel Alden, April 14, 1941. "Murder, My Sweet" by Raymond Chandler. Murder mystery, with Dick Powell, June Duprez, Mike Mazurki, June 11, 1945. Trevor as Mrs. Grayle/Velma. "Relentless" by Kenneth Perkins, with Robert Young, June 7, 1948. Trevor as Luella Purdy. "Key Largo" by Maxwell Anderson. Crime drama, with Edward G. Robinson, Edmond O'Brien, Dan Seymour, November 28, 1949. Trevor as Gaye Dawn. "Borderline" with John Hodiak, Stephen McNally, October 8, 1951. Trevor as Madeleine Haley aka Gladys La Rue. "One Last September" by Kathleen Hite. A woman returns to her family to find everyone has changed, with John Dehner, Lawrence Dobkin, Shirley Mitchell, August 31, 1953. Trevor as Elizabeth. "Mildred Pierce" by James M. Cain. A tale of murder and romance, with Zachary Scott, Hal March, Joy Terry, June 14, 1954. Trevor as Mildred Pierce. "All About Eve" by Mary Orr. A caustic story of theatrical ambition, with Ann Blyth, Betty Lou Gerson, Don Randolph, November 23, 1954. Trevor as Margo Channing.

Allegheny Uprising Premiere. Interview show over WCAE Network (Pittsburgh), with the stars of *Allegheny Uprising,* the author Neil H. Swanson, and director P.J. Wolfson. November 3, 1939. Trevor guested.

Hollywood Playhouse. NBC drama anthology. "No Common Play" by Milton Geiger, with Charles Boyer, April 3, 1940.

Don Ameche's Varieties. NBC drama variety show, with Pat Friday, the Victor Young Orchestra, April 5, 1940, to September 1940; various roles in dramas. "Manhattan Holiday" by Mark Hellinger, April 5, 1940; "Turnabout" by Mark Hellinger, April 7, 1940; "Reformation" by Mark Hellinger, April 19, 1940; "The Bribe" by Mark Hellinger, April 26, 1940; "Court Story" by Mark Hellinger, May 3, 1940; "The Gesture" by Mark Hellinger, May 10, 1940; "The Charming Lord Dusenberry" by Mark Hellinger, May 17, 1940; "The Girl Who Saved a Writer," with Vivien Bretherton, May 19, 1940. "The Ham," June 2, 1940; "Paternity Ward" by True Boardman, June 7, 1940; "The Sacrifice," June 9, 1940; "The Two of Us" by Roger Quayle Denny, June 14, 1940; "Say It with Flowers," June 28, 1940; "Errand of Mercy" by Irene Rich (Red Cross Benefit), July 12, 1940; "Absent Without Leave," July 5, 1940; "Tune in My Heart" by Frank Shane and Bill Thomas, July 14, 1940; "Just One Night in Old Havana" with Bing Crosby, July 26, 1940; "My Heart Is in the Air," August 2, 1940; "The Life of Stephen Foster," with the Victor Young Orchestra and the Sportsmen Male Quartet, August 9, 1940; "Substitute Wife," August 16, 1940; "Petticoat Strain," August 23, 1940; "The Son of Mama Posito" by Roger Quayle Denny, September 6, 1940.[3]

Red Cross Broadcast. Syndicated all-star charity appeal, with the Andrews Sisters, Judy Garland, Orson Welles *et al.*, July 1, 1940. Trevor guested. Also broadcast as "Errand of Mercy" by Irene Rich, with Don Ameche.

Silver Theatre. CBS drama. "Petticoat Fever," comedy with Red Skelton, February 11, 1941. Trevor as Irene Campton. "The Captain Had a Daughter," drama by Grover Jones and True Boardman, with Preston Foster, August 15, 1943. "Until Forever" adapted by Leonard St. Clair from a story by Elsworth Tane Beebe, August 18, 1946.[4]

The Free Company. Patriotic drama series. "The Mole on Lincoln's Cheek" by Marc Connolly. A story of academic freedom and the fight against censorship, with Charles Bickford, Burgess Meredith (narrator), Elizabeth Patterson, Robert Young, Margaret Hamilton, March 2, 1941. Trevor as Schoolteacher.

The Gulf Screen Theater. CBS drama. "High Sierra" by W.R. Burnett. With Humphrey Bogart, Oscar Bradley and His Orchestra, January 4, 1942. Trevor as Marie.

Vox Pop. CBS interview talk show discussing the subject "Hollywood at War," with Brian Donlevy, Joan Bennett, Franchot Tone, Jane Withers, Jack Holt, January 26, 1942. Trevor guested.

The Bob Burns Program. ABC variety show, May 5, 1942. Trevor guested.[5]

Soldiers with Wings. ABC Armed Forces variety show from the West Coast Air Force Training Center; (1) With Walter Pidgeon, December 12, 1942. Trevor guested.[6] (2) Interview with a returned U.S. airman, including a dramatic reconstruction of his experiences; with Ralph Bellamy, August 3, 1944. Trevor guested.[7]

The Abbott and Costello Show. NBC comedy variety show, with Freddie Rich and His Orchestra, January 14, 1943. Trevor guested. Red Network, with Connie Haines, Mel Blanc, May 11, 1944. Trevor guested.

Mail Call. AFRS variety show. With Phil Regan, Connie Haines, Edgar Bergen and Charlie McCarthy, March 31, 1943. Trevor guested. With Dick Powell, Ella Logan, Allen Jenkins, The Pied Pipers, April 4, 1945. Trevor guested, talking about *Murder, My Sweet* and taking part in the skit "Crime Does Not Pay."

Radio Reader's Digest. NBC drama. "Two for a Penny" from *The Grapes of Wrath* by John Steinbeck, with Lloyd Nolan, April 25, 1943.

The Camel Comedy Caravan. CBS comedy variety show, with Jack Carson, Connie Haines, Charles Ruggles, May 21, 1943. Trevor guested.

The Lady Esther Screen Guild Theater. CBS drama. "Whistling in Dixie" by S. Sylvan Simon. Radio detective "The Fox," with Red Skelton, Virginia Grey, May 28, 1943. Trevor as Carol Lambert. "The Amazing Dr. Clitterhouse" by Barre Lyndon, with Edward G. Robinson, Lloyd Nolan, June 5, 1944. Trevor as Jo Keller. "Flesh and Fantasy—Mardi Gras" by Ellis St. Joseph, with John Hodiak, September 3, 1945. Trevor as Henrietta. "A Night to Remember" by Kelly Roos, with Brian Donlevy, April 8, 1946. Trevor as Nancy Troy. "The Walls of Jericho" by Lamar Trotti, with Cornel Wilde, January 27, 1948. Trevor as Julia Norman.

The American Comedy Theater of the Air. CBS comedy drama. "Twentieth Century" by Ben Hecht and Charles Mulholland, with Adolphe Menjou, Hans Conried, May 28, 1943. Trevor as Mildred Plotka/Lily Garland.

The Mayor of the Town. CBS comedy drama. With Lionel Barrymore, Agnes Moorehead, May 26 to August 25, 1943. Toni McCafferty. Known episodes: "Take a Letter, Miss McCafferty," May 26, 1943. "The Pay-Off," June 9, 1943; an episode in which the mayor takes care of five cats, June 23, 1943. "Toni McCafferty Falls for Captain Bill Kennedy," June 30, 1943. Trevor as Toni McCafferty.[8]

Stars Over Hollywood. ABC drama anthology. "The Lady Was a Lawyer," October 9, 1943.

Hollywood Theater of the Air. CBS romantic drama. "The Gay Sisters" by Stephen Longstreet, October 18, 1943. Trevor as Fiona Gaylord.

Hollywood Star Time. Also known as *RKO on the Air*. Red Network variety show including interviews with current RKO players, with Frances King, Randolph Scott, June 1, 1944. Trevor guested.

Results, Inc. Mutual detective mystery series, with Lloyd Nolan, Bea Benaderet, October 7, 1944, to December 30, 1944: Thirteen episodes; only six titles known, of which only three episodes are known to have survived: "Find Me a Haunted House," October 7, 1944. "The Case of the Amorous Killer," October 18, 1944. "The Case of the Forgetful Witch," November 25, 1944. "The Case of the Desperate Doll," December 2, 1944.[9] "The Last of the Bloody Gillettes," December 16, 1944. ""The Case of the Crazy Christmas Tree," December 23, 1944. "Mummy Sitting," December 30, 1944. Trevor as Teresa "Terry" Travers.

Don McNeill & Breakfast Clubbers. NBC morning variety show, February 12, 1945. Trevor guested.

Theater of Romance. CBS drama. "Destry Rides Again," February 20, 1945. Trevor as Frenchy. "Kid Galahad" by Francis Wallace, with Wayne Morris, Jack McCarthy, Richard Arlen, January 22, 1946. Trevor as Louise "Fluff" Phillips. "An Heiress from Red Horse" by Ambrose Bierce, December 11, 1952. Trevor as Mary Jane Dement.

Edgar Bergen & Charlie McCarthy. WBEN (Buffalo, New York). "Eighth Canadian Victory Loan Drive," broadcast from Vancouver, British Columbia, with George Murphy, Dick Powell, April 29, 1945.[10]

Tommy Dorsey and Company. ABC music variety show, with Stewart Foster, July 8, 1945. Trevor guested.

Command Performance. AFRS variety show. "Victory Extra." All-star show celebrating the end of the war, with stars including Ronald Colman, Bette Davis, Carmen Miranda, Herbert Marshall, Lucille Ball, Cary Grant, Ida Lupino *et al.*, August 15, 1945. Trevor guested.

The Cavalcade of America. NBC drama. "Peggy Fancy," the story of a nurse's fight against typhoid in England, January 22, 1945. Trevor as Peggy. "The Builders of the Bridge" by D.B. Steinman. The story of the Brooklyn Bridge, with Frank Graham, November 5, 1945. Trevor as Mrs. Roebling. "Build Me Straight," a shipbuilding drama by Phyllis Parker, with Joseph Cotten, Tom Collins, January 7, 1946. Trevor as Albenia McKay. "Alaskan Bush Pilot" by Bernard Feinstein, with Dick Foran, March 18, 1946.[11]

Suspense. CBS mystery series. "A Tale of Two Sisters" by Mel Dinelli, with Nancy Kelly, Joseph Kearns; a boxer becomes an opera singer, February 8, 1945. "The Plan" by Cyril Enfield, with Elliott Lewis, Wally Maher; a convicted murderer escapes from an asylum and heads to the small town of his brother, but nothing is quite what it seems; May 16, 1946. "The Blue Hour" by Marston Schwartz, with Hans Conried, Sidney Miller, September 25, 1947; Trevor as Lois Lapaul.[12] "The Light Switch" by Richard Bodra, with Verna Felton, Wally Maher, May 12, 1949; a woman plans an explosive end for her philandering husband but things don't work out. Trevor as Mrs. Johnson. "Angel Face" by Cornell Woolrich, May 18, 1950. Trevor as Diane Tremayne.

G. I. Journal. AFRS variety broadcast, with Mel Blanc, Jack Carson, Ginny Simms, January 1946. Trevor guested.

This Is My Best. CBS drama anthology. "Beautiful Pretense" by Adeline Rumsey, January 15, 1946.

Academy Award Theater. CBS drama. "Stagecoach" with Randolph Scott, May 4, 1946. Trevor as Dallas.

Proudly We Hail. CBS Public service recruitment show for the army and air force. "Head for a Wedding," September 25, 1946. Trevor guested.[13]

The Theater Guild on the Air. ABC drama. "The Farmer Takes a Wife" by Frank B. Elser and Marc Connolly, with William Holden, Faye Emerson, June Walker, Kenny Delmar, February 2, 1947. Trevor as Molly Larkins.

Exploring the Unknown. Mutual medical program, incorporating a short drama, "Love Is a Doctor" by Sidney Lohman; the story of the advances made by science in combating cerebral palsy, with Alan Baxter, February 16, 1947. Trevor as Mother.[14]

The Hedda Hopper Show—This Is Hollywood. CBS Drama. "The Strange Love of Martha Ivers" with Van Heflin, Ida Lupino, Kirk Douglas, April 12, 1947. Trevor as Antonia "Toni" Marecheck.[15]

Screen Director's Assignment. NBC Drama. "Stagecoach" with John Wayne, Ward Bond, January 9, 1949. Trevor as Dallas.

The Philip Morris Playhouse. CBS drama. "The Dead Never Cry" by Irene Winston, February 4, 1949.

Yours for a Song. WOR (New York). Musical variety show, with Dick Haymes, April 29, 1949. Trevor guested.

Hollywood Star Theater. NBC drama, "Claire Trevor Presents Steve Brodie," with Steve Brodie, June 11, 1949. Trevor guested.

Nancy Craig. NBC interviews, January 16, 1950. Trevor guested with husband Milton Bren.

Margaret Arlett Program. CBS interview-variety show, "Antique Record Shop," January 20, 1950. Trevor guested.

Twenty Questions. Mutual quiz show. With Fred Deventer, Florence Rinard, Johnny McPhee, January 21, 1950. Trevor guested.

Hollywood Calling. Syndicated talk show (1) with host George Fisher and guests Peggy Dow, Susan Hayward, Miriam Hopkins, Jim Hayward, February 23, 1950. Trevor guested. (2) With host George Fisher and guests Mel Ferrer, Sally Forrest, Edward Dmytryk, circa 1951. Trevor guested.

Academy Awards Program. ABC live show from Pantages Theater, Hollywood, with Ronald Reagan, James Stewart, Olivia de Havilland *et al.*, March 23, 1950. Trevor guested. NBC live show from Century and Pantages Theaters, Hollywood, with Maurice Chevalier, Sal Mineo *et al.*, March 21, 1956. Trevor guested. NBC live show from Century and Pantages Theaters, Hollywood, with Anthony Quinn, Ingrid Bergman *et al.*, March 27, 1957. Trevor guested.

Adventure Is Your Heritage. Syndicated U.S. Navy broadcast. "Lifeline," 1951.[16]

Claire Trevor. Interview show broadcast over KITO (Oklahoma), January 23, 1951. Trevor guested.[17]

Jimmie Fidler Show. Syndicated Hollywood gossip show, with Tyrone Power, Jeff Chandler, Prince Ali Khan, Robert Walker, Judy Garland, June 28, 1951. Trevor guested.

Hollywood Star Playhouse. ABC-CBS-NBC drama. "Pattern in the Rug," Psychological thriller; May 15, 1950. "The Big Wave" by Pearl S. Buck, August 23, 1951. "The Frontier" by Robert Y. Libbott, with Virginia Gregg, Frank Gerstle; a family tries to make a bid for freedom, January 10, 1952. "Father's Day" by Maurice Zimm; an emotionally scarred woman tries to win custody of her adopted child, February 3, 1952. Trevor as Alice. "Nothing to Lose" with Ray Milland; a woman is trapped by an escaped convict in an isolated cabin on a mountain with her sickly child, September 10, 1952.

Tum's Hollywood Theater. NBC drama. "The Lie," a woman discovers her husband is involved in an espionage ring. October 23, 1951. "Lifeboat Number Four," a shipwreck drama set in the South China Seas, January 8, 1952.

Guest Star. Syndicated Treasury Department broadcast. "Where Are the Bullets?" with Gerald Mohr, Ronald O'Connor, the Savings Bond Orchestra, January 21, 1951. Trevor guested.

March of Dimes. Syndicated public service broadcast. One-minute celebrity spots on behalf of the National Foundation for Infantile Paralysis, with Jack Benny, Ann Sothern, Margaret Whiting *et al.*, recorded between January 1 and January 31, 1952. Trevor guested.[18]

The Martin and Lewis Show. NBC comedy variety show, with Dean Martin, Jerry Lewis, Dick Stabile Orchestra, April 4, 1952. Trevor guested.

Screen Guild Players. CBS drama anthology. "The Dark Corner" with Howard Duff, May 24, 1952. Trevor as Kathleen.

Stars in the Air. CBS Drama. "The Sun Comes Up" with Percy Kilbride, June 14, 1952. Trevor as Helen Winter. "All My Sons" by Arthur Miller, with Percy Kilbride, June 16, 1952. Trevor as Katy Keller.

The Bob Hope Show. NBC comedy show. (1) with Ida Lupino, April 15, 1953. (2) with Bill Goodwin, including skit of *The High and the Mighty*, March 31, 1955. Trevor guested.

Baker's Theater of Stars. CBS Drama. "Taos Incident" with Larry Dobkin, John Dehner; a woman visiting her brother borrows a truck to drive into town for supplies and finds herself accused of murder on circumstantial evidence, April 19, 1953.

United Jewish Appeal. Syndicated charity broadcast on behalf of the United Jewish Appeal; Six 20-second celebrity spots, with Jan Sterling, Glenn Ford, Loretta Young *et al.*, recorded May 1953. Guest.[19]

Jack Owens. ABC-KECA talk-variety show, August 18, 1953. Trevor guested.

Bud's Bandwagon. AFRS Record show presented by Bud Widom, with Jane Withers, 1955. Trevor guested.

A Cavalcade of Stars. NBC Academy Award tribute and preview, with Bing Crosby, Mary Pickford, Joan Crawford *et al.*, March 27, 1955. Trevor guested.

Nutrilite Theater. NBC drama anthology. "Runaway Flight" by Ann H. Prochnow. With series host Pat O'Brien, December 4, 1955. Trevor as Schoolteacher.[20]

Walt Disney's Magic Kingdom. ABC children's series broadcast on WXYZ (Detroit). Trevor and young son Chuck visit Disneyland Park, February 21, 1956. Trevor guested.[21]

Television

KFI-TV Grand Opening Show. KFI-TV (California) variety show. Grand opening of station KFI-TV, the first on the West Coast. With Adolphe Menjou, Art Baker, Los Angeles Mayor Fletcher D. Buron, Tom Harmon, October 6, 1948. Trevor guested.[1]

Sheilah Graham. NBC interview show, May 20, 1951. Trevor guested.

Celebrity Spots. Paramount Television: Seven 20-minute appearances by Celeste Holm, David Niven, George Jessel *et al.*, circa 1953. Trevor guested.[2]

The Ford Television Theater. NBC drama. "Alias Nora Hale" by Jerome (Jerry) Sackheim, with Warner Anderson, Roger Broaddus, Lauren Chapin, December 21, 1953. Trevor as Nora Hale. "The Summer Memory" by Rod Serling, with James Barton, William Henry, Richard Kiley, November 18, 1954. Trevor as Felicia Crandell.

General Electric Theater. CBS comedy drama. "Foggy Night" by Douglas Heyes, with Willis Bouchey, Lawrence Dobkin, Paul Frees, February 14, 1954. Trevor as Cora Leslie.

The Jack Carson Show. NBC talk-variety show, with Ricardo Cortez, Constance Towers, October 22, 1954. Trevor guested.

Lux Video Theater. NBC drama. "Ladies in Retirement" by Reginald Denham and Edward Percy, with Elsa Lanchester, Edith Barrett, Ken Carpenter, Lisa Daniels, December 9, 1954. Trevor as Ellen Creed. "No Sad Songs for Me" by Ruth Southard, with Katharine Bard, Linda Beal, William Campbell, April 14, 1955. Trevor as Mary Scott.

Climax! CBS drama anthology. "The Prowler" by F.W. Durkee, with Wallace Ford, Pat O'Brien, Cameron Mitchell, January 5, 1956. Trevor as Phyllis Talbot.

Schlitz Playhouse. CBS drama. "Fool Proof" by Ralph Rose, with Tina Carver, Walter Coy, Christopher Dark, January 6, 1956. Trevor as Mary Hunter.

Alfred Hitchcock Presents. CBS anthology series. "Safe Conduct" by Andrew Solt, with Werner Klemperer, Jacques Bergerac, Peter Van Eyck, February 19, 1956. Trevor as Mary Prescott. "A Crime for Mothers" by Henry Slesar, with Biff Elliott, Howard McNear, Gail Bonney, January 24, 1961. Trevor as Mrs. Meade.

Producer's Showcase. NBC Drama. "Dodsworth" by Sinclair Lewis, adapted from the stage play by Sidney Howard, with Fredric March, Geraldine Fitzgerald, Regis Toomey, April 30, 1956. Trevor as Fran Dodsworth.

Playhouse 90. CBS comedy crime drama. "If You Knew Elizabeth" by Tad Mosel, with Gary Merrill, Ernest Truex, Joi Lansing, Joe Sweeney; April 11, 1957. Trevor as Elizabeth Owen.

Westinghouse Desilu Playhouse. CBS drama anthology. "Happy Hill" by Barney Slater, with Edith Barrett, John Qualen, Jay C. Flippen, Ray Teal, Royal Dano, January 12, 1959. Trevor as Savannah Brown.

Wagon Train. NBC Western series. "The C.L. Harding Story" by Howard Christie and Jean Holloway, with Ward Bond, Robert Horton, Johnny Cash, October 14, 1959. Trevor as C.L. Harding.

The Untouchables. ABC crime drama series. "Ma Barker and Her Boys" with Robert Stack, Vaughn Taylor, Adam Williams, October 22, 1959. Trevor as Kate Clark "Ma" Barker.

The United States Steel Hour. CBS drama. "The Revolt of Judge Lloyd" by Joe Graham and Paul Manning, with Jeff Morrow, Laurence Hayes, Martin Huston, October 5, 1956. Trevor as Judge Leslie Lloyd.

Person to Person. CBS talk show-documentary series, with Charles Collingwood, Chuck Connors, July 14, 1961. Trevor guested with son Chuck.

The Investigators. CBS crime series. "New Sound for the Blues" with James Franciscus, Joel Crothers, Laurie Mitchell; October 19, 1961. Trevor guested Kitty Harper.

Dr. Kildare. NBC medical drama series. "The Bed I've Made" by Jean Holloway, with Richard Chamberlain, Raymond Massey, Robert Warwick, December 20, 1962. Trevor guested Veronica Johnson.

The Joey Bishop Show. ABC talk show, with

Pancho Gonzalez, Barry Lee, Ricky Nelson, October 28, 1969. Trevor guested. Lynn Anderson, Marty Britt, George Burns, November 14, 1969. Trevor guested.

All-Star Tribute to John Wayne. ABC documentary, with Frank Sinatra, Bob Hope, Glen Campbell *et al.*, November 26, 1976. Trevor guested.

The Love Boat. ABC comedy series. "The Misunderstanding," December 10, 1983. Trevor as Nancy Fairchild.

All-Star Party for "Dutch" Reagan. NBC special celebrating President Reagan's second term in office, with June Allyson, Fred Astaire, Dana Andrews *et al.*, December 8, 1985. Trevor guested.

Murder, She Wrote. ABC detective series. "Witness for the Defense" with Patrick McGoohan, Juliet Mills, Christopher Allport, October 4, 1987. Trevor guested Judith Harlan.

Breaking Home Ties. ABC movie. Director: John Wilder. With Jason Robards, Eva Marie Saint, Erin Gray, Doug McKeon, November 20, 1987. Trevor as Grace Porter.

Recordings

Stagecoach. Side 1: With John Wayne, introduced by John Ford, ABC Theater, January 9, 1949. Side 2: With Randolph Scott, CBS Academy Award Theater, August 5, 1946. Dallas. Radiola MR 1065. 1978.

Murder, My Sweet: Crime Series—No. 14: Mrs. Grayle/Velma. Radiola MR-1094, 1979.

Personality Series—No. 5: Command Performance: Victory Extra. With Bette Davis, Bing Crosby, Carmen Miranda *et al.*, with AFRS Orchestra. Recorded August 15, 1945. Guest. Radiola MR-1100, 1979.

The Gangster Single. Humphrey Bogart, James Cagney *et al.*, extracts from soundtracks. "Moanin' Low" from *Key Largo*. Vocals. RCA Records RCA 457 7" and 12" singles, 1984.

Murder Is My Beat: Classic Film Noir Themes and Scenes. "Moanin' Low" from *Key Largo*. Vocals. TCM Turner Classic Movies Music R272466, 1997. (CD)

Death in Vegas: Dead Elvis "Moanin' Low" is sampled on the track "Rocco." Vocal. CONCRETE HARD 22 LP (Two vinyl records) 1997.

Chapter Notes

Preface

1. "The Trevor Idea of It," *The North Eastern Courier* (Narrabi, New South Wales, Australia), May 25, 1939, 2.
2. "Player Rates Place She Never Attains," *Lockport Union-Sun & Journal*, August 7, 1940, 4.
3. Lucie Neville, "Too Busy to Be a Star," *The San Bernardino County Sun*, June 26, 1938, 32.

Chapter 1

1. "New York State Census, 1915," *FamilySearch* (https://familysearch.org/ark:/61903/1:1:K92F-XDP: 8 November 2014) "New York, New York City Marriage Records, 1829–1940," database, *FamilySearch* (https://familysearch.org/ark:/61903/1:1:24S5–3P2: 20 March 2015), Noel Wemlingar and Benjamina Morrison, 19 Feb 1902.
2. "United States Census, 1900," database with images, *FamilySearch* (https://familysearch.org/ark:/61903/1:1:MSPS-YZB: accessed 29 January 2017).
3. "New York, County Naturalization Records, 1791–1980," database with images, *FamilySearch* (https://familysearch.org/ark:/61903/1:1:KFXK-QSL: 6 December 2014).
4. "1900 New York Census," Family Search," https://familysearch.org/ark:/61903/1:1:MSVY-89M
5. William French, "The Lady Changes," *Movie Classic*, July 1936, 4.
6. William French, "The Lady Changes," *Movie Classic*, July 1936, 38.
7. Dennis McLellan, "Claire Trevor Bren: A Hollywood Reputation," *The Los Angeles Times*, November 5, 1995, 82.
8. Dennis McLellan, "Claire Trevor Bren: A Hollywood Reputation," *The Los Angeles Times*, November 5, 1995, 82.
9. "Claire Trevor Has Lead in Western Drama at Loew's," *Syracuse Herald-American*, April 18, 1943, 43.
10. "Trevor's Twitter," *The Des Moines Register*, July 26, 1947, 37.
11. "Hollywood Is Just a Pleasant Paycheck to Claire Trevor," *The Des Moines Register*, November 12, 1944, 43.
12. "America's "Glorified Girl," Loves Life!" *The Bulletin*, May 8, 1937, 7.
13. Martin Somers, "She Said "No," to Thalberg," *Screenland*, August 1934, 25.
14. "America's "Glorified Girl," Loves Life!" *The Bulletin*, May 8, 1937, 7.
15. "Plays Are for the College Men, Movies for the Masses, Says Claire Trevor," *Yale Daily News*, November 22, 1939, 12.
16. "Claire Trevor's Trophies," *The Los Angeles Times*, October 6, 1935, 36.
17. George Benjamin, "A Lark That Lasted," *Modern Screen*, May 1937, 46, 180–1.
18. "Hollywood," *Screen & Radio Weekly*, 1936, 12.
19. Ben Madox, "Love Is First with Me," *Silver Screen*, May 1939, 34.
20. "America's "Glorified Girl," Loves Life!" *The Bulletin*, May 8, 1937, 7.
21. Harold V. Cohen, "Notes of the Stage and Screen," *Pittsburgh Post-Gazette*, October 31, 1933, 13. Linda Lane, "Adversity Landed Many Jobs for Screen Stars," *Ellensburg Daily Record*, December 19, 1936, 10.
22. Sheilah Graham "Claire Trevor Got Her 'Oscar' and with It Leading Lady Roles," *The Milwaukee Journal*, May 30, 1949, 48.
23. George Benjamin, "A Lark That Lasted," *Modern Screen*, May 1937, 46, 180–1.
24. Hank Whittemore, "My Life in Hollywood's Golden Age," *The Reading Eagle, Parade Magazine*, February 20, 1994, 14–15.
25. "She Took Film Test to Get Stage Role," *The Hartford Courant*, August 6, 1939, A1.
26. "Claire Trevor Not a Hurler," *Harrisburg Telegraph*, August 1, 1939, 6.
27. Email to the author from Betty Lawson, Director of External Relations, The American Academy of Dramatic Art, New York, September 29, 2016.
28. Edith Dietz, "Notes on the 'Discovery' of an Actress: This Trevor Girl Makes Her Own Fame in Films," *The Long Island Sunday Press: Screen & Radio Weekly*, August 11, 1935, 5.
29. Edith Dietz, "Notes on the 'Discovery' of an Actress: This Trevor Girl Makes Her Own Fame in Films," *The Long Island Sunday Press: Screen & Radio Weekly*, August 11, 1935, 5.
30. "Claire Trevor: "Watch Your Hands," *The New Movie Magazine*, March 1935, 44.
31. "New Film Discovery a Graduate of New York Dramatic School: Claire Trevor Is James Dunn's Leading Lady in Rideau Attraction "Hold That Girl"" *The Ottawa Journal*, June 23, 1934, 12.
32. Arthur Frudenfeld "It's Fun to Have Western Role, Claire Tells Art," *The Cincinnati Enquirer*, October 8, 1950, 106.
33. "Claire Trevor Has Lead in Western Drama at Loew's," *Syracuse Herald-American*, April 18, 1943, 43.

34. Sheilah Graham, "Claire Trevor Got Her 'Oscar' and with It Leading Lady Roles," *The Milwaukee Journal*, May 30, 1949, 48.
35. "About Hollywood: Claire Trevor's Family Can't See Her as 'Fallen Woman'" *The Tuscaloosa News*, April 29, 1953, 13.
36. "Hollywood," *The Delta Democrat-Times*, November 10, 1948, 48. Martin Somers, "She Said "No," to Thalberg," *Screenland*, August 1934, 25.
37. "Drama Festival for Ann Arbor," *Detroit Free Press*, May 11, 1930, 59.
38. "Claire Trevor One of Bright Stars in Palace's Feature," *McComb Enterprise-Journal* (McComb, Mississippi), July 9, 1952, 9.
39. Earl Wilson, "It Happened Last Night: Claire Trevor Silences Critics with Comeback," *The Des Moines Register*, November 21, 1948, 57.
40. "Calls Claire "Oral Stripteaser"" *The Brooklyn Daily Eagle*, October 13, 1950, 11.
41. Alvin J. Kayton, "In the Theaters on Broadway," *Daily Star* (New York), September 29, 1930, 14.
42. A.R. "They Insist She's Shady: At Least Hollywood Does in the Case of Claire Trevor, Who's Rather Worried by It All," *The Brooklyn Daily Eagle*, January 22, 1939, 10.
43. Karen Hollis "They Say in New York," *Picture Play Magazine*, December 1932, 22.
44. ""Not Yet," Washed Up," *Variety*, October 15, 1930, 59.
45. "Internet Broadway Database: The Stalk Is Dead (1932)," https://www.ibdb.com/broadway-production/the-stork-is-dead-11629.
46. "The Stork Is Dead," *Variety*, September 27, 1932, 50, 52.
47. Martin Somers, "She Said "No," to Thalberg," *Screenland*, August 1934, 25.
48. "Vitaphone Varieties Celebrate Completion of 400th Picture," *Exhibitor's Herald-World*, December 27, 1930, 26.
49. Bradley, Edwin M. *The First Hollywood Sound Films 1926–1931*(Jefferson, NC: McFarland & Co, Inc., 2005), 416.
50. Bradley, Edwin M. *The First Hollywood Sound Shorts 1926–31* (Jefferson, NC: McFarland & Co, Inc., 2009), 119.
51. Lucie Neville: "Claire Trevor Wants to Be a Star," *San Bernardino County Sun*, June 26, 1938, 32.
52. Drummond Tell, "Three-Alarm Blonde," *Picture Play Magazine*, April 1934, 42.
53. Drummond Tell, "Three-Alarm Blonde," *Picture Play Magazine*, April 1934, 42.
54. "Where Will We Get Tomorrow's Stars," *Detroit Free Press*, August 12, 1934, 65.
55. "New Stock Company to Begin Season with Belasco Success," *St Louis Star & Times*, December 20, 1930, 10: "It's a Wise Child," *Werrenton Banner*, December 26, 1930, 8.
56. "Comedy of Divorce at Grand Central: Stock Company Presents Thompson Buchanan's Play as It's Second Bill," *The St Louis Post-Dispatch*, January 9, 1931, 19.
57. "'Broken Dishes' Amusing Play at Grand Central: Depicts Henpecked Husband's Revolt After He Is Introduced to a Gallon of Cider," *The St Louis Star & Times*, January 19, 1931, 6. "Stock Company Seen in "Broken Dishes," *The St Louis Post-Dispatch*, January 18, 1931, 28.
58. "'Broadway' Is Well Played in Stock: Wallace Ford Heads Crook Melodrama at the Grand Central," *The St Louis Post and Dispatch*, February 10, 1931, 15.
59. "'Jonesy' Is Played at Grand Central: Funny Lines Responsible for Many Laughs in Rather Slight Farce," *The St Louis Post and Dispatch*, February 16, 1931, 17.
60. Lucie Neville: "Claire Trevor Wants to Be a Star," *San Bernardino County Sun*, June 26, 1938, 32.
61. Thornton Sargent, "Can It Happen Again?" *Screenland*, July 1934, 58.
62. "Grand Central Stock in Pleasing Comedy: "Strictly Dishonorable," Well Played by Cast Nicely Suited to Requirements," *St Louis Post & Dispatch*, February 1, 1931, 15.
63. "Grand Central Players: Strictly Dishonorable," *The St Louis Daily Globe-Democrat*, February 1, 1931, 6.
64. "Nedda Harrigan in 'Gold Diggers' at Grand Central: Guest Artist Starred in Farce Which Opens Monday," *The St Louis Star & Times*, February 21, 1931, 12.
65. "$1,000 a Week and Idling," *Variety*, April 1, 1931, 2.
66. Earl Wilson, "It Happened Last Night: Claire Trevor Silences Critics with Comeback," *The Des Moines Register*, November 21, 1948, 57.

Chapter 2

1. Sheilah Graham, "Claire Trevor Got Her 'Oscar' and with It Leading Lady Roles," *The Milwaukee Journal*, May 30, 1949, 48.
2. "Theater News: Rhapsody in Black," *The Brooklyn Daily Eagle*, July 16, 1931, 12.
3. Miss Helen Galaghan, *Brooklyn Life and Activities of the Long Island Society*, July 8, 1931, 8.
4. "Players Will Perform in Guild Hall," *The East Hampton Star*, August 21, 1931, 1.
5. "The Only Trouble Is, Says He, Movies Take All the Actors," *The Brooklyn Daily Eagle*, February 14, 1932, 54.
6. Arthur Pollack, "First Nighters See 'Whistling in the Dark'" *The Brooklyn Daily Eagle*, January 20, 1932, 19 . "All New Femme Lead," *Variety*, December 8, 1931, 35.
7. Robin Coons, "Hollywood Sights and Sounds," *The Niagara Falls Gazette*, September 2, 1933, 3.
8. Alice Alworth, "Ink About Greasepaint," *The Bronxville Press*, February 12, 1932, 6.
9. "At the America: "Whistling in the Dark," Proves to Be Bright, Frank and New," *The St Louis Star & Times*, October 25, 1932, 20.
10. Edwin C. Stein, "The Stage: One of the Season's Most Amusing and Ingenious Plays Makes Its Debut," *Standard Union*, January 13, 1932, 11.
11. George Benjamin, "A Lark That Lasted," *Modern Screen*, May 1937, 46, 180–1.
12. Martin Somers, "She Said 'No' to Thalberg; Claire Trevor," *Screenland*, August 1934, 25.
13. "In Hollywood," *Argus-Leader (Sioux Falls, South Dakota)* April 25, 1948, 12.
14. "Two Claires Get Together and Read's Ears Burn!" *Woodland Daily Democrat*, August 5, 1932, 4.
15. "Read Wrote Wife, Claire, Impartially," *Oakland Tribune*, July 11, 1932, 1.
16. "Read Wrote Wife, Claire, Impartially," *Oakland Tribune*, July 11, 1932, 1.

17. "Two Claires Get Together and Read's Ears Burn!" *Woodland Daily Democrat*, August 5, 1932, 4.
18. Earl Wilson, "It Happened Last Night: Claire Trevor Silences Critics with Comeback," *The Des Moines Register*, November 21, 1948, 57.
19. "Caption Under Picture: Claire Trevor and Ernest Truex Promise Scintillating Performances in 'Whistling in the Dark'" *The Los Angeles Times*, June 11, 1932, 21.
20. George A. Leighton, "Novelist Thwarts Gangsters! Thriller Scores at Shubert's," *The Cincinnati Enquirer*, November 8, 1932, 22.
21. Wood Soanes, "Melodrama Is Made Comical by Good Acting: 'Whistling in the Dark' at Geary, Does Not Insult Intelligence of the Actors," *Oakland Tribune*, Jul 6, 1932, 21.
22. "The Private Lives of Film Stars—Claire Trevor: Beginning from the Top!" *The Mail* (Adelaide, South Australia) February 26, 1938, 1.
23. "Theatrical Notes," *The Brooklyn Daily Eagle*, February 16, 1933, Feb 16, 1933, 4.
24. John Mason Brown, "The Play: Sidney Harmon & James R. Ullman Present 'Far Away Horses' at the Martin Beck Theater," *The New York Evening Post*, March 22, 1933, 17.
25. "Play on Broadway 'The Party's Over'" *Variety*, April 4, 1933, 38.
26. Arthur Pollack, "'The Party's Over' Joins Broadway Play List Theater & Musical Events: 'The Party's Over,' a Comedy About a Breadwinner Who Gets Tired of Feeding His Family Cake, Comes to the Vanderbilt," *The Brooklyn Daily Eagle*, March 28, 1933, 10.
27. "The Private Lives of the Film Stars—Claire Trevor: Beginning from the Top," *The Mail* (Adelaide, South Australia), February 26, 1938, 1.
28. Walter Winchell, "On Broadway," *Reading Times*, May 4, 1932, 4.
29. "2 Legits Go Greeley," *Variety*, April 18, 1933, 3.
30. Robin Coons, "Hollywood Sights & Sounds," *The Niagara Falls Gazette*, September 2, 1933, 2.
31. "Private Lives of the Film Stars—Claire Trevor: Beginning from the Top!" *The Mail* (Adelaide, South Australia), February 26, 1938, 1.

Chapter 3

1. Hubbard Keavy, "Screen Life in Hollywood," *Pittsburgh Daily Press*, June 23, 1933, 6.
2. "Private Lives of the Stars—Claire Trevor: Beginning from the Top!" *The Mail* (Adelaide, South Australia), February 26, 1938, 1.
3. "A Really Good Bad Girl," Louis Reid, *Screenland*, June 1950, 70.
4. "'The Last Trail,' With George O'Brien Thrilling," *Dansville Breeze* (Dansville, New York), November 3, 1933, 7.
5. Luis Rosado, "Meet the Stars," *Big Spring Daily Herald*, August 2, 1943, 2.
6. "Film Reviews: The Mad Game," *Variety*, November 30, 1933, 30.
7. Cecilia Ager, "Going Places," *Variety*, November 14, 1933, 51.
8. "The Screen in Review: "The Mad Game," *Picture Play*, February 1934, 56.
9. "Seen and Heard: "The Mad Game"—Fox Films Put Over Another Good One: With Spencer Tracy," *Hollywood Filmograph*, October 28, 1933, 35.
10. Claire Trevor: "Watch Your Hands," *The New Movie Magazine*, March 1935, 44.
11. "Advance News Talkie Topics," *The Advance-News*, February 17, 1934, 4.
12. Curtis, James *Spencer Tracy: A Biography* (New York: Hutchinson, 2011), 215.
13. Ralph Wilk, "A "Little," from Hollywood "Lots," *The Film Daily*, December 27, 1934, 7.
14. "Picture Theaters: State—From Head Quarters," *The Age*, April 16, 1934, 9.
15. Martin Dickstein, "The Screen: "Frank Buck Brings 'Em Back Alive Again in 'Wild Cargo' at the Music Hall—'Hold That Girl' Makes Brooklyn Debut at the Fox & Cartoon," *Brooklyn Daily Eagle*, March 30, 1934, 21.
16. "Banish 1933 Blues Away at the Northport," *Northport Journal*, January 5, 1933, 1.
17. "Dialogue Man Explains How Speech Varies," *Schenectady Gazette*, November 16, 1933, 18.
18. "'Jimmy & Sally' New Film at Fox: James Dunn & Claire Trevor Head the Cast; Lou Holtz on Stage," *The Philadelphia Inquirer*, November 18, 1933, 17.
19. "Films of the Day, in Tuscaloosa," *The Tuscaloosa News*, April 18, 1934, 3.
20. "What the Picture Did for Me," *Motion Picture Herald*, March 3, 1934, 57.
21. Gladys McCardle, "What the Picture Did for Me: "Hold That Girl," Owl Theater, Lebanon, Kansas," *Motion Picture Herald*, July 7, 1934, 62.
22. Bob Oulette, "What the Picture Did for Me: "Hold That Girl," Dixie Theater, Brooksville, Florida," *Motion Picture Herald*, July 21, 1934, 61.
23. "New Program Opens at Regent Today," *Rochester Times-Union*, December 19, 1933, 24.
24. "At Elmira Theaters," *Elmira Star-Gazette*, December 16, 1933, 9.
25. Louella O. Parsons, "Dolores Del Rio Gets Drama Role," *Syracuse Journal*, September 30, 1933, 8.
26. "A Debutante Star," (Picture with caption), *Buffalo Courier-Express*, April 15, 1934, 9.
27. "Fox Studio Again Chooses Own Baby Stars," *The Los Angeles Times*, March 27, 1934, 20. "Times Square: Studio Placements," *Variety*, September 26, 1933, 59.
28. "58 Fox Features, 112 Shorts, in 1934: Musicals with Lillian Harvey," *Motion Picture Herald*, June 2, 1934, 18.
29. Louella O. Parsons, "Powell Given Lead Role in 'Thin Man'" *Times-Union*, February 13, 1934, 8.
30. Edward Schallert, "Emil Ludwig, Famous Author Coming to Hollywood," *Los Angeles Times*, September 27, 1933, 11.
31. Ralph Wilk, "A "Little," from Hollywood "Lots," *The Film Daily*, November 21, 1934, 10.
32. "Film Topics," *New Zealand Herald*, March 3, 1934, 12.
33. Ralph Wilk, "A "Little," from "Lots," *The Film Daily*, December 24, 1934, 6.
34. "Story Sales," *Motion Picture Herald*, January 12, 1935, 47.
35. Ralph Wilk, "A "Little," from "Lots," *The Film Daily*, April 3, 1934, 7.
36. "TCM Notes: Baby Take a Bow (1934)," http://

www.tcm.com/tcmdb/title/67872/Baby-Take-a-Bow/notes.html.
37. "Fox Signs Mary Brian," *Motion Picture Daily,* September 28, 1934, 15.
38. "Fox Lists 43 of 58 Total for 1934–35" *Motion Picture Daily,* May 31, 1934, 12.
39. "Fox Lists 43 of 58 Total for 1934–35: Daily Shooting Schedules-Fox," *Motion Picture Daily,* April 11, 1934, 24.
40. "49 Titles Set," *The Film Daily,* May 31, 1934, 7.
41. "Sol Wurtzel Busiest Producer on Fox Lot," *The Pittsburgh Post-Gazette,* October 23, 1933, 9.
42. "Index: Release Schedules for Features: Fox Features," *Harrison's Reports* February 16, 1935, 29.
43. "Fox Release List Is Set to July 27" *The Film Daily,* April 9, 1934, 2. "Set Louis King's Next," *The Hollywood Reporter,* April 9, 1934, 4.
44. "Claire Trevor a Star," *The Hollywood Reporter,* March 26, 1934, 3.
45. "An Appraisal of the 1935–36 Season's Pictures—No. 2 (And a Study of the Contract Terms): Fox," *Harrison's Reports,* August 10, 1935, 125. Aubrey Soloman *The Fox Film Corporation 1915–35* (Jefferson, NC: McFarland & Co, Inc., 2011) 220.
46. "Theater News: Looking Over the Local Screens: Edwards Theater," *Sarasota Herald-Tribune,* December 7, 1934, 6.
47. "Distributors' Sales Plans for 1934–35" *Motion Picture Herald,* May 5, 1934, 9.
48. "Sarasota: Exciting Love Story Shown at Princess," *Kentucky New Era,* November 15, 1934, 6.
49. Jimmy Starr, "From Hollywood," *Reading Eagle,* October 18, 1934, 21.
50. "What the Picture Did for Me: Fox: Elinor Norton," *Motion Picture Daily,* January 12, 1935, 67.
51. "Elinor Norton," *The Singapore Free Press & Mercantile Advertiser,* May 15, 1935, 2.
52. Freese, Gene Scott *Hollywood Stunt Performers: A Biographical Dictionary 1910s to 1970s* (Jefferson, NC: McFarland & Co, Inc., 2014), 232.
53. "Studio Placements," *Variety,* October 16, 1935, 24. Aubrey Soloman *The Fox Film Corporation 1915–35* (Jefferson, NC: McFarland & Co, Inc., 2011) 220.
54. Jeremy Hoffman, "Dick Powell Gets New Leading Role; Marian Marsh 'Limber Lost' Star, Random Snapshots of Hollywood Folk," *The Philadelphia Inquirer,* June 24, 1934, 6.
55. "AFI Catalog of Feature Films: Spring Tonic," http://www.afi.com/members/catalog/DetailView.aspx?s=1&Movie=5786.
56. "Slapstick Film Disconcerting to Zasu Pitts: Second Retake in "Man-Eating Tiger," Is One Too Many," *The Binghampton Press,* February 18, 1935, 16.
57. "Spring Tonic," *Variety,* June 12, 1935, 12, 41.
58. "Twentieth Century Fox: Spring Tonic: Talisman Theater, Rosedale, Miss." *Motion Picture Daily,* November 30, 1935, 85.

Chapter 4

1. Zepha Samailoff, "Nasty but Nice," *Motion Picture,* October 1936, 59.
2. "Stardust," *Spokane Daily Chronicle,* March 22, 1937, 5.
3. Sidney Skolsky, "Claire, the 'Shady Lady'" *New York Evening Post,* December 6, 1943, 23.
4. "Style Notes: Perfume Fancier": *Border Watch* (Australia), March 17, 1942, 3.
5. Sidney Skolsky, "Claire, the 'Shady Lady'" *New York Evening Post,* December 6, 1943, 23.
6. Robert Grandon, "Door Knobs Were Claire's Hobby," *Schenectady Gazette,* February 13, 1934, 12.
7. "Every Lass Needs a Hobby," *The Milwaukee Journal,* June 26, 1938, 29.
8. "Will Vie for Honors in Foreign Exhibit," *The Los Angeles Times,* June 23, 1936, 11.
9. "Plays Reporter on Radio, Gets Similar Movie Role," *The Evening News* (Harrisburg, Pennsylvania), November 27, 1937, 14.
10. Sidney Skolsky, "Claire, the 'Shady Lady' *New York Evening Post,* December 6, 1943, 23.
11. Robert Grandon, "Doorknobs Were Claire's Hobby," *Schenectady Gazette,* February 13, 1934, 12.
12. "Hollywood's Sights and Sounds," *Ogdensburg Journal,* December 29, 1934, 8.
13. Sidney Skolsky, "Claire the Shady Lady," *New York Evening Post,* December 6, 1943, 23.
14. Jimmy Starr "From Hollywood," *Reading Eagle,* March 26, 1935, 14.
15. Mack Hughes, "Goings-On in Gotham," *Modern Screen,* July 1938, 6.
16. "Coming & Going," *The Film Daily,* October 26, 1939, 2.
17. Jimmy Starr, "From Hollywood," *Reading Eagle,* August 1, 1934, 6.
18. George Shaffer "Zanuck Claims Stock List Is a Movie Evil: Declares the Fans Tire of Sameness in Casts," *Chicago Tribune,* October 5,1934, 23.
19. Malcolm Oettinger, "Kicking Over the Traces," *Modern Screen,* July 1937, 51.
20. Jimmie Fidler, "Talk of the Talkies," *Brooklyn Daily Eagle,* August 2, 1937, 8.
21. "Trevor in "Street of Chance," Opening tomorrow at Paramount," *Syracuse Herald-Journal,* December 15, 1942, 27.
22. Dennis McLellan, "Claire Trevor Bren: A Hollywood Reputation," *Los Angeles Times,* May 28, 1995, 23.
23. Jimmie Fidler. "In Hollywood," *News-Press* (Fort Myers, Florida), July 19, 1949, 4.
24. "Claire Trevor Not a Hurler," *Harrisburg Telegraph,* August 1, 1939, 6.
25. "Harry Lachman, a Film Director," *New York Times,* March 21, 1975, 23.
26. Grace Wilcox, "Gift of Laughter: Subject: Claire Trevor; Reason for Inquiry; She's Contented," *Long Island Sunday Press: Screen & Radio Weekly,* September 12, 1937, 7.
27. Edwin Schallert, "Richard Barthlemess Back: Star Signed for Krasna Picture," *The Los Angeles Times,* January 21, 1935, 13.
28. Robert Herring quoted in Halliwell, Leslie *Halliwell's Film Guide* (London: Guild Publishing Ltd, 1983), 194.
29. John Baxter (1968) quoted in Halliwell, Leslie *Halliwell's Film Guide* (London: Guild Publishing Ltd, 1983), 194.
30. Jimmie Fidler. "In Hollywood," *News-Press* (Fort Myers, Florida), July 19, 1949, 4.

31. Curtis, James *Spencer Tracy: A Biography* (New York: Hutchinson, 2011), 251.
32. Lombardi, Frederic *Allan Dwan and the Rise and Decline of the Hollywood Studios* (Jefferson, NC: McFarland & Co, Inc.,2013), 198.
33. "The Private Lives of Film Stars—Claire Trevor Beginning from the Top," *The Mail* (Adelaide, South Australia), February 26, 1938, 1.
34. Frederick C. Othman, "Voice of Americans Pains Movie Speech Teacher," *St Petersburg Times,* February 16, 1940, 18.
35. "Pneumonia Threatens Claire Trevor," *The Daily Illini,* September 24, 1935, 1.
36. "TCM Notes: My Marriage (1936)," http://www.tcm.com/tcmdb/title/84367/My-Marriage/notes.html.
37. Martin Dickstein, "Picture Parade: Some Items from Fox," *Brooklyn Daily Eagle,* October 30, 1935, 10.
38. "TCM Notes: Song and Dance Man (1936)," http://www.tcm.com/tcmdb/title/90827/Song-and-Dance-Man/notes.html.
39. "Picture Theaters Regent—Shirley Temple," *The Age* (Melbourne, Australia), June 1, 1936, 13.
40. "Blaze Ruins Stage in Hollywood Studio," *San Bernardino Sun,* November 23, 1935, 2.
41. "Film Star's Dancing Grace: Miss. Claire Trevor," *Northern Star,* September 26, 1936, 4.
42. "Claire Trevor Gathers Rhumba Records," *Oakland Tribune,* April 30, 1942, 35.
43. Gail Gardner, "Gossip from the Studios," *Santa Cruz Evening News,* May 2, 1936, 12.
44. Sheilah Graham, "Peeping at Filmdom: Stars' Insurance, Also Producers and Stories," *Auckland Star,* August 1, 1936, 5.
45. "Gowns Should Put Accent on Romanticism," *Dansville Breeze,* August 7, 1936, 1.
46. "Claire Trevor, Donlevy Win Star Assignments," *The Brooklyn Daily Eagle,* November 2, 1937, 8.
47. "Gaumont-British After Claire Trevor," *Los Angeles Times,* May 5, 1936, 15.
48. Phyllis Marie-Arthur, "When Ladies Meet: To Mary, with Love," *The Journal & Republican* (Lowville, New York), June 4, 1936, 6. Note: A Redingole is a style of French coat.
49. Lucie Neville: "Claire Trevor Wants to Be a Star," *The San Bernardino County Sun,* June 26, 1938, 32.
50. "Versatile Lady," *Evening Post,* January, 5, 1939. 16.
51. "TCM Notes: 15 Maiden Lane (1936)," http://www.tcm.com/tcmdb/title/74788/15-Maiden-Lane/notes.html.
52. "But Star Loses, Finds Borrowed Emerald in Time's Nick," *The St. Maurice Valley Chronicle,* November 19, 1936, 3.
53. Henry Sutherland, "Movie Rainmakers Face Problem in Preventing Actresses Catching Cold," *San Bernardino Sun,* August 12, 1936, 1.
54. Joe Pollack, "Claire Trevor: Sense of Style and Glamour," *St Louis Post-Dispatch,* December 30, 1982, 51.
55. Delight Evans, "The Editor's Page: An Open Letter to Claire Trevor," *Screenland,* January 1938, 11.
56. Sheilah Graham, "Cheaters of Death: Hollywood's Stunt Men Risking Life for Spectacular Effects," *Auckland Star,* July 17, 1937, 5.
57. "Odd & Interesting Hollywood Gossip," *The Los Angeles Times,* January 15, 1937, 38.
58. "Type Roles Lose Favor in Movies," *The Pittsburgh Press,* May 18, 1937, 20.
59. "Stage Tour Planned by Film Actor," *The Pittsburgh Press,* March 11, 1937, 20.
60. "Rehearsal by Wire," *The Watchman,* June 10, 1937, 3.
61. "Claire Trevor Is to Sing in Film," *Herald-Journal,* April 4, 1937, 6. "Theater Gossip," *The Evening Independent,* April 28, 1937, 4.
62. Gevinson, Alan *Within Our Gates: Ethnicity in American Feature Films 1911–60* (Berkeley, CA: University of California Press, 1997), 740.
63. "Roxy Theater," *The Daily Times,* November 20, 1937, 2.
64. "Screen News," *The Brooklyn Daily Eagle,* August 6, 1937, 9.
65. "Movies & Amusements: Lady in Black Fails to Show Up at Valentino Grave," *The St Louis Star & Times,* August 31, 1937, 16.
66. Harold V. Cohen, "The Drama Desk: The Movie Lots Beg to Report," *Pittsburgh Post-Gazette,* March 29, 1937, 18.
67. Wilson, Victoria *A Life of Barbara Stanwyck: Steel-True:1907–1940* (New York: Simon & Schuster, 2015), 498.
68. "Stars," *Cazenovia Republican,* January 28, 1937, 7.
69. Robbin Coons, "Hollywood Sights & Sounds," *The Niagara Falls Gazette,* August 7, 1940, 6.
70. "It's Easy to Get Married," *Hollywood,* April 1938, 63.
71. Harrison Carroll, "Behind the Scenes in Hollywood," *The Advance-News,* January 11, 1938, 11.
72. Dorothy Kilgallen, "Voice of Broadway: Broadway Grapevine," *Schenectady Gazette,* June 8, 1949, 16.

Chapter 5

1. "Ladies on Approval," *Screenland,* May 1934, 41.
2. "Hollywood Here and There," *Screenland,* April 1938, 65.
3. "Gale Group: Statistics": http://ic.galegroup.com/ic/uhic/ReferenceDetailsPage/ReferenceDetailsWindow?query=&prodId=UHIC&displayGroupName=Reference&limiter=&disableHighlighting=true&displayGroups=&sortBy=&zid=&search_within_results=&action=2&catId=&activityType=&documentId=GALE%7CCX3468301237&source=Bookmark&u=sand55832&jsid=ff1c546a17b62d2d1ce4007351b97724.
4. Dan Thomas, "Star Makes Business of Being Beautiful," *Ottawa Citizen,* August 22, 1935, 21.
5. Gene Handsaker, "Hollywood Sights and Sounds," *Prescott Evening Courier,* August 9, 1946, 3.
6. Lydia Lane, "Hollywood Beauty: Dyeing Hair? Analyze Skin Tone," *Nashua Review-Star,* February 18, 1953, 8.
7. Ida Jean Kain, "The Smart Set: Your Figure," *Times-Union* (Albany, New York), February 3, 1939, 9.
8. Elsie Pierce, "How to Be Beautiful Famous Beauty Elsie Pierce," *Reading Eagle,* 8 June 1936, 13.
9. Claire Trevor: "Watch Your Hands," *The New Movie Magazine,* March 1935, 44.
10. Dan Thomas, "Star Makes Business of Being Beautiful," *Ottawa Citizen,* August 22, 1935, 21.
11. Claire Trevor, "Screenland's Glamor School," *Screenland,* February 1936, 64.

12. "Hollywood Fashions," *Screenland*, October 1933, 66.
13. Margery Wells, "On Dress Parade," *Modern Screen*, March 34, 109.
14. "Gets Wardrobe as Studio Gift," *Dansville Breeze* (Dansville, New York), March 22, 1934, 5.
15. "Hollywood Sponsors Swimsuits in White Satin," *Sarasota Herald-Tribune*, August 2, 1936, 10.
16. "Especially for Women: Snapshots of Life in Hollywood Today: Latest Dance Frocks Have New "Waltz," Length," *Auckland Star*, July 22, 1937, 12.
17. Sara Day "Spring Nights: Fashions by Sara Day Sketched by Louise," *The Watchman*, April 21, 1938, 19.
18. Sheilah Graham, "White for Bridge: Famous Expert's Opinion," *Auckland Star*, August 13, 1936, 14.
19. Jimmie Fidler, "Move to Mexico Craze Strikes Prominent Film Colonists," *St Petersburg Times*, June 6, 1941, 21.
20. Claire Trevor, "Screenland's Glamor School," *Screenland*, February 1936, 54–5.
21. Lydia Lane, "Hollywood Beauty: Dyeing Hair? Analyze Skin Tone," *Nashua Review-Star*, February 18, 1953, 8.
22. "Most Beautiful Still of the Month: 'Elinor Norton'" *Screenland*, February, 1935, 15.
23. "Fashion Notes," *Spokane Daily Chronicle*, July 29, 1939, 4.
24. "Fashion Notes," *Spokane Daily Chronicle*, November 18, 1941, 9.
25. Adelia Bird "Slimming or Swimming?" *Modern Screen*, October 1936, 56.
26. "Rotogravure Section," *The Philadelphia Inquirer*, August 8, 1937, 5.
27. "Casual Note for Gowns," *The Spokesman-Review*, March 15, 1935, 3.
28. "Gowns Should Put Accent on Romanticism," *Dansville Breeze*, August 7, 1936, 1.
29. "Spiders Trim Dress," *Battle Creek Enquirer* (Michigan), May 22, 1938, 19.
30. "Little Black Dress: 1930: Coco's Great Fashion Rivalry," http://www.littleblackdress.co.uk/life-of-chanel/cocos-great-fashion-rivalry.html.
31. "Metal Fingernails," *The Mail* (Adelaide, South Australia), March 16, 1935, 23.
32. "The Ray Driscoll Collection: Hollywood's Bad Boy Designer," http://adht.parsons.edu/blog/hollywoods-bad-boy-designer-the-raymond-driscoll-collection/
33. Erskine Johnson, "Designer Sticks Neck Out Again, Picks Five Best Dressed Stars," *Elmira Star-Gazette*, March 14, 1946, 26.
34. Antoinette Donnelly, "Watching the Women's World: Always Look Your Best Is Safest Plan," *The Post-Standard* (Syracuse, New York), February 28, 1953, 8.
35. Ida Jean Kain, "The Smart Set: Your Figure," *Times-Union* (Albany, New York), 9.
36. "Wardrobe Is Modest," *The Evening News* (Harrisburg, Pennsylvania), April 23, 1948, 22.
37. Grace Wilcox, "Screen & Radio: Hollywood Bureau," *Long Island Sunday Press: Screen & Radio Weekly: The Hollywood Reporter*, July 7, 1935, 2.
38. "Helen Franklin Designed Interior Décor of Hotel," *The Desert Sun*, December 22, 1952, 20.
39. Rochelle Chadakoff, "Design for Success: Pauline Trigere Still Has a Flair for Fashion," *The Daily Gazette*, April 3, 1993, A6.
40. Lydia Lane, "Claire Trevor Gives on Topic of Youthfulness," *The Los Angeles Times*, April 15, 1951, 108.
41. Bob Thomas, "Claire Trevor Acting Age After Decade Away," *Green Bay Press-Gazette* (Wisconsin), July 11, 1982, 82.
42. Gene Handsaker, "Hollywood Sights and Sounds," *Prescott Evening Courier*, July 5, 1949, 4.
43. "Club Selects Sweetheart," *The Los Angeles Times*, February 15, 1939, 19.

Chapter 6

1. Bergan, Ronald *The United Artists Story* (New York: Octopus Books, 1986), 77.
2. Jimmy Fidler, "Talk of the Talkies," *The Brooklyn Daily Eagle*, July 27, 1937, 6.
3. Paul Harrison, "Claire Trevor Dodges into Realism," *Herald-Journal*, July 16, 1937, 5.
4. "Woman Rules Film, So Wife Refuses Role: Claire Trevor Says Name Not Big Enough," *Buffalo Courier-Express*, November 23, 1951, 14-D.
5. "Woman Rules Film, So Wife Refuses Role: Claire Trevor Says Name Not Big Enough," *Buffalo Courier-Express*, November 23, 1951, 14-D.
6. Frederick C. Othman, "Claire Trevor's Chance Comes at Long Last She Gets Big Role," *Detroit Free Press*, October 10, 1938, 11.
7. Malcolm Oettinger, "Kicking Over the Traces," *Motion Picture Daily*, July 1937, 78.
8. "Hollywood: Director William Wyler Riles Actors with His Meticulous Work on Scenes, but When They Read the Notices, They're Glad He Was So Painstaking." *Buffalo Courier-Express*, June 13, 1937, 10.
9. A. R., "They Insist She's Shady: At Least Hollywood Does in Case of Claire Trevor, Who's Rather Worried by It All," *The Brooklyn Daily Eagle*, January 22, 1939, 10.
10. "Flashes of the Cinema," *Auckland Star*, December 3, 1938, 7.
11. Louella O. Parsons, ""The River is Blue," Stars Madeleine Carroll, Fonda," *The Schenectady Gazette*, January 25, 1938, 15.
12. "'Thin Ice' Out, Henie to Make Timely History," *The Pittsburgh Post-Gazette*, May 13, 1937, 20. Ed Sullivan, "Men and Maids," 19 *The Pittsburgh Press*, April 28, 1936, 19. "The Chatterbox," *The Eugene Register-Guard*, May 24 1936, 15.
13. Eileen Percy, "Opportunity Knocks Twice for Movie People," *The Milwaukee Sentinel*, February 26, 1936, 20.
14. Harrison Carroll: "Behind the Scenes in Hollywood," *The Advance-News*, May 19, 1937, 5.
15. Sidney Skolsky, "Claire, the 'Shady Lady'" *New York Evening Post*, December 6, 1943, 23.
16. "South Carolina USTA," http://www.southcarolina.usta.com/Allied_Organizations/wilmer_hines/
17. "Wimbledon Archive," http://www.wimbledon.com/en_GB/scores/draws/archive/players/473ea10a-ff4e-45e9–81fa-4ec88a0cc24e/index.html.
18. "Hot Shots from Hollywood," *The Lewiston Daily Sun*, September 9, 1937, 4. Louella O. Parsons, "From the Studios," *The Milwaukee Sentinel*, March 25, 1937, 1.
19. Harrison Carroll, "Behind the Scenes in Hollywood," *The Advance-News*, August 24, 1937, 9.

20. Grace Wilcox, "Gift of Laughter: Subject; Claire Trevor; Reason for Inquiry; She's Contented," *The Long Island Sunday Press: Screen and Radio Weekly*, September 12, 1937, 7.
21. Robbin Coons, "Actress' Failure to Reach Stardom Puzzles Columnist," *Toledo Blade*, August 5, 1940, 25.
22. "TCM Notes: Second Honeymoon," http://www.tcm.com/tcmdb/title/89380/Second-Honeymoon/notes.html.
23. "Claire Trevor: A Movie Star in 'Real Life'" *The Los Angeles Times*, July 18, 1982, 287.
24. "Claire Trevor, Donlevy, Win Star Assignments," *Brooklyn Daily Eagle*, November 2, 1937, 8.
25. "TCM Notes: Big Town Girl," http://www.tcm.com/tcmdb/title/68736/Big-Town-Girl/notes.html.
26. "In the Cutting Room: Walking Down Broadway (20th Century-Fox) Adventures in Romance," *Motion Picture Herald*, January 15, 1938, 29.
27. "'Walking Down Broadway' Is Confusing, Cheerless Drama," *Film Exhibitor's Bulletin*, February 12, 1938, 52.
28. "Walking Down Broadway (20th Century Fox) Comedy Melodrama," *Motion Picture Herald*, August 27, 1938, 22.
29. Lucie Neville, "Too Busy to Be a Star," *The San Bernardino County Sun*, June 26, 1938, 32.
30. Thomas M. Pryor, "The "Queen of the B's," Has Abdicated," *The Newcastle Sun*, March 18, 1939, 4.
31. Jean Somers, "With Stardom Ahead," *Modern Screen* Jan 1940, 8.
32. Jimmie Fidler, "Talk of the Talkies," *Picture Parade*, October 23, 1938, 35.
33. Jean Somers, "With Stardom Ahead," *Modern Screen*, January 1940, 8.
34. "Out Hollywood Way," *Motion Picture Daily*, May 4, 1938, 8.
35. Louella O. Parsons, "Number of Theater Guild Openings," *Pittsburgh Post-Gazette*, April 12, 1937, 10.
36. "Claire Trevor, Wurtzel Form New Producing Unit," *Motion Picture Herald*, August 22, 1938, 22.
37. Lola Pertson, "Two Parties Spotlighted in Hollywood: Young Hollywood Plans Screen Actors' Guild Party," *The Los Angeles Times*, January 24, 1937, 65.
38. "TCM Notes: The Amazing Dr. Clitterhouse," http://www.tcm.com/tcmdb/title/67187/The-Amazing-Doctor-Clitterhouse/notes.html.
39. Capua, Michelangelo *Anatole Litvak: The Life and Films* (Jefferson, NC: McFarland & Co, Inc., 2015), 35.
40. "Turned Down £200,000 for Love," *The Mail*, August 20, 1938, 10.
41. "Screen News Here and There," *New York Times*, June 16, 1938, 21.
42. "Screen News Here and There," *New York Times*, January 5, 1938, 12.
43. "News of the Screen: Cantor Sells 'Sing While You Sleep,'" *New York Times*, August 7, 1937, 12.
44. Robbin Coons, "Screen Life," *Sarasota Herald-Tribune*, June 27, 1938, 4.
45. Ronald Adams Sloan, *The Times-News*, "Don't Look for 'Gamblers' Tipoff,'" January 23, 1936, 13.
46. "Actress Drives Hand Car," *The Montreal Gazette*, November 12, 1938, 10.
47. Dan Mannering,"Shooting the Lumberjacks," *Silver Screen*, October 1938, 38.

Chapter 7

1. "Radio Insures Pix Values: New Luster for Hollywood Stars," *Variety*, February 1, 1939, 55.
2. "Claire Trevor Buys Release from Agent," *Variety*, February 15, 1939, 27.
3. Whitney Williams, "Hollywood Newsreel," *Hollywood*, February 1938, 8.
4. Herbert Whittaker, "The Season of Change," *The Montreal Gazette*, May 28, 1943, 7.
5. Irene Thirer, "Screen News and Views: Film Fans Scare Claire Trevor, Not the War," *New York Post*, December 15, 1941, 22.
6. Ben Madox, "Love Is First with Me," *Silver Screen*, May 1939, 73.
7. Jimmie Fidler "Hollywood Shots," *Reading Eagle*. July 21, 1938. 16.
8. Maxine Bartlett, "Miss Trevor to Be Bride Wednesday," *The Los Angeles Times*, July 24, 1938, 60.
9. "Claire Trevor to Wed," *Reading Eagle*, April 14, 1938, 23.
10. Ben Madox: "Love Is First with Me," *Silver Screen*, May 1939, 73.
11. Don Tranter, "Radio Comment, Highlights," *Buffalo Courier-Express*, October 7, 1944, 13.
12. Malcolm H. Oettinger, "What Should Claire Trevor Do?" *Screenland*, April 1938, 54.
13. "Most Popular Radio Stars Picked in Fan Poll," *Broadcasting*, July 1, 1939, 46.
14. "New Don Ameche Show Begins: Claire Trevor Is Leading Lady of Old Gold Series," March 31, 1940, 23.
15. "New Ameche Stories," *Broadcasting*, Bcasting 57 June 15, 1940, 57.
16. "Pittsburgh Sees RKO'S "Allegheny"" *Motion Picture Herald*, November 4, 1939, 39–40.
17. "Benson & Hedges Plans," *Variety*, January 1, 1940, 73.
18. "Radio Waves," *The Waco News-Tribune*, December 12, 1946, 17.
19. "Red Cross Broadcast Blossoms into Radio's Greatest Production," *Broadcasting*, July 1, 1940, 57.
20. "The Stars Unite in War Work: Six English Actors Give Ambulances," *Evening Post*, October 5, 1940, 17.
21. Si Steinhauser, "Tech Grad Is Star of Networks," *The Pittsburgh Press*, March 4, 1940, 30.
22. "Radio Programs & Stars: Screen Stars in Connolly Drama of Lincoln Today," *The Philadelphia Inquirer*, March 2, 1941, 136.
23. "Claire Trevor on 'Playhouse'" *The Greenville News* (South Carolina), March 2, 1952, 17.
24. Walter Kirby, "Better Radio Programs for the Week," *The Decatur Daily Review* (Illinois), June 8, 1952, 44.
25. Si Steinhauser, "Air Stage Men Rate Top Stars: Screen Guild Players Judged by Workers," *the Pittsburgh Press*, March 24, 1941, 9.
26. "Friday's Highlights," *Radio and TV Mirror*, July 1940, 52.
27. Harrison Carroll: "Behind the Scenes in Hollywood," *Ogdensburg Journal*, January 12, 1949, 9.
28. Walter Ames, "Irene Dunne Set as Hostess of New Film Play Series; Local Theater Going Video," *The Los Angeles Times*, April 24, 1952, 27.
29. "Calls Claire 'Oral Stripteaser'" *Brooklyn Daily Eagle*, October 13, 1950, 11.

30. "Hollywood," *Lubbock Morning Avalanche,* October 20, 1950, 8.
31. "Ida Lupino Gives Advice to Hopefuls," *The Brooklyn Daily Eagle,* June 28, 1951, 5.
32. Irene Thirer, "Screen News and Views: Film Fans Scare Claire Trevor, Not the War," *New York Post,* December 15, 1941, 22.
33. "The Claire Trevor Collection," https://www.otrcat.com/p/claire-trevor.

Chapter 8

1. Freda Bruce-Lockhart, "Elusive Stardom: Indictment of Hollywood's Failure to Give Talent Its Opportunity: Screen Players Who Unaccountably Fail," *New Zealand Herald,* April 23, 1938, 14.
2. Eyman. Scott *Print the Legend: The Life and Times of John Ford* (New York: Simon & Schuster, 2011), 94.
3. Bogdanovitch, Peter *John Ford* (Berkeley: University of California Press, 1978), 69.
4. Interview, *DGA Action Magazine,* September-October, 1971, 33.
5. Dennis McLellan, "Memories of a Trailblazer: 60 Years Later, Claire Trevor Recounts Making of 'Stagecoach.'" *Los Angeles Times,* March 28, 1999, 56.
6. "Three Day Old Baby Youngest in Movies," *The San Bernardino Sun,* December 22, 1938, 2.
7. "Revered by Performers as Living Legend," *The Southeast Missourian,* December 4, 1971, 22.
8. Sheilah Graham, "Hollywood Gadabout," *The Milwaukee Journal,* September 3, 1939, 23.
9. Roberts, Randy & Olson, James S. *John Wayne American* (Lincoln, NE: University of Nebraska Press, 1995), 161.
10. Michael Munn *John Wayne: The Man Behind the Myth* (London: Robson Books, 2005), 62-3.
11. "Round the Studios," *New Zealand Herald,* March 11, 1939, 18.
12. "She Has Schizophrenia!" *Auckland Star,* June 24, 1939, 7.
13. Interview, *DGA Action Magazine,* Sep-Oct 1971, 33.
14. Hank Whittemore, "My Life in Hollywood's Golden Age," *Parade Magazine, Reading Eagle,* February 20, 1994, 14-15. Philip K. Scheuer, "Fates Still Fickle to Claire Trevor: Jinx Dogs Career of Actress Despite Brilliant Screen Roles," *The Los Angeles Times,* August 12, 1941, 25.
15. Michael Munn *John Wayne: The Man Behind the Myth* (London: Robson Books, 2005), 58.
16. Louis Reid, "A Really Good Bad Girl," *Modern Screen,* June 1950, 42.
17. Louella O. Parsons, "Favored Story Finally Reaches Movie," *The Deseret News,* July 5, 1939, 21.
18. "Claire Trevor," *Variety,* January 4, 1939, 29.
19. "Superb Acting," *Press,* March 31, 1939, 5.
20. Louella O. Parsons, "Movies Again Making Offer to Toscanini," *The Milwaukee Sentinel,* October 11, 1938, 14.
21. "Size-Ups," *Film Bulletin,* May 20, 1939, 10.
22. Louella O. Parsons, "Laughton Make-Up Expected to Out-Terrify Lon Chaney," *The Philadelphia Inquirer,* December 11, 1939, 8.

23. Douglas W. Churchill, "Screen News Here and There in Hollywood," *New York Times,* November 20, 1939, 21.
24. Gevinson, Alan *Within Our Gates: Ethnicity in American Feature Films 1911–60* (Berkeley, CA: University of California Press, 1997), 403.
25. "Movie World: Claire Trevor Takes a Honeymoon," *The Australian Women's Weekly,* October 15, 1938, 21.
26. "Best Performances: English Choice of Finest Players," *New Zealand Herald,* July 15, 1940, 10.
27. "In the Flesh," *The Film Daily,* May 11, 1939, 7.
28. "Devil's Isle Prisoner Is Champion Film Fan," *The Montreal Gazette,* May 9, 1939, 16.
29. Edwin Schallert, "Movieland Jottings," *The Los Angeles Times,* July 21, 1939, 15.
30. Edwin Schallert, "Grant May Be Costar of De Mille Feature," *The Los Angeles Times,* December 16, 1939, 23.
31. Edwin Schallert, "Hollywood," *The Los Angeles Times,* December 1, 1939, 18.
32. Betty Crocker, "Easy as Pie," *Hollywood,* January 1942, 44.
33. Ben Madox, "Love Is First with Me," May 1939, 73.
34. Grace Wilcox: "For Party People," *The Watchman,* February 24, 1938, 16.
35. "In Hollywood," *Arizona Republic,* May 9, 1937, 37.
36. Sidney Skolsky, "Claire, the 'Shady Lady'" *New York Evening Post,* December 6, 1943, 23.
37. Critchlow, Donald T. *When Hollywood Was Right: How Movie Stars, Studio Moguls, and Big Business Remade American Politics* (New York: Cambridge University Press, 2013), 67.
38. Edith Dietz, "Notes on the 'Discovery' of an Actress: This Trevor Girl Makes Her Own Fame in Films," *The Long Island Sunday Press: Screen & Radio Weekly,* August 11, 1935, 5.

Chapter 9

1. "TCM Notes: I Stole a Million (1939)," http://www.tcm.com/tcmdb/title/78873/i-stole-a-million/notes.html.
2. "The Shadow Stage: I Stole a Million—Universal," *Photoplay,* October 1938, 90.
3. "'I Stole a Million' Fair Melodramatic Program, *Film Bulletin,* August 26, 1939, 6.
4. "Actress, Guinea Pig in Film Experiment," *The Pittsburgh Press,* July 22, 1939, 6.
5. "Stars Go for Ice Cream Sodas," *The Times* (Hammond, Indiana), June 18, 1939, 49.
6. "Sues Universal," *Motion Picture Daily,* February 15, 1940, 8.
7. "Wife and Daughter of Late Train Robber Sue Movie Company," *Albuquerque Journal,* February 14, 1940, 1.
8. "Young Woman Asserts Film Reveals Past," *San Bernardino Sun,* February 15, 1940, 8.
9. Short, K.R.M. *Colonial History & Anglo-American Tension: Allegheny Uprising & Drums Along the Mohawk: Film Historia Vol VI No 1* (1996), 1–16.
10. Munn, Michael *John Wayne: The Man Behind the Myth* (London: Robson Books, 2005), 74.
11. Kaspar Monahan, "Show Shops: Former 'Queen of the B's' Is Premiere Queen Now," *Pittsburgh Press,* November 3, 1939, 15.

12. "Becomes Collector," *The Los Angeles Times*, December 21, 1939, 9.
13. "'It's a Pipe' Says Imitator of Dogpatch Custom: Film Star to Start Dukes in Sadie Hawkins Role," *The Pittsburgh Press*, October 27, 1939, 48.
14.{en} "'Uprising' Preen in Pittsburgh Draws Press & Radio Help," *Variety*, November 8, 1939, 8.
15. "Davis Youth Selected as Cowboy King," *The San Bernardino County Sun*, April 9, 1939, 13.
16. "Fair Finales: New York Fair Finales to $15,000,000 Gross Receipts at the Gate," *Variety*, October 25, 1939, 1, 12.
17. Robbin Coons, "Actress' Failure to Reach Stardom Puzzles Columnist," *Toledo Blade*, August 5, 1940, 25.
18. Munn, Michael *John Wayne: The Man Behind the Myth* (London: Robson Books, 2005), 360.
19. Munn, Michael *John Wayne: The Man Behind the Myth* (London: Robson Books, 2005), 75.
20. "TCM Notes: Dark Command (1940)," http://www.tcm.com/tcmdb/title/72283/Dark-Command/notes.html.
21. "Hollywood Program Notes from the Studios," *Showmen's Trade Review*, January 20, 1940, 18.
22. "Republic's $500,000 Budget for Wayne," *Variety*, October 18, 1939, 18.
23. "Round the Studios," *New Zealand Herald*, May 4, 1940, 18.
24. Douglas W. Churchill, "Screen Notes Here and There," *The Film Daily*, June 2, 1940, 21.
25. Douglas W. Churchill, "Screen News from Here and There," *The Film Daily*, March 4, 1940, 20.
26. Douglas W. Churchill, "Screen News Here and There: Virginia Replaces," *The Film Daily*, April 19, 1940, 2.
27. Louella O. Parsons, "Alan Jones Starred in Jerome Kern Musical," *St Louis Post-Dispatch*, September 8, 1940, 54.
28. Eames, John Douglas *The MGM Story* (New York: Octopus Books, 1979), 169.
29. "Claire Trevor, a 'Shady Lady' Returns," *Chicago Tribune*, March 6, 1987, 128.
30. Shirley Eder, "'Kiss Me Goodbye,' Brought Claire Trevor Back to Films," *Toledo Blade*, February 26, 1983, 16.
31. "Claire Trevor Chosen for Role in 'Achilles'" *The Pittsburgh Press*, September 9, 1941, 11.
32. Jimmie Fidler, "'Ziegfeld Girl' Ponderous, but It Dazzles with Pretty Girls," *St Petersburg Times*, April 21, 1941, 11.
33. "Claire Trevor and Brian Donlevy May Be Teamed in 'Let the Eagle Scream'" August 7, 1941 *The New York Times*, 23.
34. "Washington Holiday Dip Chips 'Out West' to $8,500," *Variety*, December 18, 1940, 51.
35. Edwin Schallert, "In Hollywood," *Los Angeles Times*, August 18, 1940, 25.
36. Jimmie Fidler, "In Hollywood," *The Los Angeles Times*, September 15, 1941, 36.
37. Anne Jeffreys, "On Hollywood Lots," *The St Louis Star & Times*, November 24, 1946, 84.
38. "'Bad Girl' Roles Are Pretty Good, Says Claire Trevor," *The Brooklyn Daily Eagle*, November 2, 1941, 5.
39. "Screen News Here and There in Hollywood," *New York Times*, December 22, 1941, 12.
40. "Production to Start on March 3 on 'Let Rafters Ring,'" *New York Times*, February 7, 1941, 14.
41. "Notes from Hollywood," *Motion Picture Daily*, December 31, 1941, 5.
42. Dennis McLellan, "Claire Trevor Bren: A Hollywood Reputation," *The Los Angeles Times*, May 28, 1995, 80.
43. "Program Notes from the Studios," *Showmen's Trade Review*, November 15, 1941, 28.
44. Harold Lamb, "Hollywood," *Ogdensburg Journal*, November 12, 1941, 10.

Chapter 10

1. Irene Thirer, "Film Fans Scare Claire Trevor, She Admits, but Not the War," *New York Post*, December 15, 1941, 22.
2. Philip F. Crosland, "Perseverance Pays: Claire Trevor—B's to Biggies," *The News Journal* (Wilmington, Delaware), December 29, 1967, 3.
3. "Day's 49 Million in Bonds High for September Drive," *Motion Picture Daily*, September 16, 1942, 7.
4. "Four Feminine Stars Will Tour for 'Women at War'" *The Film Daily*, November 17, 1942, 1, 6.
5. Virginia Vale, "Star Dust: Stage, Screen, Radio," *Fort Covington Sun*, December 4, 1941, 4.
6. Jimmie Fidler, "Hollywood Shots," *Reading Eagle*, November 30, 1941, 24.
7. Louella Parsons, "From Hollywood," *The Los Angeles Times*, December 26, 1942, 6.
8. "Hollywood Party: 60 Lerdo Cadets Dance with Actresses, the *Bakersfield Californian*, December 1, 1941, 9.
9. Wiley Padan (Cartoon), "It's True," *The Daily Banner*, September 11, 1942, 4.
10. Irene Thirer, "Film Fans Scare Claire Trevor, She Admits, but Not the War," *New York Post*, December 15, 1941, 22.
11. Janette Davis: "Ray Hagen Interview with Stacey Bean," *The Washington Blade*, August 10, 2005. http://www.janettedavis.net/p/Ray_Hagen_interview_with_Stacey_Bean.php.
12. "In Hollywood," *The Indianapolis Star*, August 6, 1944, 21.
13. "Note on Youtube Clip from *Crossroads* (1942). Https://Www.Youtube.Com/Watch?V=45tf7zYMhYI
14. Barton, Ruth *Hedy Lamarr: The Most Beautiful Woman in the World* (Lexington, KY: The University Press of Kentucky, 2010), 128.
15. Druxman, Michael B. *Basil Rathbone: His Life and Films* (South Brunswick & New York: A.S. Barnes & Company, 1975), 260.
16. "Street of Chance," *Showmen's Trade Review*, October 3, 1942, 13.
17. "In Hollywood," *The Lincoln Star (Lincoln, Nebraska)*, March 1, 1942, 30.
18. "Star Purchases Movie Wardrobe," *The News Journal*, January 2, 1943, 17.
19. "Lady Was Prepared," *The Brooklyn Daily Eagle*, March 8, 1942, 42.
20. "Fox Will Make Film About Army Glider Pilots," *The New York Times*, August 8, 1942, 22.
21. Hedda Hopper, "Looking at Hollywood," *Toledo Blade*, March 25, 1943, 36.

22. "Priscilla Lane, George Brent Will Be Starred in 'Silver Saddle'" *New York Times,* March 20, 1942, 23.
23. "The Desperadoes [Advertising]," *Motion Picture Herald,* March 20, 1943, 24.
24. "On Location," *Hollywood,* December 1942, 12.
25. Virginia Vale "Star Dust: Stage, Screen, Radio," *The Long Island Traveler & Mattituck Watchman,* September 24, 1942, 6.
26. "Filmland Fanfare," *The Knickerbocker News,* September 24, 1942, A5.
27. Jimmie Fidler "In Hollywood," *The Long Island Daily Press,* November 21, 1941, 5.
28. "Broadway Bulletin," *Wilkes-Barre Record,* October 13, 1939, 18.
29. John Truesdell, "Candidly Yours: Hollywood By," *The Philadelphia Inquirer,* October 19, 1941, 43.
30. "Claire Trevor Wins Suit," *Ottawa Citizen,* July 9, 1942, 17.
31. "Claire Trevor Gets Divorce," *St Petersburg Times,* July 14, 1942, 15.
32. "Claire Trevor, Film Actress, Divorced," *San Bernardino Sun,* July 15, 1942, 19.
33. "Claire Trevor Divorces Producer," *Pittsburgh Post-Gazette,* July 14, 1942, 3.
34. "Claire Trevor Wins Uncontested Divorce," *Daytona Beach Morning Journal,* July 14, 1942, 5.
35. Louella O. Parsons "Small Grabs Rights to Story of Famed Irish Patriot," *The Fresno Bee the Republican,* November 22, 1942, 12.
36. Irene Thirer, "Screen News and Views: Claire Trevor, Screen Star, Rushes Home to Her Charlie," *New York Post,* February 24, 1945.
37. "Called Beyond After Brief Illness," *The Los Angeles Times,* December 5, 1915, 16.
38. "Claire Trevor Wed Secretly to Officer," *Oakland Tribune,* July 25, 1943, 1.
39. "Spencer Tracy Likely to Play Will Rogers on Screen," *St Petersburg Times,* April 1, 1942, 7.
40. Hugh Dixon, "The Monday Wash," *Pittsburgh Post-Gazette,* May 3, 1943, 15.
41. "Claire Trevor in Kansas City to Visit Husband," *Del Rio News Herald,* February 15, 1944, 1.
42. Irene Thirer, "Screen News and Views: Claire Trevor, Screen Star, Rushes Home to Her Charlie," *New York Post,* February 24, 1945, 10.
43. Sidney Skolsky, "Claire, the 'Shady Lady'" *New York Evening Post,* December 6, 1943, 23.
44. Glenn Hasselrouth "At the Mayflower: Good Luck, Mr. Yates," *Eugene Register-Guard,* August 27, 1943, 10.
45. Glenn Hasselrouth "At the Mayflower: Good Luck, Mr. Yates," *Eugene Register-Guard,* August 27, 1943, 10.
46. The Three Stooges Filmography: http://threestooges.net/filmography/episode/462.
47. Hedda Hopper, "Looking at Stars of Hollywood," *Buffalo Courier-Express,* January 28, 1943, 6.
48. "Claire Trevor: A Movie Star with a 'Real Life'" *The Los Angeles Times,* July 18, 1982, 287.
49. Janette Davis Dubbers List: http://www.janettedavis.net/Dubbers/dubberslist.php.
50. Virginia Vale, "Star Dust: Stage, Screen, Radio," *Fort Covington Sun,* July 15, 1943, 4.
51. Sheilah Graham, "Claire Trevor Hates Being 'Dance Hall Belle with Heart of Gold'," *The Atlanta Constitution,* June 28, 1943, 14.
52. "Film Land Briefs," *The Los Angeles Times,* June 16, 1943, 15.
53. Louella O. Parsons "Studio Seeks Talent for Follies Film," *The Philadelphia Inquirer,* April 28, 1943, 23.
54. Mell, Eila, *Casting Might-Have-Beens: A Film-By-Film Directory of Actors Considered for Roles Given to Others* (McFarland & Co. Inc., 2005), 231.
55. Hedda Hopper, "Cowan Seeks Helen Hayes for Picture," *Buffalo Courier-Express,* April 22, 1944, 6.
56. "Three's a Family: Farce Comedy by Phoebe and Henry Ephron Will Make Its Bow at Longacre Theater," *The Los Angeles Times,* May 4, 1943.

Chapter 11

1. "Claire Trevor Goal Is Lady Macbeth," *The Brooklyn Daily Eagle,* August 9, 1942, 38.
2. "Claire Trevor Is Murder Mystery Fan," *Asheville Citizen-Times (North Carolina),* January 31, 1954, 19.
3. Ellen Keneshea & Carl Macek, "Murder, My Sweet," Silver, Alain & Ward, Elizabeth *Film Noir* (London: Secker & Warburg, 1980),192–3.
4. Philip K. Scheuer, "Fates Still Fickle to Claire Trevor: Jinx Dogs Career of Actress Despite Brilliant Screen Roles," *The Los Angeles Times,* August 12, 1945, 25.
5. Philip K. Scheuer, "Fates Still Fickle to Claire Trevor: Jinx Dogs Career of Actress Despite Brilliant Screen Roles," *The Los Angeles Times,* August 12, 1945, 25.
6. Louella O. Parsons, "Claire Trevor May Climb to New Heights This Year," *The Los Angeles Times,* April 25, 1948, 65.
7. "Jean Renoir: Interviewed by Jacques Revette and Francois Truffaut," *Sight and Sound,* Summer 1954, 34.
8. Phil M. Daly, "Along the Rialto," *The Film Daily,* February 9, 1945, 8.
9. Jewell, Richard B. & Harbin, Vernon *The RKO Story* (New York: Octopus Books, 1983), 205.
10. Hazel Hartzog, "Film Work No Bed of Roses: Cruel Gag Upsets Actress Claire Trevor," *The Pittsburgh Press,* January 28, 1945, 27.
11. Marvin Miller interviewed by Fred Remington, "Pittsburgh Gets First Look at 'Maverick' Sunday," *The Pittsburgh Press,* January 10, 1958, 41.
12. Bob Thomas, "In Hollywood," *Spokane Daily Chronicle,* August 24, 1948, 24.
13. "Bachelor's Daughters," *Daytona Beach Morning Journal,* November 26, 1946, 5.
14. A.C. Edwards, Winema Theater, Scotia, California, "RKO Radio: Crack-Up," *Motion Picture Herald,* June 7, 1947, 45.
15. Robert Porffirio "Crack Up," in Silver, Alain & Ward, Elizabeth *Film Noir* (London: Secker & Warburg, 1980), 66.
16. "Stars' Property Stolen," *Daily Examiner,* November 4, 1946, 4.
17. "Crawley's Casting Calls: Claire Trevor," http://crawleyscastingcalls.com/index.php/component/actors/index.php?option=com_actors&Itemid=56&id=4209&lettre=T
18. Bob Singer "Hollywood Films," *The Philadelphia Inquirer,* December 9, 1942, 25.
19. "Broadway Openings: 'The Big Two'" *Billboard,* January 11, 1947, 45.

20. Linton Martin, "'Big Two' a New Comedy Presented at the Walnut," *The Philadelphia Inquirer*, December 10, 1946, 40.
21. Pete Peters, "Pete Peters Recommends: Stage," *Manhasset Press*, January 27, 1947, 8.
22. Edwin Schallert, "Trevor Stage Work Praised," *The Los Angeles Times*, July 26, 1946, A3.
23. "'Goodbye Again' Detroit Draw," August 30, 1947, 42.
24. Helen Bower, Drama: "'Goodbye Again' Makes Audience Forget Heat," *Detroit Free Press*, August 7, 1947, 13.
25. "Actress Divorce Granted," *Daily Review* (Hayward, CA), August 8, 1946, 1.
26. "Actress Divorce Granted," *Medford Mail Tribune*, August 9, 1946, 5.
27. "Fan Foils Secrecy in Claire Trevor Divorce Case," *Los Angeles Times*, August 9, 1946, 13.
28. "Actress Claire Trevor Gets Divorce in California," *The Lewiston Daily Sun*, August 9, 1946, 1.
29. "Actress Claire Trevor Wins Second Divorce," *Tucson Daily Citizen*, August 15, 1947, 4.
30. Louella O. Parsons, "Doesn't Live Roles Played, Says Claire," *The Philadelphia Inquirer*, August 8, 1948, 18.
31. "Fan Foils Secrecy in Claire Trevor Divorce Case," *Los Angeles Times*, August 9, 1946, 13.
32. Dorothy Kilgallen, "Hollywood," *Pittsburgh Post-Gazette*, October 9, 1946, 21.

Chapter 12

1. "RKO Radio," *The Independent Exhibitor's Film Bulletin*, October 15, 1945, 26.
2. Jewell, Richard B. & Harbin, Vernon *The RKO Story* (New York: Octopus Books, 1983), 219.
3. "Depinet View on Censored Film," *Motion Picture Daily*, April 9, 1947, 4.
4. "Review of 'Born to Kill'" *The New York Times*, May 1, 1947, 23. "Review of 'Born to Kill'" *The New York Times*, May 1, 1947, 23.
5. Robert Porfirio "Born to Kill," Silver, Alain & Ward, Elizabeth *Film Noir* (London: Secker & Warburg, 1980), 40.
6. Richard B. Jewell *Slow Fade to Black: The Decline of RKO Radio Pictures* (University of California Press, 2016), 57.
7. "Reviews: Born to Kill," *Motion Picture Daily*, April 21, 1947, 12.
8. Robert Porfirio, "Born to Kill," in Silver, Alain & Ward, Elizabeth *Film Noir* (London: Secker & Warburg, 1980), 40.
9. Louis Reid, "A Really Good Bad Girl," June 1950, 45.
10. Marsha Hunt, Interview Q & A Noir City 5, San Francisco; Eddie Muller (host), January 2007. https://www.youtube.com/watch?v=taUMhHWY6DQ
11. "Mystery: "Follow Me Quietly"" *The Film Daily*, September 10, 1947, 5.
12. Lew Shaeffer, "'Velvet Touch' a Slick Thriller; Criterion's Weak Civil War Drama," *The Brooklyn Daily Eagle*, August 26, 1948, 4.
13. Louella O. Parsons, "Doesn't Live Roles Played Says Claire," *The Philadelphia Inquirer*, August 8, 1948, 18.
14. Sheilah Graham "In Hollywood Today," *The Indianapolis Star*, October 31, 1947, 24.
15. Hedda Hopper, "Looking at Hollywood," *The Los Angeles Times*, August 28, 1947, 16.
16. Helen Barrett, "Film and Theater Gossip," *The News Journal*, February 2, 1948, 21.
17. Helen Bower, "Star Gazing: Hughes' 'Flying Boat' Inspired Film Idea," *Detroit Free Press*, August 10, 1947, 25.

Chapter 13

1. "Jaquo: Re-Inventing Key Largo," http://jaquo.com/re-inventing-key-largo/
2. Huston, John *An Open Book* (London: Macmillan, 1981), 75.
3. Nolan, William *John Huston: King Rebel* (Los Angeles: Sherbourne Press, 1965), 87.
4. Televised interview with Claire Trevor, February 8, 2012: https://www.youtube.com/watch?v=m9WaPkrF1GU
5. Grobel, Laurence *The Hustons: The Life and Times of a Hollywood Dynasty* (New York: Skyhorse Publishing, 2014), 312.
6. Grobel, Laurence *The Hustons: The Life and Times of a Hollywood Dynasty* (New York: Skyhorse Publishing, 2014), 314.
7. Bacall, Lauren *By Myself and Then Some* (New York: Harper Collins, 2005), 115.
8. Grobel, Laurence *The Hustons: The Life and Times of a Hollywood Dynasty* (New York: Skyhorse Publishing, 2014), 311.
9. "Claire Trevor, a 'Shady Lady' Returns," *Chicago Tribune*, March 6, 1987, 128.
10. Sperber, A.M. *Bogart: The Biography* (London: Weidenfeld & Nicholson, 1997). 310.
11. Schatz, Thomas *The Genius of the System: Hollywood Filmmaking in the Studio Era* (New York: Henry Holt & Co., 1998), 417.
12. See *Recordings*.
13. Article *Movie Maker*, March 17, 2013: James Kaelan, "Humphrey Bogart Film Festival: Bogie Returns to Key Largo for This Beach Side Festival," http://www.moviemaker.com/archives/festivals/humphrey-bogart-film-festival-bogie-returns-to-key-largo-for-this-beach-side-festival-by-mm-editors/
14. "Actress Weds Producer," *The Niagara Falls Gazette*, November 15, 1948, 4.
15. "Rites Held for Film Producer Milton H. Bren," *The Los Angeles Times*, December 19, 1979, 233.
16. Hank Whittemore, "My Life in Hollywood's Golden Age," *Parade Magazine Reading Eagle*, February 20, 1994, 14–15.
17. Louis Reed, "A Really Good Bad Girl," *Screenland*, June 1950, 72.
18. ""Kiss Me," Role Fills Gap for Miss Trevor, Bridges," *The Pittsburgh Press*, January 3, 1983, B5.
19. Guy K. Austin, "Hollywood Budget," *The Sun*, March 20, 1947, 33.
20. "She Has Schizophrenia!" *Auckland Star*, June 24, 1939, 21.

21. Hedda Hopper, "News Items Hot from Hollywood," *The Pittsburgh Press,* January 22, 1948, 16.
22. George Fisher, "In Hollywood: Premature Story on Trip to Korea Angers Bob Hope," *St Petersburg Times,* September 16 1950 19.
23. "Robert Mitchum Plans a Stage Play While Waiting to Make Another Picture," *The Milwaukee Journal,* January 2, 1949, 93.
24. "Flamingo Road Adds Claire Trevor," July 17, 1948, 6.
25. Edith Gwynn, "'The Champion' Is Example of Quality, Economy," *St Petersburg Times,* March 17, 1949, 37.
26. Erskine Johnson, "In Hollywood," *The Victoria Advocate,* February 25, 1948, 8.
27. "Filmdom Chatterbox," *Toledo Blade,* May 18, 1949, 43.
28. "In and Out of the Hollywood Studios," *Ottawa Citizen,* September 3, 1949, 19.
29. Keenan, Richard C. *The Films of Robert Wise* (Lanham, Maryland: Scarecrow Press, 2007), 48.
30. "Ansco Color Film to Be Used in Five Movies," *Endicott Daily Bulletin,* January 24, 1948, 3.
31. Hedda Hopper "Gregory Peck Set to Start Job Monday in Yellow Sky," *Buffalo Courier-Express,* May 21, 1948, 10.
32. "Movieland," *Los Angeles Times,* January 26, 1948, 20.
33. Claire Trevor, "Hollywood's Mrs. Babe Ruth Talks About the Babe!" *Screenland,* September 1948, 70.
34. Harold V. Cohen, "New Film: 'Babe Ruth Story,' With William Bendix, Comes to Stanley," *Pittsburgh Post-Gazette,* September 10, 1948, 21.
35. Bosley Crowther, "The Screen: 'The Babe Ruth Story,' Starring William Bendix as Baseball Hero, Opens at Astor," July 27, 1948, 23.
36. Mrs. Babe Ruth with Bill Slocum, "The Babe and I—Conclusion," *The Evening Independent,* April 9, 1959, 3-A.
37. Oscar Fraley, "Former Yank Batboy Spanked by Bambino," *Sarasota Journal,* January 27, 1960, 12.
38. Mrs. Babe Ruth with Bill Slocum, "The Babe and I—Conclusion," *The Evening Independent,* April 9, 1959, 3-A.
39. "'Babe Ruth Story' Opens at Strand," *The Knickerbocker News* (Albany, New York), September 16, 1948, 10-A.
40. Hedda Hopper, "Zanuck Plans Lengthy Film Tour Abroad: Northwest Mounted Police Movie Sought."
41. "Hollywood Vine-Yard," *The Film Daily,* February 26, 1948, 8.
42. Edwin Schallert, "Movieland," *Los Angeles Times,* April 6, 1949, 45.
43. Edwin Schallert, "'Handle with Care' Packaged for Claire Trevor, *Los Angeles Times,* May 18, 1949, 31.
44. Edwin Schallert, "Claire Trevor for Summer Stock," *Los Angeles Times,* May 3, 1949, 31.
45. Al Salerno, "Brooklyn and Broadway Night Life," *The Brooklyn Daily Eagle,* November 5, 1950, 34.
46. Louella O. Parsons, "Hollywood," *Times-Union,* February 21, 1949, 4.
47. Edwin Schallert, "Movieland," *Los Angeles Times,* April 8, 1948, 23.
48. Thomas F. Brady, "Keyes Suspension Ends at Columbia," *New York Times,* April 20, 1949, 21.
49. Thomas F. Brady, "Reagan Refusing Role at Columbia," *New York Times,* April 21, 1949, 23.

Chapter 14

1. Virginia Macpherson, "Hilton Makes Up List of Folks He'd Take to Shangri-La," *Idaho State Journal,* April 24, 1950, 10.
2. Harrison Carroll, "Behind the Scenes in Hollywood," *Ogdensburg Journal,* June 3, 1949, 2.
3. Jimmie Fidler. "In Hollywood," *News-Press* (Fort Myers, Florida), July 19, 1949, 4.
4. "3 Big Hits with King Cole Trio at Walker Theater Sunday," *Indianapolis Recorder,* August 26, 1950, 12.
5. Erskine Johnson "Hollywood Growing Pains Hurt. Margaret O'brien Has Them," *Plattsburgh Press-Republican,* June 20, 1949, 8.
6. "In Hollywood," *Chicago Tribune,* January 29, 1950, 117.
7. Louis Reed, "A Really Good Bad Girl," *Screenland,* June 1950, 70.
8. "Barbara Fuller (Item)" *Pottsdown Barbarmercury* (Pottsdown, Pennsylvania), February 28, 1950, 4.
9. "Shooting Coup," (Picture and caption) *The Philadelphia Inquirer,* January 22, 1950, 85.
10. Louis Reed, "A Really Good Bad Girl," *Screenland,* June 1950, 70.
11. Louis Reed, "A Really Good Bad Girl," *Screenland,* June 1950, 70.
12. "Robert Donat Reported Pursued," *The Los Angeles Times,* December 3, 1949, 11.
13. Thomas M. Pryor, "Film Team Plans Two More Pics," *The Film Daily,* July 31, 1951, 32.
14. Louella O. Parsons, "Bob Taylor May Act with La Hayworth," *The Philadelphia Inquirer,* September 11, 1948, 9.
15. Cocteau, Jean *Past Tense: Diaries Vol 1* (London: Hamish Hamilton, 1987), 36.
16. Danton Walker, *The Philadelphia Inquirer,* December 4, 1950, 23.
17. "Binnie Barnes," *Los Angeles Times,* November 20, 1950, 75.
18. Edwin Schallert, "Movieland," *Los Angeles Times,* August 21, 1950, 26.
19. "Writers' Show Tosses Barbs at Hollywood," *Daytona Beach Morning Journal,* February 26, 1951, 4.
20. Louella O. Parsons, "Louella Parsons Says," *Times-Union,* February 23, 1951, 6.
21. "Ida Lupino Gives Advice to Hopefuls," *The Brooklyn Daily Eagle,* June 28, 1951, 5.
22. "No Breeze Making Tennis Champ of Toe Dancer," *The Brooklyn Daily Eagle,* July 1, 1951, 27.
23. Donati, William *Ida Lupino: A Biography* (Lexington, KY: University Press of Kentucky, 1996), 175.
24. James Padgett, *Long Beach Independent,* September 26, 1950, 29.
25. Erskine Johnson, "Claire Trevor Plays Scenes for Real," *The Saratogian,* November 18, 1950, 1.
26. Erskine Johnson "In Hollywood: Russell Thrilled at Possibility of Starring with Clark Gable," *Plattsburgh Press-Review,* October 6, 1950, 10.
27. Edith Gwynn, "Hollywood," *Pottsdown Mercury* (Pottsdown, Pensylvania), Jul 10, 1950. 4.

28. Hagen, Ray &Wagner, Laura *Killer Tomatoes: Fifteen Tough Film Dames* (Jefferson, NC: McFarland & Co, Inc., 2004), 114.
29. Erskine Johnson, "Claire Trevor Scenes for Real," *The Saratogian*, November 10, 1950, 1.
30. Erskine Johnson, "In Hollywood," *Dunkirk Evening Observer*, July 20, 1950, 15.
31. Hedda Hopper, "In Hollywood," *The Pittsburgh Press*, July 27, 1950, 21.
32. Erskine Johnson, "In Hollywood," *Plattsburgh Press-Republican*, August 25, 1950, 6. Donati, William *Ida Lupino: A Biography* (Lexington, KY: University Press of Kentucky, 1996), 173.
33. Edwin Schallert, "Movieland Jottings," *Los Angeles Times*, November 7, 1950, 43.
34. W.E.J. Martin, "Idiosyncrasy of Players in Up Any Time," *Buffalo Courier-Express*, April 15, 1951, 25.
35. "Claire Trevor Likes Lupino Directing," *Rochester Democrat & Chronicle*, June 27, 1951, 11.
36. Hedda Hopper, "Movieland Jottings," *Los Angeles Times*, May 23, 1950, 30.
37. Hedda Hopper, "Robinson Touted for Reinhardt Role," *Los Angeles Times*, August 31, 1950, 17.
38. Inez Gerhard, "Star Dust: Stage, Screen, Radio," *Cape Vincent Eagle*, September 21, 1950, 7.
39. "Claire Trevor's Son Disrupts Film Scene," *Buffalo Courier-Express*, December 10, 1950, 6-C.
40. Edwin Schallert, "'Sweet Girl' Role Desired by Claire Trevor," *The Los Angeles Times*, November 4, 1951, E3.
41. "Adler Isn't Afraid of Real Gangster Role," *The Saratogian*, October 30, 1951, 23.
42. Edwin Schallert, "Hollywood in Review: 'Sweet Girl' Role Desired by Trevor," *The Los Angeles Times*, November 4, 1951, 124.
43. Edwin Schallert, "Hollywood in Review: 'Sweet Girl' Role Desired by Trevor," *The Los Angeles Times*, November 4, 1951, 124.
44. Erskine Johnson: "In Hollywood," *Ogdensburg Journal*, March 16, 1949, 9.
45. "Irving Ravetch Dies, 'Hud' Screenwriter," *The Day*, September 21, 2010: https://www.pressreader.com.
46. Hedda Hopper, "Powell, Webb, to Star in 'Happy Scoundrel' the *Los Angeles Times*, December 12, 1952, 77.
47. Edwin Schallert, "'Odette' Starring Neagle Spy Feature of Quality," *The Los Angeles Times*, June 28, 1951, 36.
48. "Chaplin to Stay Away Six Months," *The Spokesman-Review*, November 13, 1952, 5. Hedda Hopper, "Leo Mccarey Happy Over Getting Helen Hayes for Role," *The Los Angeles Times*, Jan 31, 1951,35.
49. Edwin Schallert, "'Cabin on Hill' to Give Claire Trevor Big Role," *The Brooklyn Daily Eagle*, April 9, 1952, 11.
50. Sheilah Graham "Claire Trevor Plans a Career in Television with Her Own Show," *The Courier-Journal* (Louisville, Kentucky), July 8, 1951, 55.
51. Louella O. Parsons, "Hollywood Today: 'Letter from President' to Star Claire Trevor," *Arizona Republic*, March 10, 1952, 17.
52. "TCM Notes: My Man & I (1952)," http://www.tcm.com/tcmdb/title/1918/My-Man-and-I/notes.html.
53. *Stop, You're Killing Me* (1952) Trivia," http://www.imdb.com/title/tt0045193/trivia?ref_=tt_trv_trv.
54. "New Films Return to Damon Runyon Stop You're Killing Me," March 23, 1953, 2.
55. "Salmon Spread," *Pittsburgh Post-Gazette*, September 3, 1952, 12.
56. "Great Fire in Studio Thought to Be Arsonist's Work," *Santa Cruz Sentinel*, July 10, 1952, 12.
57. "Glamor Assignment Planned for Trevor," *Los Angeles Times*, February 3, 1951, 10.
58. Erskine Johnson "Flicker Flashes from Filmland," *The Southeast Missourian*, July 9, 1953, 4.
59. Hedda Hopper, "Hollywood: Jean Simmons Special Films Despite Battle with RKO," *Buffalo Courier-Express*, July 10, 1952, 8.
60. Edwin Schallert, "Hollywood in Review: 'Sweet Girl' Role Desired by Trevor," *The Los Angeles Times*, November 4, 1951, 124.

Chapter 15

1. "Glasgow Cinemas by Our Film Critic: Scotland Loses Screen Film School," *The Glasgow Herald*, January 10, 1955, 7.
2. Davis, Ronald L. *Duke: The Life and Legend of John Wayne* (Norman, OK: University of Oklahoma Press, 1998), 18.
3. Harold Heffernan, "Hollywood Stars Appraise Stars in 'High and Mighty' the *Long Island Star-Journal*, January 5, 1954, 13.
4. Aline Mosby, "'High and Mighty' Had Cinderella Beginning," *The Pittsburgh Press*, July 9, 1954, 11.
5. Munn, Michael *John Wayne: The Man Behind the Myth* (London: Robson Books, 2005), 166.
6. Gene Handsaker. "Hollywood Sights and Sounds," *Prescott Evening Courier*, July 5, 1949, 4.
7. "More Stars Due in Argentina," *The Indiana Gazette* (Indiana, Pennsylvania), March 1, 1954, 17.
8. Philip F. Crosland, "Perseverance Pays: Claire Trevor—B's to Biggies," *The News Journal* (Wilmington, Delaware), December 29, 1967, 3.
9. Erskine Johnson, "Hollywood: Movies—TV—Radio," *The Daily Herald* (Provo, Utah), June 20, 1954, 13.
10. "Producers Pick Up Option on 'Tycoon'" *New York Times*, June 1, 1954, 24.
11. Michael L. Schlesinger *'Johnny Guitar'* Library of Congress, nd. https://www.loc.gov/programs/static/national-film-preservation-board/documents/johnny_guitar2.pdf.
12. Eileen Mosby, "Winner of Oscar Returns to Screen for Part in 'Giant'" *Shamokin News-Dispatch* (Shamokin, Pennsylvania), October 25, 1956, 19.
13. Hedda Hopper, "Hollywood: Janet Blair May Get Part in 'Buster Keaton Story,'" *Buffalo Courier-Express*, May 17, 1956, 16.
14. "Rummage Sale Almost Real," *Eugene Register-Guard*, October 29, 1954, 5B.
15. Hedda Hopper "Hollywood: Dorothy Mcguire Booked to Star with Gary Cooper," *The Buffalo Courier-Express*, July 30, 1955, 8.
16. Sheilah Graham "Hollywood Gadabout's Diary," *Pittsburgh Post-Gazette*, August 9, 1955, 14.
17. "'Oh, Men, Oh, Women!' Next at Playhouse," *Chula Vista Star-News*, August 18, 1955, 19.
18. Edwin Schallert, "Claire Trevor Scores in 'Time

of the Cuckoo' the *Los Angeles Times*, August 12, 1955, 61.

19. "Mrs. Marberry of Carbondale Ends Vacation," *Southern Illinoisan*, September 2, 1955, 6.

20. "The Boys Get the Breaks ... the Girls? That 'One-Dimension Treatment,'" *The Singapore Free Press*, January 7, 1956, 12.

21. "The Boys Get the Breaks ... the Girls? That 'One-Dimension Treatment,'" *The Singapore Free Press*, January 7, 1956, 12.

22. Hedda Hopper, "Hollywood: Ingrid Bergman Plans Film with Yul Brynner," *Buffalo Courier-Express*, August 14, 1957, 8.

23. Curtis, James *Spencer Tracy: A Biography* (New York: Hutchinson, 2011), 695.

24. Halliwell, Leslie *Halliwell's Film Guide* (London: Guild Publishing Ltd, 1983), 562.

25. Curtis, James *Spencer Tracy: A Biography* (New York: Hutchinson, 2011), 704.

26. "Claire Trevor Gets Starring Role in "Dodsworth"" *Logansport Pharos-Tribune* (Indiana), April 22, 1956, 13.

27. Sheilah Graham, "Claire Trevor Toots Horn for Hollywood," *The Indianapolis Star*, July 8, 1951, 81.

28. Hedda Hopper, "General Bradley Paid Tribute by Columnist," *Buffalo Courier-Express*, May 24, 1951, 27. Hedda Hopper, "General Bradley Paid Tribute by Columnist," *Buffalo Courier-Express*, May 24, 1951, 27.

29. "Rising Debbie Reynolds Gets Role in Tracy Picture," *Democrat & Chronicle*, January 11, 1951, 12.

30. "Charity Group Will Hold Square Dance," *The Los Angeles Times*, May 25, 1949, 34.

31. "Lunch to Aid Vista Del Mar Home," *The Los Angeles Times*, March 7, 1952, 53.

32. "International Mother's Day Lunch," (Caption with picture), *The Los Angeles Times*, May 6, 1953, 70.

33. Charles Denton, "Claire Trevor About Ready to Retire," *News-Journal* (Mansfield, Ohio), April 22, 1956, 37.

34. Gerry Fitzgerald, "Being Bad on Film Is Good Thing to Claire," *Press & Sun-Bulletin* (Binghampton, New York), June 6, 1952, 22.

35. "Barbara Wants Out," *The Ottawa Journal*, May 18, 1957, 10.

36. Erskine Johnson, "Hollywood Today: Movies-TV-Radio," *Park City Daily News*, December 9, 1957, 3.

37. Hedda Hopper "Robert Ryan to Play Role as Captain of Freighter," *Buffalo Courier-Express*, October 7, 1957, 8.

38. Lydia Lane "Claire Trevor Gives on Topic of Youthfulness," *The Los Angeles Times*, April 15, 1951,108.

39. "Claire Trevor Inherits Estate," *The Los Angeles Times*, November 1, 1958, 32.

Chapter 16

1. "KFI Television Station Will Open Tonight," *The San Bernardino County Sun*, October 6, 1948, 2.

2. Erskine Johnson, "In Hollywood: Paramount Plans Musical with Crosby and Met's Mimi Benzell," *Plattsburgh Press-Republican*, October 4, 1950, 9.

3. Don Tranter": Comment on Radio-TV," *Buffalo Courier-Express*, September 3, 1951, 48.

4. Erskine Johnson, *Saratogian*, July 22, 1952, 22.

5. "Screen News," *The Pittsburgh Courier*, November 29, 1952, 17.

6. Dick Osgood, "Arnold Gets Excited About New TV Show," *Detroit Free Press*, May 16, 1952, 37.

7. Erskine Johnson, "In Hollywood," *Dixon Evening Telegraph*, February 6, 1952, 4.

8. Sheilah Graham "Claire Trevor Plans a Career in Television with Her Own Show," *The Courier-Journal* (Louisville, Kentucky), July 8, 1951, 55.

9. "TV Key: 9:30 Pm. Ch. 4 Ford Theater 'Summer Memory'" *Brooklyn Daily Eagle*, November 18, 1954, 20.

10. "Claire Trevor Gets Nervous on TV but Likes It," *The Call-Leader (Elwood, Indiana)*, June 21, 1956, 6.

11. "Claire Trevor Gets Starring Role in "Dodsworth"" *Logansport Pharos-Tribune* (Indiana), April 22, 1956, 13.

12. Erskine Johnson, "Johnson in Hollywood: Substitutes for Abbott Costello Use Own Routine," *Long Beach Independent*, January 18, 1954, 18.

13. "Claire Trevor Nixes Television Series," *The Pittsburgh Post-Gazette*, February 12, 1954, 20.

14. Jack Gold "TV Review: March, Claire Trevor, Excellent in 'Dodsworth'" *Buffalo Courier-Express*, May 1, 1956, 7.

15. "Claire Trevor to Appear in TV Play 'Dodsworth'" *The Los Angeles Times*, April 29, 1956, 111.

16. "Soothing Words Help Out in Dressing Stars of Shows," *Buffalo Courier-Express*, November 14, 1956, 3.

17. "Previews: Climax: "The Prowler"" *The Minneapolis Star*, January 5, 1956, 47.

18. Bill Lundigan (Letter) "TV Ballyhoo Department," *The Amarillo Globe-Times*, January 4, 1956, 14.

19. Hedda Hopper, "The Hollywood Scene," *Elmira Star-Gazette*, January 12, 1956, 32.

20. "Teacher of Blind Kidnapped in 'Foolproof' Plot," *The Daily Herald*, January 9, 1956, 16.

21. "TV Scout: JFK Addresses Nation; Tonight's Best Bet," *The Knickerbocker News*, July 28, 1961, 13A.

22. "Claire Adds 'Patsy' to Oscar and Emmy in 7 'Elizabeth' Roles," *The Philadelphia Inquirer*, April 12, 1957, 34.

23. "Claire Adds 'Patsy' to Oscar and Emmy in 7 'Elizabeth' Roles," *The Philadelphia Inquirer*, April 12, 1957, 34.

24. Walter Hawver, "TV-Radio in Review: Desilu Shows Have Stars, Little Glitter," *The Knickerbocker News* (Albany, New York), January 27, 1959, 23-A.

25. "10–11 Channel 2—Tonight—U.S. Steel Hour Drama "The Revolt of Judge Lloyd," *The Times-Herald* (Port Huron, Michigan), October 5, 1960, 30.

26. "9 PM, "Investigators"" *The Orlando Sentinel*, October 19, 1961, 40. ""The Investigators," (Adventure)" *The Indiana Gazette*, October 19, 1951, 40.

27. "Claire Trevor Guests on Thursday TV Show," *Pittsburgh Post-Gazette*, October 19, 1961, 51.

28. Erskine Johnson, "Claire Trevor, Son Combine Talents in Television Play," *The Times Daily*, November 26, 1962, 9.

Chapter 17

1. "On Broadway, Usual Optimism and More Plays than Theaters," *Ottawa Citizen*, September 13, 1958, 22.

2. Mike Connolly, "New York 19 Special," *The Desert Sun*, October 17, 1960, 4.

3. Louella Parsons, "Of Hollywood: Kathryn Grayson Returns," *Pittsburgh Post-Gazette,* June 11, 1960, 28.
4. Mike Connolly, "The Best of Hollywood," *The Philadelphia Inquirer,* August 12, 1961, 10.
5. Godard, Jean-Luc, Jean Narboni & Tom Milne [Eds] *Godard on Godard* (New York: Da Capo Press, 1972), 64.
6. Sheilah Graham, "Liz and Burton Team Again After 'Cleo'" *The Deseret News,* January 8, 1962, 7.
7. Erskine Johnson, "Claire Trevor, Son, Combine Talents in Television Play," *The Times Daily,* November 26, 1962, 9.
8. Elizabeth Mehrens, "Minnelli Remembered with a Sense of Love," *The Gainsville Sun,* September 21, 1986, 7B.
9. Verswijer, Leo, interview with Pat Boone in *Movies Were Always Magical: Interviews with 19 Actors, Directors and Producers from the Hollywood of the 1930s Through the 1950s* (Jefferson, NC: McFarland & Co, Inc., 2003),.
10. Mell, Eila, *Casting Might-Have-Beens: A Film-By-Film Directory of Actors Considered for Roles Given to Others* (Jefferson, NC: McFarland & Co. Inc., 2005), 231.
11. Hedda Hopper, "Claire Trevor Thinks Stars Aren't Real People; She Charges That Lazy Actors Have Ruined the Film Studios," *The Los Angeles Times,* July 24, 1962, 46.
12. Harold Heffernan, "Stars Need Social Introduction," *Toledo Blade,* June 15, 1962, 23.
13. Halliwell, Leslie, *Halliwell's Film Guide* (London: Guild Publishing, 1983), 393.
14. Philip F. Crosland, "Perseverance Pays: Claire Trevor—B's to Biggies," *The News Journal* (Wilmington, Delaware) December 29, 1967, 3.
15. Barney Glazer, "Off the Grapevine: Hollywood," *Toledo Blade,* February 22, 1968,.
16. Leonard Lyons, "The Lyons Den," *The Pittsburgh Press,* November 16, 1967, 23.
17. William Glover, "Claire Trevor to Make Stage Return," *The Montreal Gazette,* January 16, 1968, 14.
18. William Glover, "Claire Trevor to Make Stage Return," *The Montreal Gazette,* November 17, 1967, 34.
19. Sheilah Graham, "Hollywood," *Waterton Times* (Wilmington, Delaware), December 26, 1967, 21.
20. "Filmland's Favorite Tough Girl, Claire Trevor, Returns to the Stage," *Advance-News,* January 14, 1968, 16.
21. "Theater Potpourri," *The News* (Frederick, Maryland), January 8, 1968, 4.
22. Henry S. Humphries, "Soap Opera Star "Killed Off," In Puzzling Shubert 'Comedy'" *The Cincinnati Enquirer,* January 16, 1968, 13.
23. Gary Salt, "Review: 'Sister George' Is Dead," *The Stanford Daily,* March 1, 1968, 7.
24. Baddeley, Hermione *The Unsinkable Hermione Baddeley* (London: William Collins Sons & Co. Ltd, 1984), 214–5.

Chapter 18

1. "Miss Trevor, Chuck Connors on 'Person to Person' Tonight," *Niagara Falls Gazette,* July 12, 1961, 15.
2. Family Search: 1: Charles D. Bren, 27 & Katharin A. Nauss, 24, married at Orange County, CA, May 22, 1971: https://familysearch.org/ark:/61903/1:1:V6VV-XNG 2: Charles Dunsmoor Bren, 30 & Betty J. Jefson, married October 6, 1974, Clark, Nevada: "Nevada Marriage Index, 1956–2005,".
3. Hedda Hopper, "Diana Lynn's Charm Keeps Her in Demand," *The Spokesman-Review,* February 23, 1958, 36.
4. Hedda Hopper, "Claire Thinks Stars Aren't Real People: She Charges That Lazy Actors Have Ruined the Film Studios," *The Los Angeles Times,* July 24, 1952,.
5. Hedda Hopper "Broadway Stars Sought for 'Compulsion' Roles," *Buffalo Courier-Express,* May 28, 1958, 4.
6. "Claire Trevor," *Poughkeepsie Journal* (Poughkeepsie, New York), August 5, 1962, 12C.
7. "Claire Trevor, the 'Shady Lady' Returns *Chicago Tribune,* March 6, 1987, 128.
8. George Fisher, "In Hollywood," *St Petersburg Times,* September 15, 1950, 27.
9. Philip F. Crosland, "Perseverance Pays: Claire Trevor—B's to Biggies," *The News Journal* (Wilmington, Delaware), December 29, 1967, 3.
10. "Actress to Speak at Reagan Luncheon," *The Los Angeles Times,* May 19, 1966, 146.
11. Philip F. Crosland, "Perseverance Pays: Claire Trevor—B's to Biggies," *The News Journal* (Wilmington, Delaware) December 29, 1967, 3.
12. "Screen Stars to Aid with Voter Sign-Ups," *The Los Angeles Times,* January 14, 1966, 95.
13. "Santa Ana High School," *The Los Angeles Times,* February 25, 1966. 97.
14. Shirley Eder, "Claire Trevor Still Looks Good at 72" *Detroit Free Press,* January 29, 1983, 19.
15. "Tyrone Power: King of Twentieth Century-Fox," http://www.tyrone-power.com/johnbrown.html.
16. Monica Sullivan, "Movie Magazine International: Claire Trevor Tribute," April 12, 2000. http://www.shoestring.org/mmi_revs/claire-trevor.html.
17. "Stage Review: 'Brown's Body' Resurrected," *The Los Angeles Times,* May 6, 1976, 109.
18. Sylvie Drake "Points of the Compass," *The Los Angeles Times,* April 30, 1976, 190.
19. Sylvie Drake "Points of the Compass," *The Los Angeles Times,* April 30, 1976, 190.
20. Hudson, Rock, with Davidson, Sara *Rock Hudson: His Story* (New York: Da Capo Press, 2007), 142.
21. "Despite Hazard Warning Over Tower, Two Planes Collide Over San Diego," *The Spokesman-Review,* September 26, 1978, 1.
22. "Jetliner Crew Blamed in Crash," *Lawrence World-Journal,* April 21, 1979, 1.
23. Davis, Ronald L. *Duke: The Life and Legend of John Wayne* (Norman, OK: University of Oklahoma Press, 1998), 299.
24. Munn, Michael *John Wayne: The Man Behind the Myth* (London: Robson Books, 2005), 345.
25. Munn, Michael *John Wayne: The Man Behind the Myth* (London: Robson Books, 2005), 365.
26. "Rites Held for Film Producer Milton H. Bren," *The Los Angeles Times,* December 19, 1979, 233.
27. Earl Wilson, "Paula Prentiss Has a Beef—In Fact, She Has Several," *Detroit Free Press,* March 13, 1980, 29.
28. Joe Pollack, "Claire Trevor: Sense of Style and Glamour," *St Louis Post-Dispatch,* December 30, 1982, 51.
29. "Claire Trevor: A Movie Star with a 'Real Life'" *The Los Angeles Times,* July 18, 1982, 287.

30. "'Kiss Me Goodbye' Brought Claire Trevor Back to Films," *Toledo Blade*, February 26, 1983, 16.
31. Mason Wiley, "Director Mulligan Hasn't Gotten Credit He Deserves," *Star-News*, July 3, 1992, 5D.
32. Christopher Hicks, "Claire Trevor Only Retired from 'Junk'" *The Deseret News*, December 27–28, 1982, 17.
33. "Some Actors Mean Business in Hollywood," *The Brooklyn Daily Eagle*, November 16, 1952, 29.
34. "People in the News," *Los Angeles Times*, November 12, 2000, 21.
35. Eddie Muller, "Queens of Mean," *Los Angeles Magazine*, March 1999, 99.
36. Wagner, Robert J. & Eyman, Scott *Pieces of My Heart: A Life* (New York: Harper Collins, 2008), 301.
37. Bob Thomas, "Oscar and Emmy Winner Claire Trevor Passes Away," *Philippine Daily Inquirer*, April 15, 2000, 14.

Epilogue

1. "Claire Trevor Wouldn't Change a Thing," *Los Angeles Times*, February 15, 1972, C1 Part IV.
2. "Some Blondes Prefer Work," *Radio Mirror*, June 1938, 65.
3. Philip S. Crosland, "Perseverance Pays: Claire Trevor—B's to Biggies," *The News Journal* (Wilmington, Delaware), December 29, 1967, 3.
4. Harrison Carroll, "Hollywood Sights and Sounds," *Ogdensburg Journal*, December 29, 1934, 8.

Appendix

Theater

1. Alvin J. Kayton, "In the Theaters on Broadway," *Daily Star*, September 29, 1930, 14. "$1,000 a Week and Idling," *Variety*, April 1, 1931, 2.
2. "No Money to Guide Her Given Friday Evening," *The East Hampton Star*, July 24, 1931, 9.
3. Miss Helen Gahagan, "Benefit for Wadham Memorial at Westhampton Country Club," *Brooklyn Life and Activities of the Long Island Society*, August 24, 1931, 9.
4. Edwin Schallert, "Coward Cycle Re-Triumph; 'Family Album' Cheered," *The Los Angeles Times*, August 8, 1940,.

Radio

1. "Radio Today," *Altoona Tribune*, October 4, 1938, 10.
2. "Radio," *The Des Moines Register*, January 28, 1939, 13.
3. "Radio," *The Evening Times* (Sayre, Pennsylvania), September 6, 1940, 10.
4. "Claire Trevor Is 'Silver Theater' Star at 4:00 Pm Today," *The Times* (Shreveport, Louisiana), August 18, 1946, 17.
5. "Radio," *The Decatur Daily Review*, May 5, 1942, 14.
6. "Radio," *The Philadelphia Inquirer*, December 12, 1942, 24. 5. "Radio Highlights," *The Aniston Star*, August 3, 1944, 8.
7. "Radio Highlights," *The Aniston Star*, August 3, 1944, 8.
8. "The Airwaves," *Arizona Daily Star*, June 9, 1943, 7.
9. "Radio Highlights," *Albany Herald & Democrat*, December 2, 1944, 6.
10. Guest. Don Tranter, "Radio Comment, Highlights," *Buffalo Courier-Express*, April 29, 1945, 14C.
11. "'Alaskan Bush Pilot' Is 'Cavalcade' Story for Monday," *The Times* (Shreveport, Louisiana) March 17, 1946, 17.
12. "Writes Radio Script," *The Post-Standard (Syracuse, New York)*, September 25, 1947, 5.
13. "Radio Program Notes," *The Mason City Globe-Gazette*, September 25, 1946, 2.
14. Don Tranter: Radio Comment, Highlights, *Buffalo Courier-Express*, February 16, 1947, 14C.
15. Hedda Hopper, "Looking at Hollywood," *The Los Angeles Times*, April 16, 1947, 13.
16. "Old Time Radio Transcription Discs," http://cdn.vintagesourceentertainment.com/catalogs/old-time-radio-list-1.pdf.
17. "Radio Log," *San Bernardino Sun*, January 23, 1951, 8.
18. Listed in Library of Congress Catalog, https://lccn.loc.gov/2003645062.
19. Simon Wincelberg, "Report from Hollywood: No One Ever Had an "All-Star Cast," Like UJA," *The National Jewish Post*, May 15, 1953, 10.
20. "Radio Programs," *Times Signal* (Zonesville, Ohio), December 4, 1955, 52.
21. "Free Press Radio, Television Guide: Radio Program Notes," *Detroit Free Press*, February 21, 1956, 23.

Television

1. "KFI Television Station Will Open Tonight," *The San Bernardino County Sun*, October 6, 1948, 2.
2. Simon Wincelberg, "Report from Hollywood: No One Ever Had an "All-Star Cast," Like UJA," *The National Jewish Post*, May 15, 1953, 10.

Bibliography

Aaker, Everett. *George Raft: The Films.* Jefferson, NC: McFarland, 2013.

Alvarez, Max. *The Crime Films of Anthony Mann.* Jackson: University of Mississippi, 2013.

Atkinson, Barry. *Six-Gun Law: The Westerns of Randolph Scott, Audie Murphy, Joel McCrea & George Montgomery.* Baltimore, MD: Midnight Marquee Press, 2004.

Bacall, Lauren. *By Myself and Then Some.* New York: HarperCollins, 2005.

Baddeley, Hermione. *The Unsinkable Hermione Baddeley.* London: William Collins Sons & Co., 1984.

Baker, Aaron. *Contesting Identities: Sports in American Film.* Urbana: University of Illinois Press, 2003.

Barton, Ruth. *Hedy Lamarr: The Most Beautiful Woman in the World.* Lexington: The University Press of Kentucky, 2010.

Bartsch, Tom, ed. *Standard Catalog of Vintage Baseball Cards.* Iola, WI: Krause Publications, 2015.

Basinger, Jeanine. *Anthony Mann: New and Expanded Edition.* Middleton, CT: Wesleyan University Press, 2007.

Basinger, Jeanine. *The Star Machine.* New York: Knopf, 2007.

Beck, Robert. *The Edward G. Robinson Encyclopedia.* Jefferson, NC: McFarland, 2002.

Behlmer, Rudy, selector and ed. *Memo for Darryl F. Zanuck: The Golden Years at Twentieth Century-Fox.* New York: Grove Press, 1993.

Berard, Jeanette M., and Klaudia Englund. *Radio Series Scripts, 1930–2001: A Catalog of the American Radio Archives Collection.* Jefferson, NC: McFarland, 2006.

Berg, A. Scott. *Goldwyn: A Biography.* London: Hamish Hamilton, 1989.

Bergan, Ronald. *The United Artists Story.* New York: Octopus Books, 1986.

Bernstein, Matthew. *Walter Wanger: Hollywood Independent.* Minneapolis: University of Minnesota Press, 2000.

Berry, Sarah. *Screen Style: Fashion & Femininity in 1930s Hollywood.* Minneapolis: University of Minnesota, 2000.

Bloom, Ken. *Broadway: An Encyclopedia.* London: Routledge, 2004.

Blum, Daniel. *A Pictorial History of the Talkies.* London: Spring Books, 1964.

Blumberg, Joe, and Sandra Grabman. *Lloyd Nolan: An Actor's Life with Meaning.* Albany, GA: Bear Manor Media, 2016.

Boardman, Gerald. *American Theater: A Chronicle of Comedy and Drama 1930–69.* New York: Oxford University Press, 1996.

Bogdanovitch, Peter. *John Ford.* Berkeley: University of California Press, 1978.

Bradley, Edwin M. *The First Hollywood Sound Shorts 1926–31.* Jefferson, NC: McFarland, 2009.

Bronner, Edwin. *The Encyclopedia of American Theater 1900–75.* New York: A.S. Barnes & Co., 1980.

Bryant, Roger. *William Powell: The Life and Films.* Jefferson, NC: McFarland, 2006.

Buscombe, Edward, ed. *The BFI Companion to the Western.* New York: Atheneum Books, 1988.

Buxton, Frank, and Bill Owen. *The Big Broadcast 1920–50,* 2d ed. Lanham, MD: Scarecrow Press, 1997.

Capua, Michelangelo. *Anatole Litvak: The Life and Films.* Jefferson, NC: McFarland, 2015.

Cardullo, Bert. *Screening the Stage: Studies in Cinedramatic Art.* Bern, Switzerland: Peter Lang, 2006.

Champlin, Charles *A Conversation with John Frankenheimer.* Burbank, CA: Riverwood Press, 1995.

Cocteau, Jean. *Past Tense: Diaries Vol 1.* London: Hamish Hamilton, 1987.

Convie, Peter, gen. ed. *World Filmography 1967.* London: Tantivity Press, 1977.

Corman, Emily. *Independent Stardom: Freelance Women in the Hollywood Studio System.* Austin: University of Texas Press, 2015.

Critchlow, Donald T. *When Hollywood Was Right: How Movie Stars, Studio Moguls, and Big Business Remade American Politics.* New York: Cambridge University Press, 2013.

Crow, Jefferson Brim, III. *Randolph Scott: A Film Biography.* Madison, NC: Empire Publications, 1994.

Curtis, James. *Spencer Tracy: A Biography.* New York: Hutchinson, 2011.

Custen, George F. *Twentieth Century's Fox: Darryl F. Zanuck & the Culture of Hollywood.* New York: Basic Books, 1997.

Darby, William. *John Ford's Westerns: A Thematic Analysis with a Filmography.* Jefferson, NC: McFarland, 1996.

Davis, Ronald L. *Duke: The Life and Legend of John Wayne.* Norman: University of Oklahoma Press, 1998.

Day, Barry, ed. *The Essential Noel Coward: The Very Best of His Life and Times.* London: Methuen Drama, 2009.

Dick, Bernard F. *Forever Mame: The Life of Rosalind Russell.* Jackson: University of Mississippi Press, 2011.

Dmytryk, Edward. *Odd Man Out: A Memoir of the Hollywood Ten.* Carbondale: Southern Illinois University Press, 1996.

Donati, William. *Ida Lupino: A Biography.* Lexington: University Press of Kentucky, 1996.

Douglas, Kirk. *The Ragman's Son: An Autobiography.* New York: Simon & Schuster, 1998.

Druxman, Michael B. *Basil Rathbone: His Life and Films.* New York: A.S. Barnes, 1975.

Dunning, John. *The Encyclopedia of Old Time Radio.* New York: Oxford University Press, 1998.

Durgnat, Raymond. *King Vidor, American.* Berkeley: University of California Press, 1992.

Eames, John Douglas. *The MGM Story.* New York: Octopus Books, 1979.

Eames, John Douglas. *The Paramount Story.* New York: Octopus Books, 1985.

Essoe, Gabe. *The Films of Clark Gable.* New York: Lyle Stuart, 1972.

Etling, Laurence. *Radio in the Movies: A History & Filmography: 1926–2010.* Jefferson, NC: McFarland, 2011.

Everson, William K. *The Bad Guys: A Pictorial History of the Movie Villain.* New York: Citadel Press, 1964.

Eyman, Scott. *John Wayne: The Life and Legend.* New York: Simon & Schuster, 2015.

Eyman, Scott. *Print the Legend: The Life and Times of John Ford.* New York: Simon & Schuster, 2011.

Fagen, Herb. *The Encyclopedia of Westerns.* New York: Facts on File, 2001.

Fane-Saunders, Kilmeny. *Radio Times Guide to Films.* London: BBC Worldwide, 2000.

Fiell, Charlotte. *1930s Fashion: The Definitive Sourcebook.* London: Carlton Books, 2015.

Fiell, Charlotte, and Emmanuelle Dirix. *1940s Fashion: The Definitive Sourcebook.* London: Carlton Books, 2014.

Ford, Dan. *The Unquiet Man: The Life of John Ford.* London: William Kimber & Co., 1982.

Ford, Peter. *Glenn Ford: A Biography.* Madison: University of Wisconsin Press, 2011.

Freese, Gene Scott. *Hollywood Stunt Performers: A Biographical Dictionary 1910s to 1970s.* Jefferson, NC: McFarland, 2014.

Gansberg, Alan L. *Little Caesar: A Biography of Edward G. Robinson.* Lanham, MD: Scarecrow, 2002.

Gates, Philippa. *Detecting Women: Gender and the Hollywood Detective Film.* Albany: State of New York Press, 2011.

Gevinson, Alan. *Within Our Gates: Ethnicity in American Feature Films 1911–60.* Berkeley: University of California Press, 1997.

Godard, Jean-Luc, Jean Narboni, and Tom Milne, eds. *Godard on Godard.* New York: Da Capo Press, 1972.

Grant, Barry Keith, ed. *John Ford's Stagecoach.* New York: Cambridge University Press, 2003.

Griffin, Mark. *A Hundred or More Hidden Things: The Life and Films of Vincente Minnelli.* New York: Da Capo Press, 2010.

Grobel, Laurence. *The Hustons: The Life and Times of a Hollywood Dynasty.* New York: Skyhorse Publishing, 2014.

Guiles, Fred Lawrence. *Tyrone Power: The Last Idol.* New York: Doubleday, 1979.

Gussow, Mel. *"Don't Say Yes Until I Finish Talking": A Biography of Darryl F. Zanuck.* London: W.H. Allen & Co., 1971.

Hagen, Ray, and Laura Wagner. *Killer Tomatoes: Fifteen Tough Film Dames.* Jefferson, NC: McFarland, 2004.

Haley, Jack, and Mitchell Cohen, ed. *Heart of the Tin Man: The Collected Writings of Jack Haley.* Santa Ana, CA: Seven Locks Press, 2002.

Halliwell, Leslie. *Halliwell's Film Guide.* London: Guild Publishing, 1983.

Hanson, Patricia King, and Anny Dunkleberger. *AFI: American Film Institute Catalog of Motion Pictures: Feature Films 1941–50.* Berkeley: University of California Press, 1999.

Higham, Charles. *Merchant of Dreams: Louis B. Mayer: M.G.M. and the Secret Hollywood.* London: Sidgwick & Jackson, 1993.

Hill, Ona L. *Raymond Burr: A Film, Radio and TV Biography.* Jefferson, NC: McFarland, 1999.

Hirsch, Foster. *The Dark Side of the Screen: Film Noir.* Philadelphia: A.S. Barnes & Co., 1981.

Hirschorn, Clive. *The Columbia Story.* New York: Hamlyn, 1988.

Hirschhorn, Clive. *The Universal Story.* New York: Octopus Books, 1983.

Hirschhorn, Clive. *The Warner Brothers Story.* New York: Octopus Books, 1979.

Hischak, Thomas S. *American Literature on Stage and Screen: 525 Works and Their Adaptations.* Jefferson, NC: McFarland, 2012.

Horton, Andrew, and Stuart Y. McDougal. *Play It Again, Sam: Retakes on Remakes.* Berkeley: University of California Press, 1998.

Howsden, Gordon. *Collecting Cigarette and Trade Cards.* London: New Cavendish Books, 1997.

Hudson, Rock, with Sara Davidson. *Rock Hudson: His Story.* New York: Da Capo Press, 2007.

Huston, John. *An Open Book.* London: Macmillan, 1981.

Hyams, Joseph. *Bogie: The Biography of Humphrey Bogart.* New York: New American Library, 1966.

Jewell, Richard B. *RKO Radio Pictures: A Titan Is Born.* Berkeley: University of California Press, 2012.

Jewell, Richard B. *Slow Fade to Black: The Decline of RKO Radio Pictures.* Berkeley: University of California Press, 2016.

Jewell, Richard B., and Vernon Harbin. *The RKO Story.* New York: Octopus Books, 1983.

Jones, J.R. *The Lives of Robert Ryan*. Middleton, CT: Wesleyan University Press, 2015.

Jorgenson, Jay, and Donald L Scroggins. *Creating the Illusion: A Fashionable History of Hollywood Fashion Designers*. Philadelphia, PA: Running Press, 2015.

Kanfer, Stefan. *Tough Without a Gun: The Life & Extraordinary After Life of Humphrey Bogart*. New York: Alfred A. Knopf, 2011.

Kasson, John F. *The Little Girl Who Fought the Great Depression: Shirley Temple and 1930s America*. New York: W.W. Norton & Co., 2014.

Kear, Lynn, and James King. *Evelyn Brent: The Films of Hollywood's Lady Crook*. Jefferson, NC: McFarland, 2009.

Keenan, Richard C. *The Films of Robert Wise*. Lanham, MD: Scarecrow, 2007.

Keyes, Evelyn. *Scarlett O'Hara's Younger Sister*. London: W.H. Allen & Co., 1978.

Lachman, Marvin. *The Villainous Stage: Crime Plays on Broadway and the West End*. Jefferson, NC: McFarland, 2014.

Landis, Deborah Nadoolman. *Dressed: A Century of Hollywood Costume Design*. London: HarperCollins Group, Harper Designs, 2007.

Langman, Larry. *The Media in the Movies: A Catalog of American Journalism Films, 1900–96*. Jefferson, NC: McFarland, 2000.

Leemann, Sergio. *Robert Wise on His Films: From Editing Room to Director's Chair*. Hollywood, CA: Silman-James Press, 1995.

Leese, Elizabeth. *Costume Design in the Movies: An Illustrated Guide to the Work of 157 Great Designers*. New York: Dover Publications, 1991.

Leider, Emily W. *Myrna Loy: The Only Good Girl in Hollywood*. Berkeley: University of California Press, 2006.

Lev, Peter. *Twentieth Century Fox: The Zanuck-Skouras Years 1935–1965*. Austin: University of Texas Press, 2013.

Levy, Emmanuel. *Vincente Minnelli: Hollywood's Dark Dreamer*. New York: St. Martin's Press, 2009.

Lombardi, Frederic. *Allan Dwan and the Rise and Decline of the Hollywood Studios*. Jefferson, NC: McFarland, 2013.

MacKenzie, Harry. *The Directory of the Armed Forces Radio Service Series*. Westport, CT: Greenwood, 1999.

Maltin, Leonard. *The Great American Broadcast*. New York: Dutton Books, 1997.

May, Larry. *The Big Tomorrow: Hollywood and the Politics of the American Way*. Chicago: University of Chicago Press, 2002.

McBride, Joseph. *Searching for John Ford: A Life*. New York: St. Martin's Press, 2001.

McCann, Graham. *Bounder! The Biography of Terry-Thomas*. London: Aurum Press, 2008.

McElhaney, Joe, ed., with Raymond Bellow and Jean-Loup Bourget. *Vincente Minnelli: The Art of Entertainment*. Detroit, MI: Wayne State University Press, 2008.

Meade, Marion. *Lonelyhearts: The Screwball World of Nathanael West and Eileen McKenny*. New York: Mariner Books, Houghton, Muffin, Harcourt, 2010.

Mell, Eila. *Casting Might-Have-Beens: A Film-By-Film Directory of Actors Considered for Roles Given to Others*. Jefferson, NC: McFarland, 2005.

Miller, Don. *"B" Movies: An Informal Survey of the American Low-Budget Film, 1933–45*. New York: Ballantine Books, 1987.

Minnelli, Vincente. *I Remember It Well*. London: Angus & Robinson, 1974.

Montalban, Ricardo, and Bob Thomas. *Reflections: A Life in Two Worlds*. New York: Doubleday & Co., 1980.

Mordden, Ethan. *All That Glitters: The Golden Age of Broadway 1919–1959*. New York: St Martin's Press, 2015.

Moss, Marilyn Ann. *Raoul Walsh: The True Adventures of Hollywood's Legendary Director*. Lexington: University Press of Kentucky, 2011.

Munden, Kenneth W., executive ed. *The American Film Institute Catalog of Motion Pictures: Feature Films 1931–40*. Berkeley: University of California Press, 1993.

Munn, Michael. *John Wayne: The Man Behind the Myth*. London: Robson Books, 2005.

Nolan, William. *John Huston: King Rebel*. Los Angeles: Sherbourne Press, 1965.

Nollen, Scott A. *Glenda Farrell: Hollywood's Hardboiled Dame*. Baltimore, MD: Midnight Marquee Press, 2014.

Nott, Robert. *The Films of Randolph Scott*. Jefferson, NC: McFarland, 2004.

Oller, John. *Jean Arthur: The Actress Nobody Knew*. New York: Limelight Editions, 2004.

Parish, James Robert. *The Fox Girls*. New York: Arlington House, 1971.

Parish, James Robert. *The RKO Gals*. New York: Arlington House, 1976.

Parish, James Robert, and Ronald L. Bowers. *The MGM Stock Company: The Golden Era*. London: W.H. Allen & Co., 1971.

Quinlan, David. *The Illustrated Directory of Film Stars*. London: B.T. Batsford, 1982.

Quirk, Lawrence J. *The Films of William Holden*. New York: Citadel Press, 1973.

Roberts, Randy, and James S. Olson. *John Wayne American*. Lincoln: University of Nebraska Press, 1995.

Robinson, Edward G., and Leonard Spigelglass. *All My Yesterdays: An Autobiography*. London: W.H. Allen & Co., 1974.

Schatz, Thomas. *The Genius of the System: Hollywood Filmmaking in the Studio Era*. New York: Henry Holt & Company, 1998.

Schickel, Richard. *The Men Who Made the Movies*. New York: Atheneum Books, 1975.

Schickel, Richard, and George Perry. *Bogie: A Celebration of the Life and Films of Humphrey Bogart*. New York: St. Martin's Press, 2006.

Schiller, Ralph. *The Complete Films of Broderick Crawford*. Raleigh, NC: CP Books, 2016.

Siegel, Joel E. *Val Lewton: The Reality of Terror*. London: Secker & Warburg in Association with the British Film Institute, 1972.

Sennett, Ted. *The Old Time Radio Book*. New York: Pyramid Publications, 1976.

Sennett, Ted. *Masters of Menace: Greenstreet and Lorre*. New York: E.P. Dutton, 1979.

Shearer, Stephen Michael, and Robert Osbourne. *Beauty: The Life of Hedy Lamarr*. New York: St. Martin's Griffin, 2013.

Shipman, David. *The Great Movie Stars: The Golden Years*. New York: Hamlyn, 1971.

Shrimpton, Jayne. *Fashion in the 1940s*. London: Shire Publications, 2014.

Siegel, Scott, and Barbara Siegel. *The Guinness Encyclopedia of Hollywood*. London: Guinness Publishing, 1990.

Sikov, Ed. *Dark Victory: The Life of Bette Davis*. New York: Henry Holt & Co., 2007.

Silver, Alain, and Elizabeth Ward. *Film Noir*. London: Secker & Warburg, 1980.

Sinyard, Neil. *A Wonderful Heart: The Films of William Wyler*. Jefferson, NC: McFarland, 2013.

Soloman, Aubrey. *The Fox Film Corporation 1915–35*. Jefferson, NC: McFarland, 2011.

Sperber, A.M. *Bogart: The Biography*. London: Weidenfeld & Nicholson, 1997.

Terrace, Vincent. *Radio Program Openings and Closings, 1931–72*. Jefferson, NC: McFarland, 2003.

Thomas, Bob. *Joan Crawford: A Biography*. London: Bantam Books, 1978.

Thomas, Bob. *Golden Boy: The Untold Story of William Holden*. London: Weidenfeld & Nicholson, 1983.

Thomas, Tony. *The Dick Powell Story*. Burbank, CA: Riverwood Press, 1992.

Thomas, Tony, and Aubrey Soloman. *The Films of Twentieth Century Fox*. Secaucus, NJ: The Citadel Press, 1979.

Tranberg, Charles. *Fredric March: A Consummate Actor*. Albany, GA: Bear Manor Media, 2013.

Tranberg, Charles. *Fred MacMurray: A Biography*. Albany, GA: Bear Manor Media, 2007.

Turudich, Daniela. *1940s Hairstyles*. Long Beach, CA: Streamline Press, 2001.

Tuttle, Frank, and John Franceschina, ed. *They Started Talking*. Albany, GA: Bear Manor Media, 2004.

Vermilye, Jerry. *Buster Crabbe: A Biofilmography*. Jefferson, NC: McFarland, 2008.

Verswigver, Leo. *Movies Were Always Magical: Interviews with 19 Actors, Directors and Producers from the Hollywood of the 1930s Through the 1950s*. Jefferson, NC: McFarland, 2003.

Vieira, Mark A. *George Hurrell's Hollywood Glamour Portraits*. Philadelphia PA: Running Press.

Vieira, Mark A. *Majestic Hollywood: The Greatest Films of 1939*. Philadelphia, PA: Running Press, 2013.

Vinson, James, ed. *The International Dictionary of Films and Filmmakers: Actors and Actresses*. New York: Macmillan, 1986.

Wagner, Robert J., and Scott Eyman. *I Loved Her in the Movies: Memories of Hollywood's Legendary Actresses*. Philadelphia, PA: Running Press, 2016.

Wagner, Robert J., and Scott Eyman. *Pieces of My Heart: A Life*. New York: HarperCollins, 2008.

Walker, John, ed. *Halliwell's Who's Who in the Movies*. 14th ed. London: HarperCollins Entertainment, 2011.

Wallace, Stone. *George Raft: The Man Who Would Be Bogart*. Albany, GA: Bear Manor Media, 2015.

Wayne, Aissa, with Steve Delsohn. *John Wayne: My Father*. Lanham, MD: Taylor Trade, 1998.

Wellman, William, Jr. *Wild Bill Wellman: Hollywood Rebel*. New York: Pantheon, 2015.

Wertheim, Albert. *Staging the War: American Drama and World War II*. Bloomington: Indiana University Press, 2004.

Wilson, Victoria. *A Life of Barbara Stanwyck: Steel-True: 1907–1940*. New York: Simon & Schuster, 2015.

Young, Jordan R. *Reel Characters*. Beverly Hills, CA: Moonstone Press, 1986.

Index

Numbers in *bold italics* indicate pages with illustrations

Abbott, Bud 130
Abbott & Costello 61
Abdulla Cigarettes 44
Abel, Walter 78
Academy Awards 1, 47, 48, 52, 106, 108, 125, 126, 139, 140
Achilles 74
Adams, Clay 49
Adler, Luther 108, 118, ***119***
The Adventures of Martin Eden 76–77
The Adventures of Robin Hood 55
The Adventures of Sam the Ship Builder 83
Advice to the Lovelorn 18
The African Queen 107
Agnes of God 147
Aherne, Brian 69
Airport 126
Alfred Hitchcock Presents 118, 136
"Alias Nora Hale" 133–134
Alice Through the Looking Glass (1928) 51
All About Eve 101
"All About Eve" (radio) 62
"All About Fairfax Avenue" (skit) 114
All My Sons 94
Allegheny Uprising 61, 71–72, 112
Alton, John 100
Alworth, Alice 10
The Amazing Dr. Clitterhouse 53, 54–55
Ameche, Don 53, 61
American Academy of Dramatic Art (AADA) 5–6, 26
American Girl 114
Ames, Adrienne 22
Ames, Leon 101
Anderson, Maxwell 104
Anderson, Milo 45
Anderson, Warren 134
Andrews, Clark 55, 59–60, 69, 82
Angel Cake 8
Anglin, Margaret 6
Ann Arbor, MI 6
Ann-Margret 67
"The Anniversary Waltz" 140
Any Number Can Play 108
Appointment in Tokyo 81
Archainbaud, George 30, 86
Argentine Film Festival 126
"Argentine Swing" 51

Arnaz, Desi 129
Arnold, Edward 10
Arthur, Jean 76, 146
As Good as New 8
Ask the Dust 122
Astaire, Fred 31
Astor, Mary 62
Atlas, Leopold 101
Aurelia Cigarettes 44
The Awful Truth 74
Ayres, Lew 12, 23
Ayres, Rosemary 18

The Babe Ruth Story 108–110, 123
Baby Face 134
Baby, Take a Bow 19, 29, 132
Bacall, Lauren 105, 106, 107, 145
The Bachelor and the Bobby-Soxer 94
The Bachelor's Daughters 91
Back to Bataan 88
The Bad and the Beautiful 139
Bad Angel 75
Baddeley, Hermione 143–144
Bakewell, Billy 49
Ball, Lucille 129
Balsam, Martin 131
Bancroft, George 76
Bankhead, Tallulah 95, 114, 136
Banton, Travis 102–103
Barbed Wire 108
"Barcarolle" 8
Bari, Lynn 34, 51, 53
Barker, Jess 83
Barker, Ma 137
Barrett, Edith 134, 136
Barrie, Wendy 21, 67
Barry, Joe 56
Barrymore, Ethel 7
Barrymore, Lionel 11, 61, 106
Barton, James 134
Bassermann, Albert 83
Bautzer, Greg 49
Baxter, Anne 136, 146
Baxter, John 29
Baxter, Warner 19, ***33***, 34
The Beast with Five Fingers 39
Beatty, Warren 141
Beau Geste 71
Beauty's Daughter 29
Beckett, Scotty ***28***
"The Bed I've Made" 138
Bedoya, Alfonso 124

Behrman, S.N. 7
Bekassy, Stephen 128
Belasco, David 8
Bellamy, Ralph 30, 40
Beloved Over All 108
Bend of the River 101
Bendix, William 108–110
Benét, Stephen Vincent 146
Bennett, Constance 34, 36, 78
Bergerac, Jacques 128, 136
Bernhardt, Curtis 80
Best of the Badmen 117, 118
"The Best Things in Life Are Free" 34
Beutel, Jack 118
Beymer, Richard 141
Beyond Tomorrow 68
The Bickersons 133
Bickford, Charles 54, 110
Bide-a-Wee Homes 130
The Big Street 94
Big Town 59, 60, 63
Big Town Girl 50
The Big Trees 56
"A Bird in a Gilded Cage" 56
Bisset, Jacqueline 142
The Black Curtain 81
The Black Gang 30
"Black Maria" 8
Black Sheep 22, 45
Blackmer, Sidney 125
Blair, Janet 84
Blane, Sally 18
Blondell, Joan 55, 67, 70, 114
Blood on the Moon 116
The Blue Bird 4
Blystone, John 19
Blyth, Ann 124
Bogart, Humphrey 47, ***48***, ***53***, 54, 55, 62, 105, 106, 107, 130
Bogart, Stephen 107
Boles, John 18, 19, 26
Boles, Mrs. 26
Bomberg, J. Edward 35, ***49***, 50
Bond, Ward 137
Boone, Pat 141
Boone, Richard 127
Booth, Charles Gordon 90
Booth, Shirley 128
Border Incident 101
Borderline 111, 112–113, 114
Borgnine, Ernest 124
Born to Kill 91, 96–99, 150

Boul de Souf 64
Boy Meets Girl 75
Boyer, Charles 104
The Boys from Brazil 142
Breaking Home Ties 148
Bren, Donald H. 108, 149
Bren, Marian (née Newbert) 108
Bren, Milton H. 95, 106, 107–108, 112, 113, 114, 145, 146, 149
Bren, Peter 108
Brewer, Betty 85
Brian, David 125, **126**
"The Bribe" 61
Bridges, Jeff 148
Brisson, Frederick 102
Brittany, Morgan 148
Broadway 8
Broken Dishes 8
Broken Lance 129
Brolin, James 142
The Bronxville Press 10
Brooks, Phyllis 40, 51, **52**, 78
Brooks, Richard 104
"Brother, Can You Spare a Dime" 23
Brown, Frederick 92
Brown, Melville 23
Brown, Tom 22
Brown, Wally 125
Bruce, Virginia 73
Bruce-Lockhart, Freda 64
Brute Force 134
Buchanan, Edgar 76, 82, 84
Bukowski, Charles 122
Burke, Billie 91–92
Burke, James 31
Burkett, James S. 108
Burlesque 108
Buron, Mayor Fletcher D. 133
Burr, Raymond 99, 100, 112
Buttolph, David 81

Caan, James 148
Cabot, Bruce 118
Caged 111
Cagney, James 47, 120
Cahiers du Cinema 140
Cameron, Rod 82
Canania, Marcelo 26, 69
Cannes Film Festival, 1964 142
Canyon Passage 94
The Cape Town Affair 142–143
Capone, Al 104
Capra, Frank 103, 139
The Captive City 118
Career Woman 37, 58, 59
Carey, Harry 72
Caribbean Club, Key Largo, FL 104
Carmichael, Hoagy 90
Carol, Joan 39, 40
Carpenter, Edward Childs 75
Carradine, John 64, 66
Carrefour (1938) 80
Carrefour (novel) 79
Carreras Cigarettes 44
Carroll, Madeleine 41
Carson, Jack 61, 110

Carter, Charles 123
Cash, Johnny 137
Caylor, Rose 23
Chandler, Albert B. "Happy" 110
Chandler, Chick **34**
Chandler, Raymond 87, 88
Chatterton, Ruth 135
Chekhov, Anton 9
Cheviot Hills Tennis Club 78
Christie, Agatha 22
A Christmas Carol (1938) 91
Churchill, Berton 64
Churchill, Winston 91
City Without Men 82
"The C.L. Harding Story" 137
Claire Trevor School of the Arts 144
Claire Trevor's Hollywood Sketchpad 103
Clara Kruger (character) 139–140
Clarke, Judge Thurmond 107
Clarke, Warren 144
Climax! 135
Cobb, Lee J. 131
Cocteau, Jean 45, 114
Cohan, George M. 30
Cohn, Harry 84
Colbert, Claudette 74, 147
Collins, Ray 92, 94
Collison, Anzonetta 21
Collison, Wilson 21
Colman, Ronald 54, 76
Colonna, Jerry 56
Columbia Pictures 74, 83, 84
Columbia University 5
Columbia Workshop 94
Come Back, Little Sheba 124
Compton, Joyce **34**
Connie Williams (character) 119
Connolly, Marc 62, 83
Connolly, Maureen 114
Connolly, Mike 12
Conselman, William 16
Conway, Jack 80
Cook, Elisha, Jr. 97, 98
Cooke, Alistair 36–37
Coolidge, Pres. Calvin 66
Cooper, Gary 64, 69, 110
Corey, Jeff 137
Corey, Wendell 120, **121**
The Corn Is Green 132
Cornell University 9
The Country Doctor 56
The Country Girl 124
The Country Girl (play) 120
Courtney, Inez 26, **57**
Coward, Noel 75
Crack-Up 92–94
Crain, Jeanne 127
Crashout 111
Crawford, Broderick 19, 122, 123
Crawford, Joan 1, 10, 108, 125, 127
Cregar, Laird 69
Crime and Punishment 27
"A Crime for Mothers" 118, 136
Crisp, Donald 54
The Crooked Circle 120
The Crooked Way 39

Crosby, Bing 67
Crossfire 88
Crossroads 79–80
Crowther, Bosley 97–98
Curse of the Cat People 116
Curtiz, Michael 108
Curwood, James Oliver 72
"Cute Little Rumba" 19

Dalí, Salvador 45
A Dangerous Profession 126
Dangerously Yours 40
Dano, Royal 136
Dante Alighieri 28
Dante's Inferno 28–29
The Dark at the Top of the Stairs 141
The Dark at the Top of the Stairs (stage play) 139
The Dark Command 72–73
Dark Victory 94
Darnell, Linda 78, 82
Darwell, Jane 30, **55**
Davis, Bette 1, 19, 55, 62, 114, 125, 132, 136, 139, 144
Dawn, Gaye 104, 106, 129
Dayton Co. of Minneapolis 43
Dead End 47, 48, 50, 64, 150
Dead End Kids 47
Deadlier Than the Male 96
Deane, Gregory 5
Death in Vegas 106
de Camp, Rosemary 134
Deception 132
Dee, Francis 69
De Grasse, Robert 93
De Havilland, Olivia 72
Dekker, Albert 8, 85
Dekobra, Maurice 86
Del Rio, Dolores 55
Del Ruth, Roy 110
Demarest, William 27, 127
Dempsey, Jack 34
The Desert Song 123
Design for Living 74
The Desperadoes 82
Desperate Men 124
Destry Rides Again 62
de Toth, Andre 124
Deutsch, Adolf 56
Devi, Prativa 87
The Devil Commands 88
Dewey, Sen. Thomas E. 69
Diamond, Don 112
The Dice Woman 21
Dickens, Charles 22
Dieterle, William 114
Dietrich, Marlene 10, 25, 41, 42, 64, 69, 80, 90
Dinehart, Alan 19, 50
Dionne Quintuplets 56–58
Distant Drums 110
Dmytryk, Edward 88, 129
Dr. Dafoe 57
Dr. Jekyll and Mr. Hyde 54
Dr. Kildare 137
"Dodsworth" 133
Domino Parlor 108

Index

Don Ameche Old Gold Radio Show 61
Don Juan Quilligan 70
Dona Flor and Her Two Husbands 148
Donat, Robert 114
Donlevy, Brian 12, **32**, 33, 51, 53, 71, 72, 74, 76, 110, 111, 118, 119
Donnelly, Ruth 31
Dorn, Philip 94
Double Indemnity 102, 108
Douglas, Kirk 127, 139–140
Douglas, Paul 110
"Down Around Malibu Way" 35
Drake, Claudia 82
Dreier, Hans 39
Drew, Ellen 111
Driscoll, Ray 45
Du Maupassant, Guy 64
Dumont, Margaret 123
Dunbar, Dixie 51
Dunn, James 16–18, 19, **20**, 21, 31
Dunne, Irene 46, 74, 130
Dunsmoor, Charles (Chuck) 83, 95, 118, 137–138, 145, 147
Dunsmoor, Cylos 83
Dunsmoor, Lt. Cylos, Jr. 83, 89, 91, 95
Dunsmoor, Marilla 83
Duprez, June 86
Durkee, F.W. 135
Dvorak, Ann 91
Dwann, Alan 23, 23, 36

The Eagle Has Two Heads 114
Eagle-Lion Films 99
Earhart, Amelia 41
Earth vs. the Flying Saucers 134
East Side of Heaven 55, 67
"Eat Marlowe's Meats" 16
Eilers, Sally 16, 26, 83
Einstein, Albert 63
Elam, Jack 121
Elinor Norton 20, 21, 25, 44
Elmer Gantry 111
Emmy Awards 2, 133, 134, 138
"En Mi Soledad" 64
Enright, Ray 84
Equal Rights Party 63
Erickson, Leif 146
Erwin, Stuart 50
Escape from San Quentin 134
Escape Route Cape Town 142
The Ethel Barrymore Theater 133
Ethel Barrymore Theater, NY. 104
Evans, Gene 136
Evans, Jay 128
Excess Baggage 7

The Fabulous Dorseys 134
Fadden, Tom 100
Fair Wind to Java 120
The Fake 87–88
"Family Portrait" 75
Fante, John 122
Far Away Horses 10
Farewell, My Lovely 87

Farewell to Fifth Avenue 21
Farmer, Frances 48
Farrell, Glenda 73, 82
Farrow, John 135
"Father's Day" 62
Faye, Alice 18, 21, 31, 40, 53, 54
"Feelin' High" 39
Ferber, Edna 7
Ferrer, Jose 94
Fidler, Jimmie 75
Field, Betty 67
Field, Sally 147
Fifteen Maiden Lane 35–37, 58
Film Noir 94
Film Weekly 68
The First Baby 18
The First Rebel 71
Fisher, Carl 104
Fisher, Steven Gould 69
Fitzgerald, F. Scott 127
Fitzgerald, Geraldine 135
Five of a Kind 56–58
Flamingo Road 108
Fleet, Jo Van 140, 141
Fleming, Rhonda 137
Fleming, Susan 34
Florey, Robert 39, 136
Flynn, Errol 62
Foch, Nina 120
Fodor, Dr. Frenz 63
"Foggy Night" 134
Follow Me Quietly 101
Fonda, Henry 48
Fontaine, Joan 46, 74, 75, 114
Fontanne, Lynn 14
Fool Proof 135
Ford, Corey 113
Ford, Glenn 75–76, **77**, 82
Ford, John 64–67, 70
Ford, Wallace 8, 92, 127, 135
Ford Television Theater 134
Forrest, Sally 114–116, **115**
Foster, Lewis R. 111
Foster, Preston 18
Foster, Stephen 64
Four Freshmen 128
Fournier, Claire 135
The Foursome 8
Fox Film Corp. 1, 12, 14–24, 25–40 passim, 41, 43
Fox Movietone Follies of 1934 19
Foy, Eddie 85
Francis, Arlene 145, 147
Franciscus, James 137
Frankenheimer, John 136
Franklin, Helen 46
Frederick, Pauline 30
Fredericks, Ellsworth 141
The Free Company 62
Freed, Ralph 39
Freeman, Y. Frank 145
Fremont, Douglas 120
French Guiana 68
"Frere Jacques" 57
Frontier Marshall 68
Fuller, Leslie 86
Fullerton Federation of Republican Women 146

Fun on a Weekend 92
Furness, Betty 40

Gable, Clark 69, 73, 108
Gage, Jack 102, 103
Gallaher Cigarettes 44
Garbo, Greta 42, 69
Gardner, Ava 130
Gardner, Roy 70, 71
Gargan, Ed 93
Garland, Judy 45
Garmes, Lee 68
Gaudio, Tony 55
Gaumont-British Studios 33
Geary Theater, San Francisco 144
General Electric Theater 134
Genn, Leo 101
The Gentleman Misbehaves 76
Gents Without Cents 84
George, Gladys 42
Georgie, Leyla 86
Giant 127
Gielgud, Irwin 110
"Girl of My Dreams" 47
Glennon, Bert 66
Godard, Jean-Luc 139
Gold, Alfred 40
Gold Diggers 9
Gold Rush of 1934 15
Goldsmith, Jerry 141
Goldwyn, Sam 47, 108
Gomez, Thomas 106
Gone with the Wind 68
Good Housekeeping 30
Good Luck, Mr. Yates 83–84
Good Times 8
Goodbye Again 94
Gorney, Jay 16, 19, 23
Gould, William 76
Grable, Betty 108
Graham, Sheila 47, 104, 139
Grant, Cary 69, 76
Grant, Ulysses S. 63
Grayson, Kathryn 123
The Great Diamond Robbery 40
Great Guy 47
The Great Victor Herbert 91
Green, Alfred E. 134
Greene, Eve 96
Greenstreet, Sydney 102, 103
Greer, Jo Ann 137
Greiling Cigarettes 44
Grey, Zane 14
Guinan, "Texas" 94
Gunn, James 96

Hagen, Jean 120
Hagen, Ray 78
Hal Roach Studios 107
Hale, Alan 56
Hale, Barbara 120
Haley, Jack 8, 23, 24
Halfway to Nowhere 118
Hall, Porter 86
Hall, Thurston 54
"The Hand That Rocks the Cradle" 137
Handle with Care 76, 110

Index

"Happy Hill" 136
Hard, Fast and Beautiful 114–118, 150
The Harder They Fall 108
Hardwicke, Sir Cedric 54, 71
Harmon, Tom 133
Harris, Phil 126
Harris, Robin 40
Hasso, Signe 90
Hawk of the Desert 23
Haycox, Ernest 64
Hayward, Susan 94
Hayworth, Rita 29, 74
Head, Edith 127
Hecht, Ben 23
Hedda Gabler 102
Heflin, Van 114
Hefti, Neal 142
Hellinger, Mark 42, 51, 61
Hell's Kitchen 48
Henderson, Robert 6
Hepburn, Katharine 42
Herbert, F. Hugh 69
Here Comes Trouble 30
Hersholt, Jean 57
Heston, Charles 127, **128**
The Hidden Room 89
Higgins, John C. 101
The High and the Mighty 125–126
"High Sierra" 55
Highway 301 91
Hill, Virginia 118
Hilton, James 112
Hines, Wilmer 49
His Kind of Woman 122
Hitchcock, Alfred 87, 116
Hitler's Children 94
Hively, Jack 81
Hodiak, John 81, 120
Hoffman, Samuel 100
Hold That Girl 17–18, 43
Holden, William 75–76
Holloway, Sterling 54
Hollywood Filmograph 15
Hollywood Hotel 59
Hollywood Pattern Co. 44
Honky Tonk 73–74, 77
Hoodlum Empire 114, 118–120
Hoover, Herbert 69
Hope, Bob 61
Hopkins, Miriam 25, 34, 69
Houghton, James 148
House of Wax 124
Houseman, John 146
"How Can I Tell Her?" 128
How Green Was My Valley 120
How to Murder Your Wife 142
Howard, Esther 57, 88, 96, **97**
Hud 120
Hudson, Rock 144, 146, 147
Hughes, Howard 114, 115
Hull, Henry 86
Human Cargo 32–33
Hunt, Marsha 99, 101
The Hunted Woman 72
Hunter, Ian 33
Hunter, Kim 120
Hussey, Ruth 74, 78

Huston, John 104–106
Hutton, Betty 94

"I Don't Have a Thing to Wear" 97
"I Hate to Talk About Myself" 39
I Love the Author 53
I Married a Communist 111
I Stole a Million 70–71
I Will Be Faithful 32
Ibsen, Henrik 6
"I'll Get By" 110
"I'm a Heavy Tipper" 85
I'm Going to Maxeme's 123
Imitation of Life (1934) 40
Immodest Violet 10
The Imperfect Lover 8
In Old Chicago 142
Incendiary Blonde 94
Inge, William 139, 141
International Settlement 55
The Investigators 137
Ireland, John 100
It Can't Last Forever 40
It Happened One Night 74
It's a Small World 21
It's a Wise Child 8
"It's the Irish in Me" 16
"I've Got You at the Top of My List" 18, 19

Jagger, Dean 35
"Jane Eyre" 62
Janofsky, Jan 70–71
"Jeannie with the Light Brown Hair" 64
Jefson, Betty J. 145
Jenkins, Allen 47, 54
"Jerusalem, the Holy City" 85
Jewell, Isabel 37, 96
Jimmy and Sally 16, 17, 33
Joan of Arc 146
John Brown's Body 146
Johnny Angel 90–91, 150
Johnny Guitar 127
Johnson, Amy 41
Johnson, Erskine 123
"Join the Party" 31
Jonesy 8
Juarez 19
Juarez and Maximilian 19
"The Judge" 101
Judge, Arlene 30, 35
June Buckridge (character) 143–144

Kafka, John H. 78
Kalloch, Robert 74, 80
Kane, Joseph 120
Kaper, Bronislau 80
The Kate Smith Hour 60
Kaufman, George S. 7
Kazan, Elia 139
"Keep Young and Beautiful" 42
Kefauver, Sen. 118
Keighley, William 56
Kellogg, Virginia 111
Kelly, Gene 69, 118, 131–132

Kelly, Grace 130
Kelly, Paul 30–31, 125
Key Largo 1, 19, 104–107, 108, 129, 150
"Key Largo" (radio) 62
Keyes, Evelyn 76, 82
Keystone Cops 30
Kid Glove Killer 101
Kilbride, Percy 85
Kiley, Richard 134
The Killing of Sister George 143–144, 146
The King and I 124
King Kong 66
King of Gamblers 19–20, 136
Kirby, Klayton 31–32
Kiss and Wake Up 23
Kiss Me Goodbye 147–148
Klotz, Florence 45
Koerner, Charles 89–90
Kohner, Paul 147
Korda, Alexander 114
Kottow, Hans 7
Kraly, Hans 69
Krasner, Milton 70
Kruger, Otto 88
Kyne, Peter B. 56

Lachman, Harry 28, 29
Ladd, Alan 46
Ladies in Love 36
"Ladies in Retirement" 134
The Lady Claire 107
Lady Cop 19
Lady Esther Screen Guild Theater 62
Lady of Deceit 99
Lady Windermere's Fan 6
The Ladykillers 54
Laguna Beach Playhouse 94
Laine, Frankie 127
Lake, Veronica 86
Lamarr, Hedy 79
Lambert, William 33
Lamour, Dorothy 78, 111
Lanchester, Elsa 134
Lane, Allan 49
Lane, Burton 39
Lane, Priscilla 82
Lang, Fritz 111
Lang, June 26
Langford, Frances 133
Lansbury, Angela 103, 144, 148
Lassie (television series) 81
The Last Trail 14, 143
The Last Tycoon 127
Laurel & Hardy 29, 111, 113, 143
Laurents, Arthur 128
Leonard, Jack 122
Leonard, Sheldon 123
Let the Eagle Scream 75
"Let the Rest of the World Go By" 123
"Let's Get Going Baby" 31
The Letter 55
Letter from the President 120
Levine, Sam 75, 110
Lewis, Harry 106

Index

Lewis, Jerry 61
Lewis, Joseph H. 137
Lewis, Sinclair 15, 111, 135
Lewton, Val 98
Leyton, Drue 18
Lieberson, Goddard 113
The Life and Times of Grizzly Adams 81
Life in the Raw 14
The Life of Rafael Sabatini 114
"The Life of Stephen Foster" 61
"The Light Switch" 62
Lightner, Fred 110
"Lila Dale" 64
Lindsey, Judge Benjamin B. 40
A Lion Is in the Streets 120
List, Eugene 91
The Little Lady in the Big House 114
Litvak, Anatole 54
Litvinov, Mrs. 78
Livingston, Jay 128
Livingston, Walter 10
Llewellyn, Richard 120
Lockhart, Gene 119
Lombard, Carole 48
London, Jack 76, 114
The Long Straw 69
Longacre Theater, NY 86
Loper, Don 130
Lord, Robert 54
Los Angeles Symphony Orchestra 49
The Loss of Roses 141
Lost Horizon 112
Louise, Anita 72
Loving Cup 115
Lowe, Edmund 22, **23**
Loy, Myrna **33**
Luciano, "Lucky" 104, 105
The Lucky Stiff 111
Lucy Gallant 127–128
Lundigan, William 101
Lupino, Ida 61, 63, 114–118, 125, 129, 134
Lupino, Stanley 117
Lux Radio Theater 62

"Ma Barker and Her Boys" 137
Macauley, Richard 96
MacDonald, Jeannette 78
Maclane, Barton 118
MacMurray, Fred 112, **113**
Macpherson, Aimee Semple 111
MacRae, Gordon 123
The Mad Game 15, 21, 43
Madman's Holiday 92
Maeterlinck, Maurice 4
Magnificent Obsession 127
Main, Marjorie 47, 72
Main Street After Dark 101
Mains, Marion **85**
Makelim, Hal 124
The Maltese Falcon 54
Maltin, Leonard 107
The Man from Colorado 76
Man Without a Star 127
The Manchurian Candidate 136

Mander, Miles 87–88
Mann, Anthony 99, 101, 111
Mann, Danny 120, 129
Marble, Alice 114
March, Fredric 135
Marcus, Frank 143
Marin, Edwin L. 91
Marjorie Morningstar 131–132
Marry the Girl 40
Marseilles 86
Marshall, George 75
Marshall, Herbert 92, **93**, 94
Martin, Dean 61
Martineau, Pierre-Martin 68
Marvin, Lee 124
Marx Bros. 24, 123
Massey, Raymond 138
Matisse, Henri 29
Mature, Victor 82
Maximilian and Carlotta 19
Mayehoff, Eddie 142
Mayer, Norma 149
Mayerling 54
The Mayor of the Town 61
Mazurki, Mike 87, 88
McCambridge, Mercedes 127
McCarthy, Sen. Joseph 62
McCoy, Herschel 43, 58
McCrea, Joel 47, 110
McCullough, Lester 110
McDonald, Dr. 49
McEwen, Doug 148
McFadden, Hamilton 22
McGoohan, Patrick 148
McGrane, Mr. 3, 5
McGuire, Dorothy 129
McHugh, Frank 56, 86
McKay, Alexander 10
McLaglen, Victor 67, 76
The Meal Ticket 8
Meek, Donald 64, 66, **67**
Meet the Girls 53
"Memphis in June" 90
Menjou, Adolphe 91, 133
Meredith, Burgess **80**, 81
Merivale, Philip 75
Merrill, Gary 136
Metro Goldwyn Mayer 9, 103, 107
Metty, Russell 127
Mildred Pierce 45, 62
Milestone, Lewis 67
Miller, Arthur 94
Miller, Marvin 90, 91
Mills, Juliet 148
Minnelli, Vincente 139–141
The Miracle Woman 111
Miss Lonelyhearts 18
Miss Private Eyeful 133
Mr. Angel Comes Aboard 90
Mr. Smith Goes to Washington 111
Mr. Twilight 76
Mitchell, Cameron 135
Mitchell, Thomas 61, 64, **68**, 94
Mitchum, Robert 88, 124
"Moanin' Low" 19, 105–106
"Modern Beauties" BAT Cigarette series 44
Modern Screen 25

Moise, Nina 29
"The Mole on Lincoln's Cheek" 62
Monet, Claude 29
Montalban, Ricardo 120
Montez, Lola 82
Montgomery, Robert 94
Moody, Helen Wills 114
Mooney, Martin 111
"Moonlight Sonata" 91
Moorehead, Agnes 5, 61
Morgan, Frank 73
Morris, Chester 67, 72
Morris, Wayne 54, **55**, 56
Morrison, Charles (uncle) 5
Morrison, Mary Chambers (grand-mother) 3
Morrison, Robert (grandfather) 3
Morrow, Jeff 137
Mother of a Champion 115
Moulin Rouge 45
The Mountain 120, 129–130
Mulligan, Robert 147
Muni, Paul 104
Munson, Ona 59
Murder for Two Cents 55
Murder, My Sweet 45, 87–90, 91, 129, 150
"Murder, My Sweet" (radio) 62
Murder, She Wrote 148
Murphy, Sen. George 78
Mutual Radio Network 60
My Forbidden Past 101
My Man and I 120–122, 150
My Marriage 30, 86
Myron, Helen 43

The Naked Spur 101
The Narrow Margin 122
The National Repertory Theater 133
Nauss, Katharin A. 145
Navy Wife 19, 29–30
Neal, Tom 83
Negri, Pola 68
Never Fear 116
Neville, Lucy 14
"New Sound for the Blues" 137
New York World's Fair (1939) 72
New Zealand Herald 64
Newley, Anthony 143
Newton, Robert 125, **126**
"Niagara Falls" 84
Nichols, Barbara 131
Nichols, Beverly 69
Niessen, Gertrude 109
Nijinsky, Vaslav 118
No Money to Guide Her 10
"No Sad Songs for Me" 134
Nocturne 91
Nolan, Lloyd **36**, 37, 38, 60, 101
None But the Lonely Heart 86
Norris, Kathleen 29
Not Wanted 115
The Notorious Mr. Monks 120
Novarro, Ramon 26
Now, Voyager 132

O'Brien, Edmond 62, 114
O'Brien, George 14, 15, 49, 71

O'Brien, Pat 55, 76, 92, 93, 94, 108, 135
Obsession 89
Oettinger, Malcolm H. 59
Of Mice and Men 67
Oh Dad, Poor Dad ... 142
O'Hara, Maureen 78
O'Keefe, Dennis 99
Oligny, Hugette 123
"On a Holiday in My Playpen" 31
"One Last September" 61
One Mile from Heaven 39–40
One Minute to Zero 124
One Touch of Venus 112
An Open Book 104
Oppenheimer, George 114
Orange County Arthritis Foundation 146
Orlova, Gaye 104
Orsatti, Ernie 26
Orsatti, Vic 26
Our Relations 29
Our Very Own 108
Our Wife 74
Out West It's Different 75
Outrage 116
The Outsider 29
"Over a Cup of Coffee" 35

Paal, Alexander 118
Pacific Liner 67
Paige Sisters 8
Painted Lady 21
Palance, Jack 129
Pallette, Eugene 22
Palmer, Lilli 110
Paramount Studios 39, 48, 101, 145
Pardon Our Nerve 53
Paris When it Sizzles 142
Parker, Jean 68
Parker, Lew 133
Parliament Cigarettes 61
Parrish, Robert 127
The Party's Over 12, 18
Pathé Newsreels 49
Patrick, Dorothy 101
Patterson, Pat 18
Patterson, Robert 134
Patton 142
Payne, John 111
Pearl, Jack 8
Peck, Gregory 129
Petticoat President 63
Phantom Footsteps 10
Photoplay 43
Picasso, Pablo 29
Pick-Up on South Street 142
Pickford, Mary 126
Picnic 141
Picture Play 15
Picturegoer 68
Pidgeon, Walter 72, **73**, 74
Pier's End 107
Pitts, ZaSu 24
"The Plan" 62
Planet of the Apes 142
Platt, Louise 64, 65
Playhouse 90 136

Plunkett, Walter 66
Pocketful of Miracles 139
Poe, Edgar Allan 87
Pogany, Willy 29
Poison Pen Letter 120
"Poor Polly" 85
Porffirio, Robert 94
Potter, Hank 10
Powell, Dick 87, 88, **89**, 90
Powell, William 79
Power, Tyrone 49, 74, 145
Presley, Elvis 143
Price, Vincent 133
Primrose Path 88
"The Prowler" 135
Pursuit 107

Qualen, John 57, 136
Quiet Please 69
Quine, Richard 142
Quinn, Anthony 129

Race Street 91
Radio Mirror 60, 61
Raft, George 48, 70, 76, **90**, 91, 110
Raines, Ella 110
Rambeau, Marjorie 111
Rapper, Irving 132
Rathbone, Basil 79, 80
Rathbone, Ouida 80
Ratoff, Gregory 53
Raven, Judith 19
Raw Deal 99–101
Ray, Leah 51, 52
Read, Alfred C. 11
Reagan, Ronald 146
Redheads on Parade 18
Reed, Ione 22, 82
Reflected Glory 36
Regan, Jayne 51, 52
Reid, Beryl 143, 144
Reid, Louis 41
Reinhardt, Max 118
Reis, Irving 94
Renoir, Auguste 29
Renoir, Jean 89
Republic Pictures 72, 120
Results, Inc. 60
Reunion 56
"The Revolt of Judge Lloyd" 137
Reynolds, Adeline de Walt **80**, 81–82
Rhapsody 107
Rhapsody in Black 10
Rhinehart, Mary Roberts 22
Rice, Craig 111
Rice, Florence 23
Riggs, Bobby 114
Ritter, Thelma 127, 142
RKO Pictures 71, 72, 90, 98, 135
Roach, Hal 67
Roach, Leonard 145
The Roaring Twenties 96
Robards, Jason, Jr. 148
Roberts, Roy 112
Robin, Leo 39
Robinson, Bill 40

Robinson, Edward G. **53**, 54, 59, 70, **107**, 118, 139–140
Rockwell, Norman 148
Rogers, Ginger 45, 125, 128
Roland, Gilbert 21, 128
Romeo and Juliet 78
Romero, Cesar 36, 40, 43, 56, **57**
Rooney, Mickey 137
Roosevelt, Franklin D. 66, 69
Rosa, Lee 65
Rose, Paul 38
Rosenbloom, Maxie **53**, 55
Rosza, Miklos 86
The Royal Family 7
Royer, Louis 43
Rubinstein, Arthur 26
Ruman, Sig 24
Russell, Connie 80
Russell, Gail 91
Russell, Lillian 82
Russell, Rosalind 5, 45, 74, 101–103
Ruth, Herman "Babe" 109, 110
Ruth, Mrs. 110
Rutherford, Ann 78
Ryan, Anthony Bentley 49
Ryan, Robert 116, **117**, 118, 120, 129

"Safe Conduct" 136
Saint, Eva Marie 148
St. Louis Cardinals 26
Salome 6
San Quentin Prison 101
Sanders, George 71, 114
Santa Ana High School 146
Santa Fe Trail 72
Sargent, Thornton 8–9
Saville, Victor 123
Sawtell, Paul 97, 99
Saxon, Grace 19
Scaasi, Arnold 46
Schiaparelli, Elsa 45
Schlesinger, Michael 127
Schlitz Playhouse of Stars 135
Schulberg, Budd 78
Scott, Lizabeth 114
Scott, Randolph 61, 68, 72, 82, 83, 124
Screen Actors Guild 54, 146
Screen Guild Theater 62
Screen Writers Guild 114
Screenland 41, 43
The Search for Bridey Murphy 127
The Seagull 7
Second Honeymoon 49
Seiter, William A. 112
Selznick, David O. 64
The Sentence 73
Separate Rooms 75
Serisawa, Sueo 145
Serling, Rod 135
The Set-Up 108, 116
Seven Cities of Gold 143
7 Women 66
The Seventh Victim 116
77 Sunset Strip 137
Seymour, Dan **107**
Shakespeare, William 78, 129
Shanghai Deadline 55

Shanghai Madness 15
She Learned About Sailors 21
"She May Have Seen Better Days" 65
Sheehan, Winnie 41
Shelton, John 94
Shepard, Kathleen 32
Sheridan, Ann 45
Sherman, Harry 86
Sherriff, R.C. 114
"She's More to Be Pitied Than Censured" 65
Shirley, Anne 88
Side Street 101
Sidney, Sylvia 47
Silver Queen 82
Silvers, Harry 7
Simon, Simone 26
Simpson, Fred C. 72
Sinnott, Patricia 143
The Sisters 54
Six Girls and Death 51
Slezak, Walter 96, 97
Sloane, Everett 131
Smith, Alexis 108
Smith, Sir C. Aubrey 75
Smith College 5
The Snake Pit 54
Sokoloff, Vladimir **53**, 54
"Something's Gotta Give" 142
Somewhere in the Night 81
Song and Dance Man 30, 35, 103
Sorry, Wrong Number 54, 108
South of St Louis 108
Sparkuhl, Theodore 81
Spawn of the North 48
Sperling, Milton 110
Spillane, Mickey 87
Splendor in the Grass 141
Spring Tonic 23–24
Springfield Rifle 124
Stack, Robert 125, 126
Stage Door 51
Stage to Lordsburg 64
Stagecoach 1, 59, 62, 64–69, 70, 71, 144, 145, 150
Stalin, Joseph 91
Stand Up and Cheer 19
Stanwyck, Barbara 1, 40, 69, 108, 125
Star for a Night 34, 35
Starr, Jimmy 21
Stars in My Crown 111
State of the Union 103
The Steel Trap 91
Steiger, Rod 135
Steinbeck, John 67
Steiner, Max 54
Stephens, Harry 12
Sterling, Jan 108, 125, **126**
Stetson Hat Co. 6, 44
Stevens, George 127
Stevenson, Edward 89
Stewart, James 111
Stone, Andrew 91
Stone, Lewis 72
Stop, You're Killing Me 19, 122–123
The Stork Is Dead 7

Storm Center 108
The Story of GI Joe 101
"The Story of Ruth Taylor" 60
The Stranger Wore a Gun 123–124
Street of Chance 80–82, 150
A Streetcar Named Desire 120
Streisand, Barbra 145
Strictly Dishonorable 8
The Stripper 141–142
Sturges, Preston 8, 86
Sullavan, Margaret 134
Sullivan, Barry 85
Sullivan's Travels 86
"The Sun Comes Up" 62
Suspense 62
Swanson, Gloria 114
Swanson, Neil H. 70
Sweeney, Joseph 136
Sweet Bird of Youth 139
The Sweet Smell of Success 131
"Swing Low, Sweet Chariot" 19, 29
Sylva, Carmen 82
Synanon 142
The Syndicate 110

T-Men 101
"Take Me Out to the Ball Game" 109
Talbot, Lyle 8, 50
A Tale of Two Cities 80
The Talk of the Town 76
The Tall Target 101
Tamiroff, Akim 38, **39**
Taurog, Norman 74
Taylor, Kent 30
Temple, Shirley 19, **20**, 41, 132
Tennant, Eleanor "Teach" 114–115
Terry-Thomas 142
Texas 75–76, 77
Thalberg, Irving 11, 107
"Thanks for the Memory" 55
They Drive By Night 96
This Gun for Hire 70
Thomas, Bob 125, 145
Three for Bedroom C 113, 118
365 Nights in Hollywood 21
Three's a Crowd 76
Three's a Family 86
Thurber, Kent 7
Tierney, Gene 78–79
Tierney, Lawrence 96, 97, **98**, 99, 118
Time of the Cuckoo 128
Time Out for Romance 37–38
Tiompkin, Dimitri 126
To Mary—With Love 33–35, 59
Toll, Charles E. 83
Tomorrow, the World! 101
Tone, Franchot 108
Tonight at 8:30 75
"Tonight There's a Spell on the Moon" 23
Too Young to Love 10
Torvay, Jose **113**
Tourneur, Jacques 94, 111
Tracy, Spencer 5, 15, 18, 21, 28, 29, 103, 125, 129
"Trade Winds" 62

"Trail to Mexico" 64
The Treasure of the Sierra Madre 48
Trigere, Pauline 46
Truex, Ernest 10, 136
Truman, Harry S. 91
Tucker, Forrest 118
Tunis, John R. 114
Turner, Lana 73
The Turning Point 118
Tuttle, Frank 70
12 Angry Men 136
Twelvetrees, Helen 21
Twentieth Century–Fox 28–30, 33, 38, 39, 48, 51
Twenty-Four Hours a Day 21
Two Weeks in Another Town 139–141
Two Yanks in Trinidad 76

Under Pressure 23
Under the Greenwood Tree 29
Underground Cable Co. 5
The Unholy Wife 130, 135
The United States Steel Hour 137
Universal Pictures 70, 111
University of California in Irvine 149
The Unsinkable Hermione Baddeley 144
The Untouchables 137

Valley of the Giants 45, **55**, 56
Vanderbilt, Cornelius, Jr. 21
Variety 12, 15, 24, 59, 67
Variety Boys Club 145
Vassar College 5
The Velvet Touch 101–103
Venable, Evelyn 35
Venita, Benay 128
The Very Singular Miss Brown 69
"The Victim" 133
Victory Caravan 64
Villa Villa! 80
A Village in the Valley 69, 75
The Vitaphone Company 8

Wagner, Robert 129, 149
Wagon Master 66
Wagon Train 137
Wagons Westwards 72
"Wait Till the Sun Shines, Nellie" 110
Wald, Jerry 108
Walker, Mary Kathleen 66
Walker, Ray 19
Walking Down Broadway 51, 52, 53
"Walking My Baby Back Home" 8
Wallace, Irving 63
Waller, Thomas "Fats" 8
Walsh, Raoul 23, 72
Walthall, Henry B. 28
Wanger, Walter 59
Wanted 21
Warner, Jack 104
Warner Bros. 8, 53, 55, 72, 96, 103, 104, 106, 108, 123
Washington, Fredi 39–40

Wayne, John 64, *65*, 66, 71–72, 73, 94, 108, 125, *126*, 138, 147
Webb, Robert D. 142–143
Welles, Orson 60, 67, 68
Wellman, William A. 121, 125–126
Wells, Peter 7
Wemlinger, Andreas 3
Wemlinger, Bea "Benny" (née Morrison; mother) 3–5, 25, 46, 132
Wemlinger, Benjamin (grandfather) 3
Wemlinger, Clara (grandmother) 3
Wemlinger, Helena 3
Wemlinger, Noel B. (father) 3–6, 25, 46, 132
West, Mae 12, 25
West, Nathanael 18
West Side Story 141
Westinghouse Desilu Playhouse 136
Westwood Tennis Club 78
Whalen, Michael 31, 37, *38*, 49, 54
What Am I Bid? 21
"When My Baby Smiles at Me" 108
Wherever the Grass Grows 82
Whistling in the Dark 10–12, 75, 136
White, Pearl 38
Whiting, Richard 39
Wife in Name Only 7
Wilcox, Grace 112
Wild Gold 15, 18, 19
Wild Goose 147
Wilde, Cornel 82
Wilde, Oscar 6
Wilder, Thornton 60
Williams, Guinn "Big Boy" 82
Williams, Hugh 21
Williams, Tennessee 120, 139
Win-Drift 110
Winchester '73 101, 111
Windsor, Claire 11
Winters, Shelley 111, 120, ***121***
Withers, Jane 19
"Witness for the Defense" 1487
Witte, Lou 32
Woman and the Law 18
A Woman Commands 68
The Woman of the Town 84–86, 150
The Woman on Pier 13 111
Women Without Men 111
Wood, Natalie 131–132
Woodhull, Victoria 63
Woodward, Joanne 141
Woodward, William 135
Woolrich, Cornell 81
Work of Art 15
The World Within 117
Wright, Teresa 127
Wurtzel, Sol 18, 20, 21, 29, 31, 40, 52, 53
Wuthering Heights 77
Wyatt, Jane 69, 91
Wycherly, Margaret 80, 90
Wyler, William 47, 48, 64
Wylie, I.A.R. 30
Wyman, Jane 127
Wynn, Keenan 69
Wynn, Nan 84

"You Can Have Everything" 53
Young, Loretta ***49***, 50, 51
Young, Victor 72
"You're My Ever-Loving" 123
"You're My Favorite One" 35
"You're My Thrill" 16

Zanuck, Clara 140
Zanuck, Darryl F. 20, 21, 22, 25, 51, 52–53, 140

www.ingramcontent.com/pod-product-compliance
Lightning Source LLC
Chambersburg PA
CBHW081558300426
44116CB00015B/2933